CRISIS EDUCATION AND SERVICE PROGRAM DESIGNS

CRISIS EDUCATION AND SERVICE PROGRAM DESIGNS

A Guide for Administrators, Educators, and Clinical Trainers

Miracle R. Hoff and Lee Ann Hoff

Routledge
Taylor & Francis Group
New York London

Routledge
Taylor & Francis Group
711 Third Avenue
New York, NY 10017

Routledge
Taylor & Francis Group
27 Church Road
Hove, East Sussex BN3 2FA

Printed in the United States of America on acid-free paper
Version Date: 20110726

International Standard Book Number: 978-0-415-88899-8 (Hardback)

Library of Congress Cataloging-in-Publication Data

Hoff, Miracle.
Crisis education and service program designs : a guide for administrators, educators, and clinical trainers / Miracle R. Hoff, Lee Ann Hoff. -- 2nd ed.
p. ; cm.
Rev. ed. of: Creating excellence in crisis care / Lee Ann Hoff, Kazimiera Adamowski. 1st ed. c1998.
Includes bibliographical references and index.
ISBN 978-0-415-88899-8 (hardcover : alk. paper)
1. Crisis intervention (Mental health services)--Study and teaching. 2. Crisis intervention (Mental health services)--Study and teaching. I. Hoff, Lee Ann. II. Hoff, Lee Ann. Creating excellence in crisis care. III. Title.
[DNLM: 1. Crisis Intervention--methods. 2. Crisis Intervention--education. 3. Mental Health Services. WM 401]

RC480.6.H63 2011
616.89'025--dc23 2011018663

Visit the Taylor & Francis Web site at
http://www.taylorandfrancis.com

and the Routledge Web site at
http://www.routledgementalhealth.com

To David

and

to people worldwide who are struggling but still there for others in crisis

Contents

SECTION II EDUCATION AND TRAINING PROGRAM DEVELOPMENT AND IMPLEMENTATION

List of Figures

List of Tables

Foreword

C. Everett Koop, MD, ScD

For all human beings, life is the experience of pursuing basic needs: food, shelter, stable and loving relationships, meaningful work—a pursuit most possible in a climate of peace. But each year, millions of people are thrust outside of this fundamental pursuit into the pain and chaos of crisis and thwarted in their need for safety, shelter, and social support. Instead of the joy of friendship, family, and community, some are victimized by the treachery of false friends, the violence of a wronged lover, the meanness of a parent, and the brutality of random vengeance. For others, the crisis may be intensely personal: an interior tragedy that attacks and devours its own host.

Good intentions—the outpourings of human charity—are needed for us to begin and to persevere; but such intentions, by themselves, are simply not enough. For the professional person in the fields of public health and social service, human charity is only the beginning of the process, not the end. And the process is not simple. If we are truly dedicated to bringing relief to a person in crisis, we must do our work in an organized, effective manner, one that promotes the physical, mental, and emotional healing processes. Therefore, we need to apply the knowledge and skills of all relevant disciplines to the human service we perform. There's nothing elementary about personal crisis, and there should be nothing elementary about our response to it either.

I especially favor having health and social service personnel look beyond the immediate crisis event and develop the means with which to prevent a repetition of the crisis. Preventive service, often delivered simultaneously with treatment, also requires clarity of purpose and good organization to be effective over the long term.

The person in crisis, therefore, must receive service that is not only immediate and caring—but also capable. And capability in service requires broad-gauge, systematic thought and action. Fortunately, over the past several decades, crisis leaders in our respective professions of public health, medicine, nursing, social service, law enforcement, and psychology have constructed a firm base of theory and practice upon which we can individually build strong and effective protocols for patient/client assessment, treatment, and follow-up. The emotional chaos that may immobilize a person in crisis must not be mimicked by the individual or the agency providing vital service to that person. Quite the opposite: We must make sure that we meet—and overcome—the potential anarchy of personal crisis with the structure and rationality of appropriate organization and well-trained crisis managers.

That's what this book, *Programs for People in Crisis*, is all about, and I commend it to you.

June 1987

C. Everett Koop, MD, ScD
Surgeon General
U.S. Public Health Services

Reprinted from *Programs for People in Crisis: A Guide for Educators, Administrators, and Clinical Trainers* (1987) by Lee Ann Hoff and Nina Miller.

Foreword

Richard Ramsay, MSW

Timing is crucial in the response actions of crisis practitioners. Split-second decisions can contribute to critically big differences, frequently involving matters of life and death. The authors know this. Crisis practitioners know this. Now those engaged in the nonclinical side of crisis work—education and training, administration, interagency coordination, governing bodies—have a book that describes the importance of their work to the development of skilled crisis workers.

The authors' extensive knowledge of crisis work in American and Canadian agencies is shared with informative and well-placed examples throughout this book. They know that crisis work cannot be segregated into primary health care or psychosocial health care approaches. Integrated holistic approaches need to replace old Cartesian beliefs about mind–body separatism. They know that the rapidly emerging shift to community-based health care models situates crisis services in a pivotal role.

Their book is superbly timed for those involved in the nonclinical aspects of crisis work to participate fully in the development of ideal crisis care services for the 21st century. The authors have compiled an impressive array of information addressing the significance of effective interagency coordination, good access to consultation, standardized education and training, and relevant administrative approaches. Without this kind of comprehensive support, well-intentioned crisis practitioners are left frustrated and easily burned out. This is not my first encounter with Lee Ann Hoff's expertise in crisis intervention. In 1984, I was working with three mental health colleagues in a multidisciplinary partnership to develop, test, and disseminate quality-controlled suicide prevention training programs. Our first-generation efforts to design a standardized training curriculum met with considerable resistance, including an imposed 6-month moratorium on 2 years of development work. Lee Ann Hoff was one of three independent evaluators selected to review our work. Thanks to their positive evaluations, the way was paved for the eventual formation of LivingWorks Education, dedicated to the development of effective gatekeeper training programs for crisis care and other frontline community caregivers around the world. The knowledge and wisdom that she used to help that innovative program continue to develop are now combined with Kazimiera Adamowski's expertise to benefit a much bigger crisis care audience dedicated to the development of a program of excellence.

This book is divided into three parts: background issues; education and training programs; and service organizations, management, consultation, and community education. The first part gives an excellent overview of crisis care services in the context of primary and psychosocial health care paradigms. It provides a clear and succinct orientation to the language and concepts associated with crisis programs. Terms like *crisis assessment*, *crisis management*, and *crisis intervention* are easily understood in the continuum of crisis care. They take the "foreign language" sound of *traumatic stress debriefing* and *posttraumatic stress disorder* and give them practical and easily understood descriptions. Whether you are an administrator, policy board member, trainer, educator, funder, crisis worker (paid or volunteer), or employee of an associated community service agency, this book gives you what you need to know about the background issues in crisis care.

The education and training section evokes many memorable images. I started my crisis training career 30 years ago as cofounder of the Ottawa Distress Centre. Two things were ominous at the time. Volunteer crisis workers were viewed by the professional community with a great deal of skepticism. Crisis line volunteers required special training to give them confidence and a practical guide to be effective crisis workers when there was no one but their colistener on duty. Huge improvements in professional attitudes and methods of training have occurred since then. This book captures these changes and provides the nonclinical members of crisis organizations with a comprehensive understanding of key concepts and training issues, standards for crisis training programs, core content for education and training, and much more.

Evaluation of education and training programs is a major challenge for administrators, program planners, trainers, policy makers, and program funders. One discovers in this book that evaluation is more than outcome measures. The diversity of crisis workers has to be accommodated. Community and cultural contexts have to be factored into good evaluation studies. Training has to be tailored to the needs of the crisis worker. This book gives nonclinical members of crisis organizations an excellent sense of how they can contribute to the challenge of establishing effective evaluation policies and approaches.

The material in the third part of this book is probably the least attended to but perhaps among the most important in terms of ideal crisis care. To be effective, crisis service organizations cannot rely solely on well-managed agencies and highly skilled professionals and volunteers. They must be prepared to participate in fully supported community-based interagency communication activities. My experience at this level of crisis care work has covered a wide spectrum of activities as a crisis center board member, member of a large urban crisis care coordinating committee, and ministerial appointee to Alberta's provincial suicide prevention advisory committee and, more recently, the new government-supported Alberta Centre for Injury Control and Research. All of these activities gave me firsthand experience of how important the issues discussed in this third part of the book are for everyone involved in the nonclinical facets of crisis programs. This discussion reflects the often undervalued importance of an interdisciplinary approach to crisis care involving professionals and volunteers committed to interorganizational communication networks of cooperation, coordination, and collaboration at the agency-to-agency as well as the crisis worker–to–crisis worker level. The kind of information contained in this section should be readily available to both the clinical and nonclinical members of all crisis care organizations. Needs and resource assessment, the organizational structure of telephone crisis services, and staff screening and selection guidelines are thoroughly discussed; issues as diverse as staff burnout, chronic callers, and certification of services are all covered.

Without the full support and competent participation of everyone involved in the nonclinical aspects of these programs, even well-prepared crisis care practitioners can be left frustrated and prone to early burnout. Those pitfalls can be avoided by giving the same careful and considerate attention to the delivery of ideal crisis care that Lee Ann Hoff and Kazimiera Adamowski gave to the preparation of this book.

Richard Ramsey, MSW
LivingWorks Education Professor
Faculty of Social Work
University of Calgary
Calgary, Alberta, Canada

Reprinted from *Creating Excellence in Crisis Care: A Guide to Effective Training and Program Designs* (1998) by Lee Ann Hoff and Kazimiera Adamowski.

Foreword

Leona L. Eggert, PhD, RN

Everyone, at one time or another, is certain to experience a situational crisis—an emotionally hazardous event, a dilemma, or a disaster—that places us as human beings at a turning point, in dire straits and with pressing needs for an immediate, expedient end to the human suffering that is felt. These crises may arise from physical or emotional abuse, a sexual assault, a suicide, a mass homicide, a psychiatric emergency, or a natural disaster that devastates an entire community, to name but a few examples. Such crisis events typically leave us feeling shattered, in anguish, and tormented with grief. Naturally we may feel depressed, experience emotional pain, sorrow, or perhaps even shame. At such times, what all human beings need is support, comfort, and guidance. Direction in how to cope with situations that are beyond our scope of experience is in order. Encouragement and an infusion of hope that the despair currently felt will subside are essential. To carry on in the face of loss, immediate help that is competent, caring, and effective is required on a 24-hour basis as critical events usually occur with little or no warning.

In the best of all worlds, family and friends—our natural network of support persons—would provide the solace, help, and guidance needed in a crisis situation. But this is often not the case. The support of family and friends may be insufficient or missing; alternatively, everyone may be in need of each other's help simultaneously as in the case of a widespread disaster or a youth's suicide at school. For these and other reasons, community-based crisis services are a vital aspect of primary health care today. The place of crisis services in the prevention of violence, in the care of rape victims, or in the aftermath of a natural disaster or suicide is as important today as it was when these services were first designed and implemented. The goals remain the same: to prevent physical and emotional disorders due to poor or inadequate resolution of a crisis and to provide immediate, accessible, and competent care to persons in acute psychosocial distress.

The work of professional crisis practitioners is not a simple matter; nor do crisis services occur in a vacuum. They are, as Lee Ann Hoff and Kazimiera Adamowski remind us, one of several health services to be integrated within a community or comprehensive health care plan. This interdisciplinary book has needed to emerge from the upheaval of our social and health care reforms. It is just the right book at the right time to deal with the growing need for understanding how crisis services should round out, not replace, comprehensive health care services, and how ideal crisis care is to be achieved. The authors are adept at supporting the claim that crisis services cannot be a panacea. With cogent, rational assertions, we are led to understand that in the current climate of health care reforms, crisis services cannot and should not, in the name of cost containment, become a substitute for long-term mental health care or ongoing treatment needs. Consequently, the implications for practitioners, administrators, and policy makers are cogent and timely.

With precision and clarity, this book serves as a superb guide to directing the future of crisis services in our communities. What is inspiring is its central message: To provide superior and effective crisis interventions, training of practitioners is fundamental and a supportive administrative structure is crucial. It fills many gaps in our knowledge related to training professionals and volunteers and designing crisis services. What is unusual about the book is the integration of a well-grounded crisis model with the essentials for training program and service designs for implementing and evaluating core crisis content. What excites me is that at every level, the authors consistently present education, training, and program designs that advance crisis prevention and care across a variety of health and human service settings. The book emphasizes prevention as well as care; it stresses collaboration across disciplines—the health, social service, and legal professions—and across human service settings. The content of this book, with its examples from many agencies and settings throughout the United States and Canada, is timely and realistic; the organization is eminently useful.

This book is destined to be a success in many arenas—in crisis service agencies, academia, health insurance organizations, the advisory board room, and related community settings. Undoubtedly it will help crisis workers learn more about the interface between empirically supported crisis modes and the ongoing training and support they need to provide excellent crisis care. Administrators in crisis service and related agencies will appreciate the sound, practical guidelines for meeting their charge of planning programs and supportive structures that foster ideal crisis services. Educators and trainers will benefit from the content, organization, and multiple resources this book provides as they use it to prepare practitioners in crisis care across multiple disciplines. Not insignificantly, members of local advisory and policy boards, health insurance executives, and legislators can benefit from this book; the pragmatics and wisdom portrayed can reinforce the need for crisis services as a vital element of a comprehensive health care plan as well as the traditional role crisis services have always played in mental health services. Last but not least, consumers interested in the quality of crisis care provided in their own community will find this book informative and of worth.

In short, this is an exceedingly valuable book for all who are connected to and interested in the prevention of crises and the provision of ideal care to those currently in need of crisis services. Lee Ann Hoff—a nurse and forerunner in the field of crisis care and prevention—has joined forces with Kazimiera Adamowski to bring us a highly relevant book that will help us create excellence in crisis care. Wholeheartedly, I commend it to you.

June 1998

Leona L. Eggert, PhD, RN
Spence Endowed Professor
Developer and Director, Washington State Youth Suicide Prevention Program
Principal Investigator, Reconnecting Youth Prevention Research Program
Psychosocial and Community Health Department
University of Washington School of Nursing
Seattle, Washington

Reprinted from *Creating Excellence in Crisis Care: A Guide to Effective Training and Program Designs* (1998) by Lee Ann Hoff and Kazimiera Adamowski.

Preface

This book addresses the *nonclinical* facets of crisis programming. It emphasizes the importance of preparing crisis workers and developing programs that will facilitate high-quality crisis and psychosocial care. In other words, it provides the *infrastructure* necessary for effective practice. The most expert and best intentioned crisis practitioner (whether paid or volunteer) can be enormously frustrated in achieving clinical service goals when administrative supports are lacking or ineffective. Despite the vast number of *clinical* texts available to assist clinicians in understanding and helping individuals and families in crisis, there is a noticeable absence of published works to assist administrators, educators, and clinical trainers on how to develop and maintain crisis programs. Successful crisis programming requires appropriate education and training, intentional organization and management, smooth interagency coordination, and access to consultation.

In an era of health care reform, which emphasizes primary care and cost containment, the ability to provide effective crisis service, by both primary health care professionals and mental health care providers, will continue as a critical issue. Although "crisis care" has been historically neglected by mainstream policy makers, program planners, and practitioners, the terminology is more common in various reform documents, partially because of its expedient means to cost containment, but more importantly because of its traditional role as one of *several* essential mental health services.

Although crisis care is increasingly recognized for its important place on the continuum of proper psychosocial care, it is important not to promote this vital service as an *inappropriate fill-in* (when funds are short) for other essential services such as transitional housing, psychotherapy, and long-term rehabilitation counseling. Health reform has seen a shift to community-based health care—a movement that situates crisis services, which are typically community based, at center stage for their enhanced role in comprehensive health care. To avoid the inappropriate use of crisis services, it is necessary to provide broad education, such as through a book like this, about how crisis and psychosocial care fit within the array of crucial physical and mental health care services.

Despite a century of history indicating the significant role of crisis prevention and intervention, there are notable gaps in systematic training and preparation among health and human service professionals specific to this area. The inclusion of crisis content in the health and social services professions' curricula is still incidental despite pronouncements and position papers from nursing, medical, and various specialty practitioners as to its importance. This book is intended to serve as a guide to administrators, educators, and clinical trainers, who may otherwise feel ill prepared to teach crisis theory and practice. It provides a framework for more systematic inclusion of crisis content (e.g., critical life events, violence, victimization, suicide, and psychiatric emergencies) in the formal preparation of health and human service professionals. Further, it offers criteria for developing programs and practice protocols that balance attention to the psychosocial and biomedical needs of people in distress and crisis.

A unique contribution of this book is the attention to the interconnectedness between normal but stressful life events, catastrophic events like violence and disaster, and serious emotional and mental disabilities. Another hallmark of this interdisciplinary book is that it recognizes both the biomedical parameters of psychiatric disturbance and the sociocultural context of most emotional crises and mental upheavals. Overall, it provides a holistic view on developing educational and crisis service programs for a wide range of people in need, not just those suffering from serious and persistent mental illness or who are victims of disaster. In addition, although diversity issues continue as a central element in crisis services, various training and program development examples and case scenarios are provided that contribute to the book's cultural relevance in programs serving a variety of population groups.

By clearly delineating *what crisis care is and is not*, our proposed book shows that this facet of mental health care is neither a mere "band-aid," as previously thought, nor a panacea for what ails the health care system; rather, it is an essential element of the total health service delivery system that recognizes the whole human being, not only his or her medical or psychiatric diagnosis. This book aims to (a) fill the current gaps in knowledge and training across disciplines; (b) contribute to a more holistic, collaborative, and integrated practice by all health and human service workers; and (c) help heal the historic mind–body split in our approach to distressed people.

Audience

This book is intended to serve as an interdisciplinary guide to administrators, educators, and clinical trainers. It is written to help readers facilitate the delivery of ideal crisis care across disciplines, in particular:

- Educators in universities and certificate programs who are preparing future health and human service practitioners, supervisors, administrators, and trainers
- Administrators and program planners concerned with proper development, accreditation, and maintenance of crisis programming as an element of comprehensive health service
- Clinical trainers working in diverse crisis service delivery programs, such as health, mental health, and social service agencies, as they develop culturally relevant crisis programming and provide in-service training
- Paid or volunteer crisis workers (specialists), including first responders such as police, firefighters, and emergency medical teams, who need to be informed of training and service ideals and the infrastructure supports required for their pivotal role in providing quality crisis care
- Health and mental health professionals (generalists) in governmental, nongovernmental, and faith-based agencies who seek to expand their knowledge in the crisis field and work collaboratively with crisis programs
- Policy boards responsible for ensuring that crisis service delivery accords with current international standards
- Governmental entities charged with setting standards and policies ensuring basic crisis care to constituents
- Health insurance agencies interested in providing cost-effective care without compromising quality
- General readers and consumers concerned about access to and the quality of the crisis care they and their families may need

Organization

The book is divided into four parts. Section I (Chapters 1 and 2) presents background issues and an overview of the crisis field along with examples illustrating key concepts and training issues, and comprehensive service needs around life crisis examples. It sets the tone and provides the theoretical framework for succeeding chapters. Section II (Chapters 3 through 5) addresses education and training program development and implementation, including standards, core content, and differential application. Section III (Chapters 6 through 8) deals with service organization, management, and delivery including program planning, essential elements, and evaluation. Section IV (Chapters 9 and 10) bridges the gap between essential knowledge, attitudes, and skills in service delivery, including the presentation of ideal programs and the significance of consultation and community education in the provision of crisis care.

Historical Connections

In preparing the final manuscript for this book, we are both struck by the relevance of preceding editions. We therefore feel the book's true history is important to share. Our book's foundation was as a single chapter, first published in *People in Crisis* (1978) by Lee Ann Hoff. When the need to extend this basic content for new readers was fully realized, it was expanded to a book-size manuscript entitled *Programs for People in Crisis: A Guide for Educators, Administrators, and Clinical Trainers* (1987) by Lee Ann Hoff and Nina Miller. Another revision was published in 1998 and entitled *Creating Excellence in Crisis Care: A Guide to Effective Training and Program Designs* by Lee Ann Hoff and Kazimiera Adamowski.

In considering the foundational content for this revised edition, we are equally stunned by how pertinent the forewords by C. Everett Koop (1987), Richard Ramsey, and Leona L. Eggert (1998) remain. Their wisdom and recommendations about the urgency of crisis care across the disciplines they represent (medicine, public health, social work, and nursing) are as relevant today as decades ago. Despite significant advancements in the field, the inclusion of *nonclinical* facets of crisis care in education and training programs continues to lag behind. Although most agree it is foolish to "reinvent the wheel," the inclusion of essential content such as this book provides is witness to correcting the continued fragmentation within the health sector. We hope our book will contribute to at least partial closure of that gap as we envision a future of holistic, integrated, and collaborative crisis care.

March 2011

Miracle Hoff
Fargo, ND

Lee Ann Hoff
Boston, MA

Special Appreciation

The seeds that eventually grew into this book were planted at Johns Hopkins University (Psychiatry, Public Health, and Sociology) and the Los Angeles Suicide Prevention Center. I am deeply indebted to my professors and clinical supervisors at these institutions for a National Institute of Mental Health (NIMH)–sponsored interdisciplinary fellowship program that introduced me to crisis and suicidology as distinct fields of study and practice that led in part to the body of knowledge that characterizes crisis theory and practice today. As a return for this privileged educational experience, we were urged to incorporate what we had learned into the curricula of our respective disciplines.

Special thanks are also due the scholars and clinicians who over the years have advanced the field through their research, practice, and writing. But without the dedicated unpaid work of an army of volunteers—noted as the "real professionals" in the field—staffing hundreds of crisis hotlines in the United States, The Samaritans International, and other services worldwide, crisis care practice likely would not have thrived and survived as the necessary community-based service it is today on life's front lines. From these sources I learned two key principles informing the field: (a) Crisis intervention is *everyone's business*, not the specialty of any particular discipline, and (b) teamwork in 24/7 timelines is *essential to save one's own and other lives* in high-risk crisis situations.

These collaborative principles led to recruitment of coauthors for the 1987 and 1998 predecessors to this book. As I moved from full-time direct crisis care and clinical supervision to academe and a research program on violence issues, the role of a coauthor from the front lines of crisis work was self-evident. Nina Miller of the Suicide Prevention and Crisis Service in Ithaca, New York, most admirably filled that role for the 1987 work. The same principle applied for the 1998 edition, for which Kazimiera Adamowski, social worker and chief domestic violence trainer of physicians and nurses at the Ottawa General Hospital Emergency Department, assumed the role of coauthor. And for this book, Miracle Hoff, mental health and substance abuse counselor, graciously accepted the role of lead author. Without Miracle's spirited and competent dedication to the first-author role, this updated version of the book may not have seen the light of day! For this I am deeply grateful to you, Miracle; your husband, David; and your children, who understood when Mom had to do her "homework."

Complementing the work of these coauthors, special thanks go to the community-based crisis specialists in the Greater Boston area who contributed descriptions of their ideal services featured in Chapter 9. We hope that their example of expert service delivery and training of student interns across disciplines will inspire educators and other clinicians and trainers to help close the gap between theory and practice toward systematic versus "incidental" coverage of crisis content in the formal preparation of health and social service providers.

Special thanks also go to the anonymous reviewers of our book proposal and the manuscript who have helped us make this a better book. Last but not least, we thank Anna Moore at Routledge Mental Health for her timely editorial guidance and support through the production process.

Lee Ann Hoff
Boston, MA
2011

In addition to the above acknowledgments, I would like to thank those agencies who graciously answered my call for updated information and provided me with a more thorough understanding of the inner workings of their crisis program. In particular, special thanks to Karen Gooden at Some Other Solutions Society for Crisis Prevention, Stacie Loegering and Cindy Miller at FirstLink, and Jan Eliassen at Gladys Ray Shelter for the many hours you dedicated to helping me make this a solid book.

Lee Ann, my deepest appreciation for turning this "project" over to me and trusting in my professional abilities to see this through to completion. Thank you for letting me struggle through the process so that I might get the full view of what it takes to be an author. I am honored to work with you.

To my husband, David, and my wonderful children, Kyle, Joe, Brandon, Mason, and Jasmine~ THANK YOU. Thank you for letting me turn the kitchen table into my office, thank you for giving me my space when I needed to get some work done, thank you for letting me monopolize the computer, and most importantly, thank you for graciously reminding me of my priorities when I went into tunnel vision mode. I know it is hard for you to understand why I busy myself with extra projects. My hope is that someday you too will find your passion and dedicate yourself to a larger purpose.

Miracle Hoff
Fargo, ND
2011

I

BACKGROUND AND OVERVIEW OF THE CRISIS FIELD

The two chapters in this section lay the book's foundation in research, theory, policy, and practice arenas over several decades of development by interdisciplinary players in the field. The five life examples in Chapter 2 address key concepts and the services needed by a diverse sample of people in crisis across the array of community and clinical settings in which crises are experienced. Together, these chapters show the relevance and application of theory to excellence in crisis care practice.

Chapter 1

The Significance and Urgency of Crisis and Psychosocial Care

Chapter Outline

A Biopsychosocial Approach to Human Services
The Crisis Model in Human Services
Key Issues and Events Affecting Crisis and Psychosocial Care
Crisis Service Delivery: Differential Approaches
Evaluating the Content and Context of Training, Education, and Service Programs

Centuries ago, Hippocrates said, "It is better to know the man who has the disease, than the disease the man has." Yet, even in the new millennium while taking into consideration the essential interconnectedness of body, mind, emotion, and spirit and their impact on health, we continue to find ourselves swimming against the tide of biological paradigms that tend to give only lip service to the psychosocial facets of health care.

A Biopsychosocial Approach to Human Services

Although authors of most reputable texts tout a "biopsychosocial" approach to health care, the reality in practice is that the psychosocial facet of care is often shortchanged in the context of economic constraints and "managed care" service delivery models. Most health practitioners *want* to listen to their clients and tend to the psychosocial parameters of health, but listening takes more time than writing a drug prescription, and is poorly reimbursed. Health practitioners' goodwill and theoretical convictions about holistic health care must be blended with policy mandates and reimbursement systems that move beyond the age-old bias against those with mental and emotional problems or illness.*

This book addresses the issues that many health professions educators and practitioners face in their attempt to balance the psychosocial and biomedical elements of health care. After discussion and illustration of these issues in the first two chapters, we present education, training, and service delivery models that facilitate moving from theoretical conviction about holistic care to implementation in various education and practice arenas. Although psychiatric emergency treatment is included, we emphasize its connection to sociocultural meanings, and the *prevention* of these medical and psychiatric episodes through psychosocial support and timely crisis care. Central to our approach is the smooth coordination of service components across the spectrum of agencies needed for comprehensive health care. Our experience and that of many others reveal that individualistic, competitive, profit-driven, or uncoordinated services constitute some of the greatest hazards to health care in general, and crisis and psychosocial care in particular.

The Crisis Model in Human Services

Many family members and human services professionals will be familiar with the following crisis situation.

* We recognize that definitions of mental "illness" vary cross-culturally, and that the psychiatric and mental health field is neither entirely scientific nor neutral. Rather, it is influenced by sociopolitical processes, values, and such issues as cost containment and profit. Among those who apply psychiatric diagnoses, the term *disorder* is commonly used (as in *adjustment disorder, adult type with depressed mood* or *bipolar disorder*). However, because bias against the "mentally ill" or disabled is still very much alive, and because a psychiatric label can have damaging results, we use terms such as *cognitively impaired* and *emotionally distressed* when referring to those with serious and persistent mental health problems.

Example: David Jones

> At 11:00 p.m. a police officer calls the 24-hour telephone crisis program. The crisis team's professional crisis workers (a volunteer and a mental health professional, both formally trained in crisis intervention) make an outreach visit to the home of David Jones, whom the police and the Jones family believe to be acutely suicidal and in need of assessment for possible psychiatric hospitalization. Mr. Jones has refused police and family recommendations for treatment. The outreach team spends nearly 2 hours with Mr. Jones and his family in their home. Mr. Jones finally agrees to go to the emergency department of a community hospital, where he will be examined by psychiatric liaison staff for treatment planning. Following the assessment of Mr. Jones and his family situation, he remains overnight in the emergency department crisis unit. Outpatient therapy begins the following morning for Mr. Jones and his family at the community mental health center, where follow-up of such crisis situations is provided. The family is given the telephone number of the 24-hour crisis outreach program the police had originally called on behalf of this family. (Adapted from Hoff & Wells, 1989.)

This example highlights the similarity of response to such a crisis by family members and mental health professionals, for example listening and making judgments and decisions about what to do. In situations like this one and others, the work of the "natural" (family) and "formal" (professional) crisis workers is complementary (Hoff, Hallisey, & Hoff, 2009).

However, there are some differences. In this situation, the crisis outreach workers and mental health professionals are linked to formally established programs offering crisis services. These workers possess knowledge and skills—acquired, presumably, through professional education or training—that go beyond what "everybody knows" about distressed people's needs.

Timely responses to life crises have occurred since the beginning of recorded time (Hansell, 1976). Humans possess the capacity to create a culture of caring and concern for people in distress. Helping people in crisis is intrinsic to the nurturing side of human character. Thus, crisis intervention can be seen as natural human action embedded in culture and the process of learning how to survive through stressful life events among our fellow human beings.

In many traditional societies, assistance and support to distressed people were available through the extended family, indigenous community leaders such as a tribal chief or healer, and formal rites of passage (van Gennep, 1909/1960). A truism about the human condition is the community's recognition that most individual members cannot manage stressful or traumatic life events alone if they are to avoid potential pathologies or fatal outcomes. As an organized body of knowledge and practice, the crisis field, although nearly a century old, continues to gain momentum with major developments in the mental health and public health arena (Agar-Jacomb & Read, 2009; Golan, 1978; Hoff et al., 2009; Parad, 1965).

Nevertheless, individuals in contemporary industrialized societies are still frequently left to their own devices when troubled, traumatized, or facing the challenge of normal life passages. There is a seeming paradox here: Because people have "naturally" been handling crises through the ages, many may think that "formal" preparation in crisis care is unnecessary despite research and clinical evidence suggesting otherwise (Joint Commission on Mental Health and Illness, 1961; Lindemann, 1944; Ross, Hoff, & Coutu-Wakulcyzk, 1998; Woodtli & Breslin, 1996, 2002). How else do we explain why decades after spending many millions of dollars instituting and demonstrating the program and cost-effectiveness of comprehensive community mental health services (including 24-hour crisis response), such services are not systematically included in the health care delivery and professional training landscape (Dorfman, 2000; Marks, 1985; Marks & Scott, 1990; Morgan & Hunt, 2008; Roberts, Cumming, & Nelson, 2005; Stein & Test, 1980)?

At the macro level, one obvious explanation is the political process in which mental health needs have rarely commanded a priority position—due in part to historic bias against those with emotional or mental health needs (Capponi, 1992; Chandler, 1990; Johnson, 1990; Levine, 1981; Ustun, 1999). And it appears that history is repeating itself (Hoff & Morgan, 2011). Another is the dominant individualistic (vs. communitarian) ethic so prevalent, especially in the American psyche (Bellah, 1985). Individualism run amok can sabotage crisis prevention programs and decrease the ability of people with insufficient psychosocial "supplies" (Caplan, 1964) to survive the trauma of critical life events. Such individuals are more vulnerable to crisis and, without well-orchestrated community supports and timely intervention, may require costly institutional care (Hoff, 1993b; Test & Scott, 1990). Although health reform efforts in Canada and the United States are in process, with continued emphasis on community-based primary care, the need for cost containment, and moves toward profit-based health care delivery, compound an already complex issue (see Hoff & Morgan, 2011; Whitaker, 2010).

Case consultations and the clinical dilemmas presented by students in formal crisis courses suggest that the following scenario is commonplace in health and mental health practice across settings, countries, and provider disciplines.

Example: Jane Warren

Jane Warren, age 54, has been widowed for 6 months. She has entered "brief therapy" for 10 sessions focused on unresolved grief and a history of excessive dependency on her husband. A mental health professional with no formal crisis care training concludes a therapy session with Ms. Warren during which she expressed suicidal ideation. Following a very brief discussion of suicide risk, a "no suicide contract" is negotiated together with a referral to the local hotline should Ms. Warren feel suicidal before the next week's appointment. Over the weekend, Ms. Warren calls the hotline; during a 45-minute session, the telephone counselor assesses her suicide risk as low, suggests she consider a widow-to-widow local support group, and urges her to be more forthright with her therapist regarding her various concerns. When Ms. Warren returns for her next therapy appointment, she does not disclose the session with the telephone worker, and the therapist does not inquire beyond determining that Ms. Warren is at low risk for suicide this week. Several weeks later, Ms. Warren's name is entered on the "repeat callers" list of the crisis line; in the meantime, therapy has been terminated with no record of communication or planning between the two service agencies.

With the current interest in the crisis model and an extensive knowledge base to support it, this scenario invites serious reflection by all health, psychiatric, and social service providers. For instance, the questionable practice of developing a "no suicide contract" has been popular among some but provides *no legal protection to the practitioner* and usually serves to help the provider feel better about the situation rather than to aid the client in resolution of suicidal feelings. The only benefit of the "no suicide contract" is that, when genuinely approached, it can communicate caring and concern for the client's well-being and lead to a concrete safety plan. Additionally, seamless collaboration between health and mental health providers and the crisis service agencies they refer their clients to is essential (see Chapter 7). This matter is complicated by confidentiality laws and the anonymous nature of hotline services.

Development of the crisis field has been an uneven and complicated process. The growth of professionalism emphasizes the training of various experts across work settings and provider disciplines. A major outgrowth of this trend is the development of the crisis model as a distinct body of knowledge and practice, including certification of crisis workers. However, few health and other human service professionals receive more than a few hours of training regarding crisis theory and practice during their formal preparation (Cassidy, 1995; Haddad et al., 2005). Likewise, exposure to formal curricula is incidental rather than systematic (Ross et al., 1998; Woodtli & Breslin, 1996, 2002), a finding that complements an earlier U.S. national survey (Berman, 1983) revealing that few professional schools include formal coursework on crisis theory, violence prevention, and practice. As members of the human community, we all know something about helping people in crisis, so it is easy for health and social service professionals to avoid, through rationalization, the need for special training. In addition, the recent popularity of crisis practice has been fueled not only by the service needs of distressed people but also by cost containment issues. It is thus seen as an expedient and, at face value, less expensive form of "treatment," if for no other reason than its brevity.

The language used by writers and practitioners contributes to some of the major issues and problems in the crisis field: crisis intervention, crisis therapy, crisis management, crisis counseling, solution-focused brief therapy (SFBT), emergency psychiatry, critical incident stress debriefing (CISD), crisis work, crisis service, crisis program, and "managed care." Complementing this array of terms for services rendered are various descriptions of the people who deliver these services to people in crisis: crisis counselor, crisis therapist, crisis worker, crisis manager, professional, nonprofessional listener, and paraprofessional crisis workers. These interchangeable and sometimes confusing descriptions of the work and workers involved in the field reveal it as a young area of human service practice. For example, crisis counseling has always been brief and "solution focused" rather than psychodynamically oriented to personality change. The emergence of solution-focused brief therapy suggests that a piece of the crisis field has been excerpted and renamed partly because the body of knowledge about crisis has been addressed in piecemeal fashion.

Another example has been the use of critical incident stress debriefing—a term popularized through the work of Jeffrey Mitchell and the International Critical Incident Stress Foundation. For decades, crisis practice has included immediate support to individuals affected by the traumatic stress of disaster and other extraordinary or catastrophic events. These include war combatants, police officers, firefighters, ambulance attendants, classmates after a teen suicide or murder, rescue workers, and others witnessing or dealing with horrific events beyond most everyday experience. If practitioners of such emotional first aid are not grounded in a more comprehensive approach to the crisis resolution *process* and interconnections between traumatic stress and psychiatric vulnerabilities, CISD can degenerate from a humanistic to a mechanical process (see Hoff et al., 2009, ch. 13; Hoff, 2010a, ch. 11; see also www.crisisprograms.org).

The various terminologies used to describe the crisis field point to beliefs and assumptions about distressed people and what can be done to assist them toward growth and empowerment. As a basis for shared meaning, as an aid to development of the field, and to clarify the various terminology used throughout this book, refer to the glossary (Caplan, 1964; Golan, 1969; Hoff, 2010a; Hoff et al., 2009; Hoff & Wells, 1989; Mawby & Walklate, 1994; McCullough, 1995; Whitaker, 2010).

Every person working in health and human services—professional, paraprofessional, or lay volunteer—should understand the basic concepts and practices of the crisis model. Crisis intervention is not merely a "band-aid" version of psychotherapy. *It is an organized approach to helping distressed people that can be mastered by professionals and lay people through a systematic education and training program.* Though goodwill and peer support are necessary, they are not sufficient. As persons with serious and persistent mental health problems and histories of psychiatric hospitalization are increasingly referred to hotline services for after-hours care, it is crucial that volunteers who staff these programs have access to consultation and linkage networks. Yet to have credibility, mental health professionals who provide consultation to frontline workers must have both training and experience in crisis outreach work. Thus, educators and trainers need to examine their curricula for inclusion of crisis and psychosocial concepts and practice strategies needed by future practitioners in health and human services.

Key Issues and Events Affecting Crisis and Psychosocial Care

The U.S. Joint Commission, Evidence-Based Practice, and Recovery

The report of the U.S. Congress's Joint Commission on Mental Health and Illness, *Action for Mental Health* (1961), laid the foundation for the community mental health movement in the United States. Through 5 years of study, it documented that people were not getting the help they needed, when they needed it, and where they needed it: close to their natural social setting. The report revealed the following:

- Distressed people were tired of waiting lists.
- Professionals were tired of lengthy and expensive therapy that often did not help because sometimes it came too late.
- Large numbers of people (42%) went initially to a physician or to clergy for *any* problem.
- Long years of training were not necessary to learn how to help distressed people.
- Volunteers and community caretakers (for example, police officers, teachers, and ministers) were a large untapped source for helping people in distress.

A similar report, *Putting People First* (Ontario Ministry of Health, 1993), found similarities to the U.S. findings in Ontario, Canada's most populous province. As a result of *Action for Mental Health* (Joint Commission on Mental Health and Illness, 1961), the Community Mental Health Act was passed in 1963 to provide federal funding for community mental health centers, resulting in widespread deinstitutionalization of seriously ill patients. A half century later the findings of this report are still relevant.

In 2003 the New Freedom Commission's report *Achieving the Promise: Transforming Mental Health in America* (U.S. Department of Health and Human Services, 2003) provided a framework to reform a system that was often fragmented and inadequate for persons with serious mental illness living in community settings. Central to this transformation was the implementation of a "recovery" orientation along with the promotion of evidence-based practice (EBP). Combining these two concepts, however, seemed contrary, because EBP represented a medical model and recovery represented a consumer-centered model (Solomon & Stanhope, 2004). Ustun (1999) identified a need to bridge the gap between science and service through continued research on the efficacy, effectiveness, cost-effectiveness, and generalizability of mental health interventions.

The Institute of Medicine (IOM) defines *evidence-based practice* as "the integration of best-researched evidence and clinical expertise with patient values" (Institute of Medicine Committee on Quality of Health Care in America, 2001). With the pressures of accountability from managed mental health care, there is a major push toward evidence that interventions produce the greatest therapeutic gain in the shortest amount of time and with the fewest financial and human resources (Dziegielewski & Roberts, 2004). Morrison (2004) noted that many service providers believed that the rigor needed to meet the standards of evidence-based treatments left them out of reach and very challenging to implement in a "real" clinical environment, particularly a community-based setting serving persons with serious and persistent mental illness. Yet, Morrison concluded that EBPs could be implemented with commitment, culture change, and clinical discipline. The Institute of Medicine, however, reported a 15- to 20-year delay between research findings and their translation into routine clinical practice (Institute of Medicine Committee on Quality of Health Care in America, 2001).

The adoption of recovery language challenges the prevailing view within the mental health industry that mental illness is a chronic condition with treatment focusing solely on symptom management and reduction. The concept of recovery represents a significant shift away from the medical model, which focuses on symptoms and pathology, toward the needs of the individual—who may have very different goals than those presented by the clinician (Solomon & Stanhope, 2004). Anthony (1993) described recovery as a multidimensional concept that involves the changing of one's attitudes, values, and feelings while living a satisfying and hopeful life that includes finding new meaning and purpose.

There has been considerable debate about whether EBP and the concept of recovery are compatible. Criticisms leveled by recovery advocates speak to the limitations of EBPs in which measures fail to consider the view of the consumer's quality of life, empowerment, sense of hope, or connection and functioning within the community, which is important from the recovery perspective. The New Freedom Commission identified that fragmentation within the mental health system was the major barrier to systems intervention and mental health reform. This fragmentation, from a recovery perspective, is evidence of a system that does not reflect how mental illness and recovery involve all aspects of people's lives (Solomon & Stanhope, 2004). Although EBPs are valuable for persons very disabled by illness, as conditions improve and symptoms decrease, consumers should have more control over their treatment options and access to a broader range of services—evidence based or otherwise (Frese, Stanley, Kress, & Vogel-Scibilia, 2001).

The Patient Protection and Affordable Care Act (ACA) became law in the United States on March 23, 2010, in an attempt to make health insurance coverage more affordable. According to the U.S. Department of Health and Human Services (2010a), when fully implemented, the law will provide access to coverage for an estimated 32 million uninsured Americans. At the time ACA passed, it was estimated that one fifth to one third of uninsured citizens had mental health and/or substance abuse disorders. ACA will create a fundamental shift in the availability of services to individuals with mental health and substance abuse disorders and will enhance community-based service options, serving to further solidify the role of mental health within the context of general health care, rather than as a separate system. The Prevention Council, which was created as part of this legislation, has identified that one of the 10 leading strategies will be to focus on behavioral health.

The book by James Hillman and Michael Ventura, *We've Had A Hundred Years of Psychotherapy and the World's Getting Worse* (1993), and Robert Whitaker's *Anatomy of an Epidemic* (2010) suggest the need for a critical new look at what we are doing to meet the needs of people in distress and how psychotherapy and pharmacotherapy are related to broader sociocultural issues.

It is also noteworthy that the National Institute of Mental Health (NIMH) in the United States published the proceedings of its 1970 national conference to chart the course of suicide prevention and crisis intervention in the 1970s (National Institute of Mental Health, 1973). The NIMH document, *Suicide Prevention in the Seventies*, formed the basis for such programs as LivingWorks in Calgary, Alberta, a suicide intervention gatekeeper program used worldwide, in addition to more than 100 crisis programs in the United States, Canada, and Australia currently certified by the American Association of Suicidology (AAS). Certification of crisis practitioners is explored in Chapter 3. This pioneering work is still relevant at the dawn of the new millennium because the national agenda for suicide prevention and crisis intervention was displaced by issues of greater political popularity. Meanwhile, historical but largely unaddressed concerns of tribal, ethnic, and First Nations groups have continued to command greater attention as we develop education and service programs with sensitivity to the traditions and values of diverse groups.

Over the years we have reinvented the wheel—or at least pieces of the wheel. Often this has occurred out of political or economic expediency, without serious outcome evaluations of mental health service models that were designed after years of study and the investment of many millions of dollars (Hoff, 1993b; Marks & Scott, 1990). One result is that many of the recommendations for the 1970s still require implementation in some communities. Fortunately, North American governments are addressing these critical issues as international attention focuses on adolescent suicide, physician-assisted suicide, HIV/AIDS, violence and victimization, and homelessness. Meanwhile, individuals and organizations such as AAS, the American Foundation for Suicide Prevention (AFSP), the Suicide Prevention Resource Center (SPRC), the Centre for Suicide Prevention (CSP), the Canadian Association for Suicide Prevention (CASP), victim assistance groups (such as the National Organization for Victim Assistance [NOVA]), and others continue their work in spite of limited public support.

Annual conferences among professional and paraprofessional groups in the United States, Canada, and Europe—including AAS, CASP, the International Association of Suicide Prevention (IASP), Crisis Workers Society of Ontario, CSP, NOVA, the YWCA, and various state and local mental health organizations—reveal the continuing divisions and lack of coordination between associations with similar missions and common clientele. Among those organizations with both lay and professional membership, lay members frequently feel bored or see no practice relevance of "esoteric" research papers, whereas professionals feel disconcerted about how to reconcile research and publication demands with the needs of frontline workers. Current multicultural concerns, of course, may compound the complexities and divisions.

Some of these groups struggle to stay alive, raising membership dues to do so, but often do not consider partnerships with like-minded groups who have similar missions. This is not to suggest that any of these organizations should necessarily disband, or that all should be amalgamated. Yet, the array of groups and how they function appear symbolic of the divisiveness experienced in many mental health practice settings. The human and financial costs of these divisions are incalculable. Thus, for example, one can wonder whether the physician-assisted suicide debate would have emerged if groups with crisis expertise had greater influence on mainstream health care protocols around the psychosocial needs of the dying. The ultimate loss, one's own death, is more easily prepared for if one has been supported through life's many mini-losses. Given what dying patients taught health professionals years ago in Elisabeth Kübler-Ross's classic work *On Death and Dying* (1969); what we know of hospice care through the pioneering work of Cecily Saunders (1978); and, finally, what we know about pain relief and palliative care (Morgan, 2010), it is no less than astounding that physician-assisted suicide, in most instances, is sought because of unalleviated pain due to some health professionals' withholding medication out of misplaced fear of "addicting" a dying patient! It is well past time to expand into *general* health care what crisis and suicide prevention experts have known for decades about psychosocial care.

Primary Care and Prevention

In 1978, at the conference in Alma Ata in the Soviet Union, the World Health Organization (WHO) proclaimed a goal of "health for all by the year 2000" (World Health Organization, 1981). Member countries of the United Nations (UN) outlined practical steps toward goal implementation; for example *Healthy People 2000* (U.S. Department of Health and Human Services, 1992) in the United States and *Achieving Health for All* (Health and Welfare Canada, 1986) in Canada. In 2000, The United Nations Millennium Declaration was signed by all 191 UN member states creating the UN Millennium Development Goals (MDG), which served to combat poverty, hunger, disease, illiteracy, environmental degradation, and discrimination against women by 2015 (World Health Organization, 2010). In the United States, every 10 years the Department of Health and Human Services (DHHS) reviews knowledge and insight gained in the past decade. *Healthy People 2020* reflects assessment of major risks to health and wellness, changing public health priorities, and emerging issues related to our nation's health preparedness and prevention (U.S. Department of Health and Human Services, 2010b). In Canada, each province develops and updates its own framework. For instance, within the past few years, Alberta went through major restructuring, and a joint effort between Alberta Health and Wellness and Alberta Health Services resulted in *Becoming the Best: Alberta's 5-Year Health Action Plan* (Alberta Health Services, 2010), which addresses, among other things, improved mental health services in primary care for children.

Central to this endeavor is the role of primary health care, of which crisis services, consultation, and community education are pivotal elements in prevention efforts—particularly in the psychosocial facet of care. Widespread deinstitutionalization decades ago resulted in primary care becoming the de facto mental health system (Regier, Goldberg, & Taube, 1978). Nevertheless, in many countries, the majority of money available for health has traditionally been allocated to tertiary and secondary care centered in hospitals, rather than to primary care, which focuses on addressing people's health care needs while maintaining them in their home and community (Hoff & Morgan, 2011). In both the United States and Canada, current health reform efforts aim to correct the disproportionate percentage of health care dollars traditionally spent on acute institution-based care. These reform measures provide an opportunity to direct more balanced attention toward the prevention of acute episodes in both physical and emotional realms and the sociocultural factors that are at the root of many medical problems, emotional crises, and psychiatric disturbances. The enormous cost differential between primary care and preventive approaches versus secondary and tertiary institution-based care underscores the urgency of implementing the WHO goals and its potential contribution to containing escalating health care costs (Hoff, 2010b).

Certainly, persons who have serious and persistent mental disorders should have the public and private care they need at whatever level is clinically indicated. But, there is a dual irony in the wastefulness of a human service system that does not emphasize primary prevention with other necessary care for disabled persons. First, if community education and consultation regarding psychosocial health—along with 24/7 crisis service—were available to all, much human pain in the form of depression, alcohol and other drug abuse, institutionalization, suicide, and violence against others might be avoided. Second, because the dollar costs per consumer of secondary- and especially tertiary-level care are much higher than those of primary care, the role of crisis prevention and timely intervention cannot be overstated. For instance, it may require several intensive hours of social network intervention to help a worker stay on the job, a child to stay in school or in their home, or an adult to receive care at home rather than be institutionalized, or treated only with psychotropic drugs (Whitaker, 2010). But such preventive care and crisis service are still less expensive than the alternatives of unemployment, foster care, or institutionalization. Figure 1.1 illustrates the client and cost benefits of smoothly integrated services in contrast to institution-focused care. Ideally, community education, consultation, and crisis training should interface (see Chapter 10).

However, although implementation of such primary care programs continues to expand, the contradiction between ideals and reality persists. One major reason lies in the complex interplay of cultural values and political-economic factors that sustain the emphasis on biomedical and costly technological and pharmaceutical approaches to care (McKinlay, 1979; Whitaker, 2010). A related problem in the United States, in contrast to Canada, for example, is that millions of people have no health insurance, in spite of the growth of health maintenance organizations (HMOs)—a statistic that will change with the ongoing implementation of the Affordable Care Act. Further, managed care and for-profit models in the United States, although originally implemented to contain costs, are highly controversial and have stirred outrage among many for sacrificing patient care to the profit motive (Shindul-Rothschild, Berry, & Long-Middleton, 1996). Similar concerns are being expressed in Canada as the

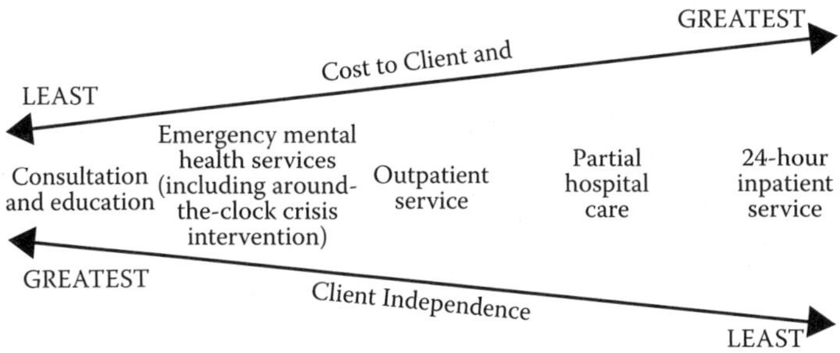

Figure 1.1 Continuum of mental health services: Cost and client independence. Assisting distressed people in their natural social roles (homemaker, paid worker, or student) through consultation, education, and crisis services is the *least* costly means of service and allows the *greatest* client independence; institution-based care is the *most* costly means and allows the *least* client independence.

national health care system is being threatened by special interest groups promoting for-profit models of health care (Armstrong & Armstrong, 1996; Rachlis & Kushner, 1994).

The basic principle of the right of *all* residents to equitable, comprehensive, and accessible health services continues to be challenged. Rising disenchantment with the current direction of health care in the United States resulting from giant for-profit takeovers of hospitals led an ad hoc committee of physicians and nurses in Boston to publish a "call to action" for the defense of health care (Lown, Woolhandler, & Avorn, 1997). For the continuing complex process of restructuring health care services in the United States and England, see McKee, Ferlie, and Hyde (2008). This movement can serve as a warning to Canadians who value their universal health care system.

The new emphasis on primary care has tremendous implications for health educators and administrators and the provision of psychosocial and crisis care. Besides the general challenge of conducting consultation and community education programs, mental health and crisis professionals face other major obstacles. Their work is often devalued because it is not generally carried out within mainstream health institution contexts such as hospitals. Also, there is often no insurance coverage for the work done; or mental health service is reimbursed at much lower rates than biomedical care. This disparity was partially addressed in the United States with the 2008 Mental Health Parity and

Addiction Equity Act, which requires that health policies offering both physical and mental health benefits must treat both benefits similarly (i.e., similar co-pays, number of allowed visits, duration of treatment, and scope of services) ("Parity," 2010). The pressure for crisis service is increased by the greater vulnerability of people who lack health insurance and so cannot obtain preventive mental health care without serious financial hardship. These obstacles and the issues contributing to them underscore the importance of sound consultation and community education programs in crisis and psychosocial care (see Chapter 10).

International Attention to Violence Prevention and Victim-Survivor Care

Past government reports in Canada and the United States on victimization by violence pointed to the necessity of expanding crisis services and assuring that health, social service, and criminal justice workers receive basic training in assisting victims in crisis (Attorney General's Task Force on Family Violence, 1984; Hoff, 1995; President's Task Force on Victims of Crime, 1982; Ristock, 1995; Rodgers, 1994; Surgeon General's Workshop on Violence and Public Health, 1986). Yet despite the fact that several decades have passed since these training recommendations were made, many faculty either feel unqualified to teach this content or cannot squeeze it into an already overcrowded curriculum, although it is increasingly recognized by some (Coretta, 2008; Hamberger, 2007; Hoff & Ross, 1993; Woodtli & Breslin, 2002). The above documents, along with numerous texts (e.g., Campbell & Humphreys, 1993; Edleson & Eisikovits, 1996; Hoff, 2010a), reveal the importance of collaboration between various human service workers (health, social service, and criminal justice). It has been observed, however, by some grassroots groups that when health professionals do take an interest in the issue of violence, they also like to take control and "professionalize" the process of working with victim-survivors and their assailants. This not only results in fragmentation of effort that ill serves those needing services but also discredits the work of often unrecognized advocates and frontline crisis workers (see also Chapter 9; Hoff, 2010a; Hoff & Morgan, 2011).

There is also growing recognition of the interplay between victimization by violence (physical, sexual, and emotional) and subsequent depression, suicidality, substance abuse, homelessness, and various physiological and psychiatric pathologies (Hoff, 2010a; Hoff et al., 2009; Stephens, 1985). We should also note that the terminology *victim-survivor* is intended to acknowledge explicitly one's victimization but simultaneously convey an abused person's potential for growth, development, and empowerment, for instance, a status beyond the dependency implied by *victim* (Mawby & Walklate, 1994; McCullough, 1995).

Attention to violence prevention is even more significant because of the life-and-death dimensions of many crisis situations. Here, the work of Morton Bard (1972) is still instructive, particularly around increased workplace violence in the United States and Canada (Runyan, 2001; see also www.crisisprograms.org). The crisis intervention training programs for police officers developed by Bard in New York City resulted in a significant reduction in the number of injuries and deaths of officers on the job. Also, when officers made appropriate referrals of distressed people to mental health facilities, most agencies had no crisis programs providing the immediate access to service demanded by these life-threatening circumstances. This situation has improved in some communities and in numerous violence prevention programs in various work settings. In fact, the (U.S.) Occupational Safety and Health Services Administration (OSHA) now offers guidelines for violence prevention and intervention protocols to be in place as a federal safety standard (see Churchill, 1995).

Clinicians in many psychiatric facilities increasingly recognize the inherent linkage between numerous clients' psychopathologies and somatic complaints and earlier crisis points, especially victimization by violence (Hoff & Morgan, 2011; Rieker & Carmen, 1986; Sugg & Inui, 1992). Clearly, if crisis care was not available as *primary* prevention, with posttraumatic stress responses predictably following (Burgess & Holmstrom, 1979; van der Kolk, 1987), it is imperative that the *original* source of distress finally be addressed in *tertiary* settings. One psychiatric hospital in Ontario reported that at least 83% of female psychiatric clients had histories of victimization that were significantly related to current psychosocial stress or psychopathology (Bourget, 1993); other studies support this finding (Hamilton, Jensvold, Rothblum, & Cole, 1995). Research now documents that victimization injury holds the potential for later psychopathologies and death when support and other assistance are not available as the first crisis response to trauma (Hoff, 1990, 2010a). The implementation of trauma-informed services for all women and appropriate training for all workers is imperative (Elliott, Bjelajac, Fallot, Markoff, & Reed, 2005).

It is also clear that mental health professionals are rarely the first to see victim-survivors of violence; rather, abused women and sexual assault victims most frequently have their *initial* contact with the health care system through emergency medical, primary care, or prenatal services. This pattern underscores the key role of *general* health care professionals at entry points in psychosocial and crisis assessment, intervention, and timely referral for *immediate* assistance during crisis from victimization (Adamowski, 1989; Hoff, 1992, 1993a, 2010a; Hoff & Morgan, 2011). Because this is a value-laden topic, however, many primary care professionals are reluctant to inquire into violence issues. As for assailants, many people now recognize the connections between violence, sex role stereotypes, learned aggressive behavior, and socioeconomic disparities based on gender. For example, despite popular misconceptions, most violence against women, male and female children, and other men is committed by heterosexual males, although rates of violence by girls and women are increasing (Ellickson, Saner, & McGuigan, 1997; Hoover & Juul, 1993, p. 28; Walker, 1993, p. 21).

The Role of Crisis Care in Suicide Prevention

After decades of research, education, and program development, suicide and parasuicide—especially among youth, older white males, substance abusers, and male veterans—remain major public health problems worldwide. In a recent U.S. national survey, 8.3 million Americans ages 18 and older indicated serious thoughts of suicide in the past year, of which 2.3 million adults made a plan and 1.1 million adults made an attempt (Office of Applied Studies, 2009). In 1999, U.S. Surgeon General Dr. David Satcher declared suicide a national health problem and put out a Call to Action for all 50 states to draft and implement their own suicide prevention plan (U.S. Public Health Service, 1999). In an effort to modify the social infrastructure, thereby altering the basic attitudes about suicide and changing the judicial, educational, social service and health care systems, the National Strategy for Suicide Prevention (U.S. Public Health Service, 2001) outlined 11 goals and 68 objectives with the intention that effective implementation would assist the United States in reaching the suicide prevention goals outlined in *Healthy People 2010*. In 2005, the National Suicide Prevention Lifeline (1-800-273-TALK) was launched. Lifeline consists of a network of more than 140 crisis centers across the United States. By 2007 the Lifeline's Suicide Risk Assessment Standards were implemented with all callers being assessed for suicide risk (Joiner et al., 2007). More information about the National Suicide Prevention Lifeline can be found at www.suicidepreventionlifeline.org.

Despite the efforts of organizations dedicated to preventing unnecessary death by suicide, programs such as 24/7 hotlines are not always well coordinated with community health and mental health services. Although depression is a major correlate (some would say cause) of suicide, there has been insufficient attention to suicide as the culmination of life's accumulated problems that appear insurmountable to the despairing person. These include somatic illness, substance abuse, victimization by violence (including sexual assault), and inadequate support in coping with life's daily problems as well as acute crises. International concern with the growing problem of suicide was addressed in a report of the WHO Division of Mental Health outlining national policy strategies from a 1993 conference held in Calgary and Banff, Alberta, Canada (Ramsay & Tanney, 1996; United Nations, 1996). This report also contained Finland's national strategy, the only known example of the time that integrated the functions of all public and private health and social service institutions toward the goal of suicide prevention.

Integrating Crisis Protocols Into Routine Health Care

Although the role of nurses, physicians, and others as first responders during crises in acute and long-term care health facilities is self-evident, their practice in this role is by no means systematic (Hoff & Morgan, 2011; Kurz & Stark, 1988). Sugg and Inui (1992), for example, cited physicians' reluctance to open "Pandora's box" through routine inquiry about battering among emergency service clients. Traditional values defining battery as a "private" matter, plus lack of formal preparation, explain this pattern in part (Dobash & Dobash, 1979). The legacy of considering violence among intimates and family members as a "private" issue may still serve as a barrier to prevention and identification of persons at risk from violence and abuse. There are two factors that feed into this lack of inquiry: the continuing "mind–body" split in medical practice and the well-known fact of the long time it takes to bring about social and attitudinal change when deeply embedded values and powerful vested interests are involved (Hoff, 2010a).

Research on violence during pregnancy by McFarlane, Parker, Loeken, and Bullock (1992), which found that prenatal clinic staff typically have failed to identify battery victims among a population whose risk rate for abuse is at least 25%, and many others led to a policy by The Joint Commission on Accreditation of Healthcare Organizations (JCAHO, 1993) requiring victimization to be included in intake health history forms as a condition of accreditation in the United States. Accordingly, many institutions are now working toward the implementation of protocols highlighting crisis assessment and intervention as supplements to current standard treatment (for instance, asking questions such as "Are there any significant new stressors in your life?" "Do you feel safe in your home?" or "Has anyone been violent with you?"). Kendall et al. (2009) confirmed the value of screening and assessment for intimate partner violence (IPV) among emergency department (ED) patients, finding that an ED intervention with advocacy counseling, safety planning, resource referral, and follow-up could assist victims of IPV to feel safer and decrease violence in their lives.

In addition to the generally increased attention to violence and its impact on health and mental health worldwide, health workers must also note any increased vulnerability to crisis experienced by individuals and communities disadvantaged as a result of bias based on race, ethnicity, age, immigrant status, sexual identity, physical or mental disability, or economic disadvantage (see Toney, 2009).

Data suggest, then, that the time is long overdue for the integration of psychosocial aspects of primary care—including *crisis assessment and intervention*—as a routine part of health service delivery. The following example illustrates that fear, rather than knowledge about crisis and psychosocial assessment and intervention, was the driving force in the care of a dying AIDS patient.

Example: Kevin Barnes

Mr. Kevin Barnes, age 35, is dying of AIDS. He tells his nurse that he wants to end his misery by jumping from a hospital window. Instead of talking with Mr. Barnes (who was physically unable to leave his bed) to ascertain the meaning of this self-destructive message and his risk for suicide (essential elements of the crisis model), the frightened nurse requests consultation with a psychiatrist. Mr. Barnes is subsequently discharged as a measure to prevent a suicide on the hospital unit. Later it is learned that the message behind Mr. Barnes's suicide threat was his desire to go home and die without the tubes and other trappings of high-technology approaches to dying people. Apparently he felt that a suicide threat was the best means of communicating his displeasure with hospital care of the dying. Mr. Barnes died naturally, at home, 2 days after hospital discharge.

Clearly, primary and acute care health providers have a pivotal role in suicide risk assessment and the prevention of suicide and possible psychopathologies. For further discussion, see Hoff and Morgan (2011), Chapters 2–5 and www.crisisprograms.org.

Collaborative Versus Hierarchical Service Delivery Models

Complementing the WHO emphasis on primary care and community-based service models is the centrality of client empowerment and collaboration in the design and delivery of health services. Besides greater attention to consumer satisfaction in general, collaborative approaches to health care received major support from the burgeoning women's health movement that began in the 1970s (Boston Women's Health Book Collective, 1992; Miller, 1986). Increasing numbers of women have been enlightened regarding the centuries-old gender bias in health care research, education, and practice, and the abuse of power at the expense of women in traditional hierarchical service delivery models. For example, historically, cancer research money was not earmarked for any "women's" cancers (such as breast or uterine cancer). In the 1970s and 1980s, public pressure from the grassroots women's health and environmental movements prompted the increase of money into medical research for female cancers.

Collaborative models not only benefit women but also are pivotal in the delivery of crisis services for several reasons. First, in crisis situations where the person has been victimized by violence or abuse, a central dynamic of the traumatic experience is the feeling of disempowerment; through physical, psychological, or sexual force, the perpetrator exerts power over another person against the individual's consent, resulting not only in physical and emotional trauma but also in profound feelings of powerlessness. Hierarchical (versus collaborative) service models therefore hold the potential of reproducing exploitative power relations and exacerbating the loss of control that a victim-survivor already feels. Implementing a recovery orientation or trauma-informed service requires changing the nature of the relationship between providers and consumers to enable power sharing. It also addresses the need for providers to have hope for their clients, to individualize recovery through client goal setting, and to promote the client's autonomy rather than foster increased dependence (Elliott et al., 2005; Jacobson, 2004). It is only when providers learn what the client wants that they can more easily see them as whole persons (Felton, Barr, & Clark, 2006).

Second, collaborative team models are necessary to ensure the safety of workers who deal with high-risk crisis situations, especially where there is potential of violence and risk to life. Third, collaborative models are among the best preventive measures for avoiding the burnout experienced by many crisis workers when they feel inadequately supported or are pressured (often for economic incentives) into facing high-risk crisis situations alone (see Chapter 8).

Another area that needs increased collaboration is between paraprofessional crisis workers and traditional psychiatric practitioners. Historically, paraprofessionals and lay people played a large role in responding to the urgent need for crisis programs. Meanwhile, traditional psychiatric agencies were pressured to lend their professional expertise to the growing need for crisis services. The 1965 call for a 24/7 crisis response through U.S. federal legislation for community mental health centers went unanswered for years in all but a few communities and was often embroiled in political conflict (Levine, 1981).

One result of these historical developments has been a false dichotomy between traditional psychiatric emergency care and crisis service arising from indigenous community sources. In some communities, this dichotomy goes so far as to suggest a clear demarcation between "clinical" crises (primarily psychiatric emergencies) and "social" crises—as though there are no *social* sources or ramifications of psychiatric upsets, and no *clinical* manifestations of a so-called social crisis like losing one's home or job. One result of this dichotomy is the designation of artificial work boundaries between those responding to "social" and "clinical" crises. These dichotomies are often exacerbated by funding bodies (for example, mental health departments) that fail to provide financial support to 24/7 hotlines responding to all kinds of crises, including those of psychiatric clients.

These false dichotomies are also visible in the imbalance between biomedical and psychosocial facets of practice and in service coordination conflicts that have detrimental effects for people in emotional distress or crisis. They highlight the need for more widespread knowledge about agency and individual practice standards, common concepts and principles guiding practice, and other interdisciplinary issues that this book addresses.

Crisis Intervention, Psychiatric Emergency Stabilization, and Brief Treatment

The blurring of these three service modalities presents additional complexities to the uneven practice of crisis intervention and the collaborative arrangements so pivotal to this work. Some of the confusion relates to the issues already discussed, including the widespread tendency to "medicalize" or "pathologize" essentially "normal" life events. One of the most obvious examples of this trend is the prescription of psychotropic drugs for people who primarily need support and crisis intervention, not pharmacotherapy. This can be seen in an instance such as when an employee experiences the psychosocial impact of job loss, a personal problem requiring individual and family resolution. The incidence of increased family violence, suicidal vulnerability, and inappropriate coping strategies leading to health risks is prime fodder for the quick drug fix to deal with the stress and anxiety accompanying this life-altering event. The broader socioeconomic and political issues underlying these major workforce changes are thereby masked.

Significantly, when the abuse of prescription drugs is noted in crisis training programs for health professionals, a typical response is "That's what people want … . They don't want to talk about their problems." Equally significant are several related phenomena: (a) the public's common acceptance of "tranquilizing" rather than working through life's problems (even for adolescents), (b) the origin of this mentality in the pharmaceutical and health care industry's profit motive and the advertising and practice that follow, and (c) the contrasting unawareness among many people of the option of nonmedical crisis care during stressful or traumatic life events. Ironically (and sadly), Rogers's (1971) assessment of the "drug abuse" issue is as relevant today as it was decades ago—"just what the doctor ordered" (see also Hamilton et al., 1995). Whitaker (2010) provides extensive documentation of national and international research revealing the abusive practices of pharmacotherapy leading to chronic illness and lifetime support on Social Security Disability Insurance (SSDI). Whitaker's mind-blowing exposé of the collusion between psychiatrists, the pharmaceutical industry, and how the National Institute of Mental Health (NIMH) in fact aided and abetted the entire process may spark the fourth revolution in the mental health field—after Freud, the crisis model, and the original psychopharmacology revolution.

These issues suggest the need for further delineation of the distinctions and overlap between crisis, psychiatric, and brief treatment modalities. Such clarification assumes the commonly accepted definition of crisis as a normative (rather than a pathological) life experience—albeit with the potential for pathology. Grof and Grof (1989) argued for a distinction between true psychiatric and psychotic disorders and a range of experiences they defined as "spiritual emergencies" that need to be worked through and not tranquilized, medicated, and pathologized. In a related vein, Perry (1990) emphasized "uncommon interventions" that contrast with biomedical models of treatment. De Jong and Kleber (2007) identified that many people deal with traumatic experiences by giving meaning to those experiences. In many non-Western societies this is accomplished through the spiritual world, a concept that most Western practitioners are uncomfortable with. In Sierra Leone, Médecins Sans Frontières utilized spiritual leaders both as advisors and for referral options in the programs they developed. Quinn (2007) found that among families living in Ghana, those in urban areas and influenced by Western beliefs were more likely to have a biomedical understanding of mental health and subsequent treatment, as compared to those families living in rural areas, where a more traditional understanding utilized "social treatment" in the healing process.

Katschnig and Konieczna (1990) noted the interchangeable use in Europe of the terms *crisis* (arising from psychosocial stress) and *psychiatric emergency* (acute psychotic, suicidal, and aggressive behaviors). Though there are obvious overlaps between these two populations in distress, the differences between the terms should be noted. For example, hotline and distress center workers routinely work with suicidal callers, but usually do not refer to them as "psychiatric emergencies." Or, a chemically dependent person may call a crisis hotline for help after a heated argument with one's spouse. Besides assessment of danger to self and others, such persons should be counseled to seek assessment and treatment for the chronic condition of substance dependence. The key definitions offered herein are intended to clarify the crisis model's distinct characteristics. Here we elaborate further on the terms *crisis intervention*, *emergency psychiatry*, and *psychotherapy* (see also the glossary).

In psychiatric emergency situations, the term *crisis stabilization* is common. During instances of such acute disturbance, chemical restraint (the use of powerful psychotropic drugs) may be indicated. This medical intervention typically occurs in hospital emergency departments. Ideally, the health facility should include 24- to 72-hour crisis or "holding" beds for those who, even with drug treatment, cannot be discharged because of serious danger to self or others. During these "crisis stabilization" periods, crisis intervention and counseling focus on protective measures and attention to the situation or event that triggered the acute crisis episode, for example, disruptive behavior in mental health transitional housing that resulted in homelessness, or failure to take psychotropic medication for bipolar illness.

In contrast to psychotherapy, crisis intervention *avoids* probing into deep-seated psychological problems; hence its main features and strategies can be understood and effectively practiced in relatively short training courses compared to the years of preparation needed for effective psychotherapy practice. But a caveat seems in order: Although crisis workers employ some of the same techniques as therapists (for example, active listening), *crisis intervention is not psychotherapy*. But neither is it a simple procedure of "balancing" people back to precrisis equilibrium. The common but static concept of "equilibrium" and general systems approaches to crisis intervention that have dominated the crisis theory literature shortchange its historic emphasis on growth, development, and people's active participation in crisis resolution (Antonovsky, 1987; Hoff et al., 2009). Ramsay (1997) elaborated further on these concepts in his discussion of crisis and chaos theory.

Fortunately, after years of enduring "band-aid" status from many quarters (Hoff et al., 2009, ch. 1), pioneers in the crisis field are gratified that this timely helping approach is now widely accepted as the "treatment of choice" for numerous clients (Roberts, 1990, p. xviii; see also Ontario Ministry of Health, 1993). But therein is implied a question: Is crisis intervention now widely accepted primarily as an *expedient cost containment device* for countless problems, or is it one of several necessary elements in a comprehensive system of care? And, is crisis intervention a "treatment," or is it both more and less than that? If crisis intervention is labeled *therapy* when a psychotherapist conducts it, what is it when a nontherapist, such as a trained volunteer, police officer, community youth worker, or surgical care nurse, conducts it? The inclusion of crisis intervention strategies on behalf of a client who becomes suicidal or assaultive during the course of hospital or longer term treatment does not warrant reconstituting crisis intervention as "therapy." Though some analysts may argue that this is mere word quibbling, language *does* reveal values, ideology, and dominant paradigms affecting practice.

Because the essential features of formal crisis intervention have not changed much since the era when mental health professionals deemed it a mere "band-aid," how do we now explain its widespread adoption? The redefinition of crisis intervention as therapy following its historical minimization may partly explain the continued reluctance of *general* health practitioners (i.e., nonpsychotherapists) to incorporate the model into routine health care practice or instances of workplace violence, for example. Understandably, most nonpsychiatric physicians and nurses do not think of themselves as psychotherapists (Hoff & Morgan, 2011).

It seems more than coincidental that the crisis movement's continued popularity has emerged in concert with several other factors. First, as noted earlier, international anecdotal evidence and national surveys in the United States and

Canada (Ross et al., 1998; Woodtli & Breslin, 1996) revealed that formal crisis courses (or specified content beyond a few hours) in health professionals' preparation are the exception rather than the rule, a situation essentially unchanged since Berman's 1983 survey addressing suicidology content. Second, fiscal constraints have tightened in the face of worldwide recession and escalation of health care costs. Third, the bias against equality of service and insurance coverage for persons with emotional and mental disabilities continues.

From our definitions of crisis intervention, it follows that assistance with life's common stressors and traumas resides essentially in the empathic and social support processes embedded in *normal* social life, that is, in "natural crisis management" (Hansell, 1976; Hoff et al., 2009). However, life is not quite that straightforward and simple; hence, the relevance of further distinctions regarding crisis service:

Catastrophic life events: Some traumatic life events, particularly victimization by violence or massive losses from disaster or catastrophe, fall outside and beyond life's "normal" ups and downs. The potential for serious emotional damage or even death from these traumatic events increases to the extent that the origin of the trauma (a) can be traced to sociocultural sources (Cloward & Piven, 1979; Gerhardt, 1979; Hoff, 1990); (b) challenges the person's attempt to derive "meaning" from the event (Antonovsky, 1979, 1987; Janoff-Bulman, 1992; Lifton & Olson, 1976); or (c) occurs coincidentally with *prior* psychopathology (as discussed next). A word of caution, however, comes from Ethan Watters's book *Crazy Like Us: The Globalization of the American Psyche* (2010) regarding the reckless application of Western mental health practices to non-Western catastrophes.

Crisis vulnerability of the seriously and persistently mentally disabled: Persons already suffering from chronic emotional and mental disorders, many of whom need longer term psychotherapy, psychotropic drug regimens, rehabilitative services, and continuing care, are at the same time more vulnerable to experiencing negative outcomes from the same stressful life events found among the general population. Hence, to prevent further debilitation and costly care, and to maximize the benefits of other service modalities required by this high-risk population, 24/7 access to crisis prevention and intervention is crucial (see "open-dialog therapy" in the glossary; Whitaker, 2010, pp. 339–344; and Watters, 2010, for cross-cultural perspective).

By contrast, as disaster workers have long noted, even individuals with severe and chronic mental or emotional disability can rise to the occasion and participate in a community crisis response to those in acute need, if they are expected and called upon to do so (Koegler & Hicks, 1972). Clearly, in a humane society, even those with serious disabilities have a social role beyond dependency. For example, a 60-year-old woman who had spent years in psychiatric treatment (including lengthy periods of hospitalization) and continuing care found great meaning and purpose in volunteering with an agency dedicated to advocacy and prevention of HIV/AIDS following the death of her son from complications of AIDS. In a similar vein, the director of the Gladys Ray Shelter, in Fargo, North Dakota, has witnessed several examples of the "guests" of this homeless shelter, which serves the most chronically mentally disabled and addicted, "taking care" of each other both on the street and in advocating for services. Evidence suggests that performing acts of "required helpfulness" (helping someone else whose immediate need is greater) can result in an increased sense of self-efficacy, increased self-esteem, social recognition, and inoculation against future stress. This is applicable to healthy individuals as well as those with psychiatric or other disabilities or illnesses (Rachman, 1990, p. 177).

As we consider intersecting service modalities for an array of crisis situations, the need for coordination and communication among various players and agencies cannot be overstated. For example, community hotline services are obviously a vital part of community response networks, but their potential impact is greatly diminished when not systematically coordinated with professional psychiatric services. When mental health professionals astutely integrate—across units and agencies—the distinctive features of crisis prevention, assessment, and intervention with behavioral, psychotherapeutic, and drug stabilization approaches, much chaos and costly institutional care can be avoided—not to mention "revolving door" episodes, staff burnout, and a vicious cycle of hopelessness among clients and staff (Whitaker, 2010). Such synthesis of helping modalities, however, requires prior analysis of the *distinctive features of each.*

Example: Debriefing Following Suicide

Following a patient suicide, an outpatient psychiatry group was debriefed by a crisis intervention–trained psychologist. The remaining patients, some of whom were actively suicidal, all opted to form a buddy system to provide mutual telephone support during the evening and night following the tragedy. They also contracted with each other to phone the nursing unit the following morning to let each other know that they were each alright. Involved staff were also debriefed. For the following 24 hours, the psychologist remained on call to (a) provide staff with a break during which to begin to recover, (b) make follow-up telephone calls on the first evening to patients assessed as highly suicidal, and (c) handle any potential crisis calls from patients or staff. Brief follow-up contacts were made with both patients and staff over the next 10 days.

Because crisis intervention is one of the newest of various mental health service modalities, some of the disarray concerning the crisis model is understandable. The human and financial costs, however, are too high to tolerate continued confusion or underuse of this essential element of comprehensive health care. Accordingly, the five life examples in Chapter 2 review and clarify how crisis assessment and intervention strategies can be integrated with routine psychosocial care and coordinated more systematically across all sectors of health and mental health service delivery.

Research and Theory Development

Research and theory development is another issue needing attention in the crisis field. Even though historically important figures like Gerald Caplan (1964) and Erik Erikson (1963) emphasized cultural and social factors influencing the crisis experience, most U.S.-based sources reflect a psychodynamic emphasis and the dominant theme of individualism in American society. Though Canada's cultural heritage is more communitarian than that of the United States, many other issues reveal similar strains across the two cultures. The social and cultural origins of many crisis situations influence the current status of crisis theory development, particularly victimization by crime and the various forms of human-made disaster. In an attempt to fill the general sociocultural gap in crisis theory, Hoff (1990) developed, from her research with battered women, a crisis paradigm discussed further in Chapter 2. The psychosociocultural perspective of this paradigm, along with complementary works, exhibits the dominant theoretical underpinnings and values of this sourcebook, as well as the interface between routine crisis work and psychosocial care in general and specialized health care arenas.

The core elements of theory and practice in crisis and psychosocial care must be identified, regardless of professional discipline and service setting. Thus, although most communities have always cared for distressed members, the systematic approach to crisis care by educators, practitioners, and administrators as an organized body of knowledge and practice is just a few decades old. Therefore, we urge educators and practitioners to examine critically the concepts they choose for training and guiding service (see www.crisisprograms.org). The practice implications of theory selection are illustrated in Figure 1.2, depicting the relationship between educational or service philosophy, objectives, content, methods (of education and training or service delivery), and evaluation. The broad parameters of a comprehensive approach might include information based on a particular philosophy about psychosocial stressors and the crisis experience, the people experiencing these, and the human service delivery system.

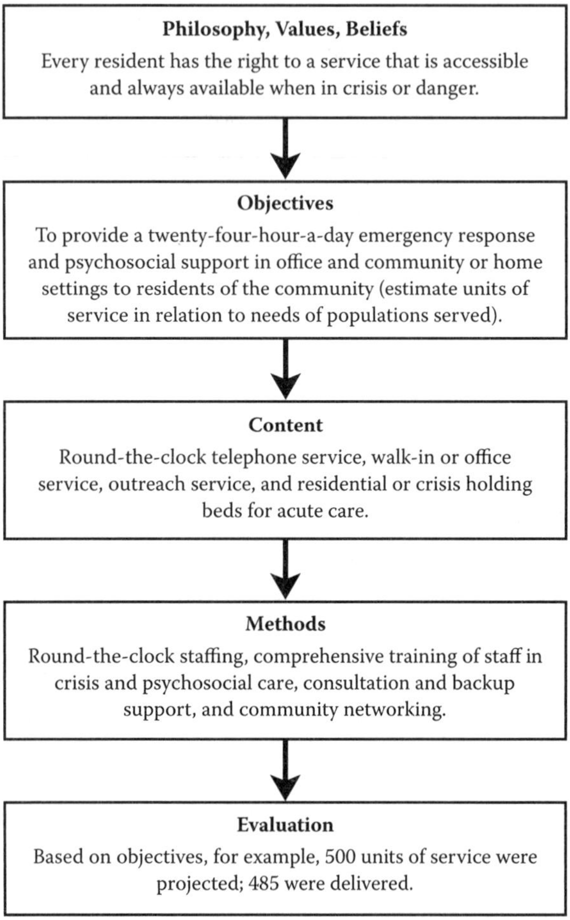

Figure 1.2 Crisis program elements. Chart illustrating how program elements flow from philosophy. Reprinted by permission of Hoff and Miller (1987).

Crisis Service Delivery: Differential Approaches

We have already stated that psychiatric or indigenous community groups deliver crisis service with particular attention to the sociocultural roots and ramifications of many crisis situations. Now, we elaborate on the different approaches that can be used in crisis work while preserving the core aspects of the crisis model that distinguish it from other forms of service, regardless of the person delivering it. This discussion lays the foundation for later presentation of core content and its application to different groups and in various settings (see Chapters 3 and 5). Regardless of different approaches to crisis prevention, intervention, and counseling, four essential steps characterize the process of helping people in distress or crisis:

1. Psychosocial assessment of the individual, family, or community in crisis. This always includes assessment for victimization trauma, and evaluation for the risk of suicide and/or assault on others. Some health professionals may wish to add a diagnosis at this stage of the helping process. When doing so, the least stigmatizing of DSM-IV-TR diagnoses is recommended (American Psychiatric Association, 2000). See Hoff and Morgan (2011), Chapter 2, "Mental Health Assessment and Service Planning," for an overview and critique of assessment approaches, including psychiatrist McHugh's "perspectives."
2. Development of a plan with the distressed person, family, or group, based on assessment data.
3. Implementing that plan by drawing on personal, social, and material resources.
4. Follow-up and evaluation of the service plan and helping process, including resolution of problems or crisis by the individual, family, or community in crisis.

Generically, these steps correlate with the "problem-solving process," which is employed by all trained people in health and human service domains. In this book, a client-centered empowerment approach is promoted.

Individuals or family members in natural settings, formally prepared professionals, or trained crisis workers in telephone, office, college residence hall, nursing home, social agency, community, mobile unit, hospital, or other settings can implement these steps. The essentials of care for distressed people can be offered in specialized settings for crisis service, or be integrated with psychotherapy or other forms of human interaction. For example, in *natural* situations, parents who know the warning signs of suicide (usually through public health education programs) can respond effectively with their own child during the normal process of parent–child interaction.

In *formal* settings, trained volunteers and others can implement the basics of crisis care as a specialized service or with other kinds of needed service, for example:

- Medical treatment of an accident victim (paramedics, nurses, physicians)
- Death notification or rescue of a sexual assault victim (police)

- Comfort of suicide survivors* (clergy, nurses, social workers)
- Long-term treatment of emotionally and mentally disabled people (mental health workers)
- Social service to abusive parents (social workers)
- Support of battered women and other survivors of abuse (various victim advocates)
- Support of people with acute illness, such as HIV/AIDS, and their families, including friends or significant others (everyone)
- Support of people suffering job loss, disaster, and all that these events entail (everyone)

These examples underscore the artificiality of classifying some crises as "social" and others as "clinical," as discussed earlier. Being clear about the crisis model and its myriad applications aids in its successful integration with the general psychosocial care and treatment of the physically ill or emotionally or psychiatrically disabled, and people distressed by normal and catastrophic life events (Hoff et al., 2009; Whitaker, 2010).

The creative application of these basic elements of the crisis model will vary according to personal style and will be influenced by factors such as professional training in particular disciplines. Regardless of these individual variations, crisis trainers and practitioners should recognize the influence of their values and historical sources on their teaching and practice with people in crisis. Also, everyone involved in the crisis field needs to acknowledge the crisis approach's limits and the cultural meaning of the popularity of the crisis model during an era of fiscal constraint. There is no substitute for 24/7 local response to people in acute distress. However, the crisis model needs revitalization as *one* aspect of "primary prevention" as promulgated by WHO and originally proposed by Caplan (1964), while avoiding rigid formulas and remembering its importance in secondary and tertiary prevention, especially among those already more vulnerable from abuse or psychiatric disability.

Crisis intervention must not be regarded as a panacea for all social, emotional, and mental problems. For example, if adequate psychiatric care is not provided for seriously disabled people out of a misplaced concern for cost containment or profit making, the psychiatric patient discharged too early with only a drug prescription and without necessary community support may feel forced to "invent" a ticket to hospital admission by a serious suicide attempt.

* *Suicide survivors* in this book refers to those people (e.g., family and friends) left behind by a person who has died by suicide. The term is sometimes mistakenly taken to mean people who have survived a suicide attempt.

Such suicidality clearly is "iatrogenic" (that is, caused by the provider or by agency policy) or "socially constructed" as a result of inadequacies in the mental health care system.

The limitations of crisis intervention and the need to see it in larger socio-cultural and political perspective are dramatically illustrated in the following vignette. McKinlay (1979) discussed the futility of tinkering with "downstream" versus "upstream" endeavors:

> My friend, Irving Zola, relates the story of a physician trying to explain the dilemmas of the modern practice of medicine: "You know," he said, "sometimes it feels like this. There I am standing by the shore of a swiftly flowing river and I hear the cry of a drowning man. So I jump into the river, put my arms around him, pull him to shore and apply artificial respiration. Just when he begins to breathe, another cry for help. So back in the river again, reaching, pulling, applying, breathing, and then another yell. Again and again, without end, goes the sequence. You know, I am so busy jumping in, pulling them to shore, applying artificial respiration, that I have *no* time to see who the hell is upstream pushing them all in." (p. 9)

Evaluating the Content and Context of Training, Education, and Service Programs

The Accreditation Committee of the AAS, a group that stresses the importance of national standards for crisis service and training, has addressed some of these issues in recent decades. In 1976, it launched a program to certify/accredit comprehensive crisis programs in the United States. Accreditation ensures consumers that the services provided by an accredited crisis program meet at least the minimum standards in administration, training, and service delivery recommended by national crisis experts—the *content.*

For crisis trainers and administrators, the 10th edition of the *Organization Accreditation Standards Manual* (American Association of Suicidology, 2011), originally the *Certification Standards Manual* (Hoff & Wells, 1989), represents a skeleton of standards, whereas this book adds substance to the bones in developing specific educational and training or service programs, evaluating their work, and preparing for national accreditation (see Chapter 3 and www.crisisprograms.org). The need exists for an exchange of ideas and strategies with people either contemplating new crisis training and service programs or wishing to evaluate their programs in light of others' experience and national standards.

The task of evaluating the *context* of various education, training, and service programs is tailored much more to the unique needs and resources of individual settings (urban, rural) and agencies. Though *content* and *context* represent different aspects of a total process, one depends on the other. Thus, the core elements of a curriculum or crisis program (the *content*) can be identified and recognized internationally, whereas its distinctive features depend on the program's individual *context* and philosophy, including, for example, the concerns and values of particular ethnic or tribal groups served.

As we evaluate the content and context of crisis training and service programs, we need to remember that our objectives, content, and methods of training and service delivery flow from the following:

- The nature and values of people in distress or crisis
- The society or environment in which these people reside, including their cultural and spiritual heritage
- The characteristics of the teaching and learning process
- The elements of the service delivery process

These beliefs vary from person to person and in different cultural settings. But whatever the beliefs and values are, it is important to be explicit about them, as they will inevitably affect work done with the client.

The remaining chapters address largely the *content* to be considered for such a developmental and evaluation process within the general framework of crisis and psychosocial care. Where content is not provided in detail, see www.crisisprograms.org.

References

Adamowski, K. (1989). *Family violence training project: Final report.* Toronto, Canada: Ontario Ministry of Health.

Agar-Jacomb, K., & Read, J. (2009). Mental health crisis services: What do service users need when in crisis? *Journal of Mental Health, 18*(2), 99–110.

Alberta Health Services. (2010). *Becoming the best: Alberta's 5-year health action plan.* Edmonton, Canada: Alberta Health and Wellness Communications.

American Association of Suicidology. (2011). *Organization accreditation standards manual* (10th ed.). Retrieved from http://www.suicidology.org/c/document_library/get_file?folderId=234&name=DLFE-306.pdf

American Psychiatric Association. (2000). *Diagnostic and statistical manual of mental disorders* (4th ed., text rev.). Washington, DC: Author.

Anthony, W. A. (1993). Recovery from mental illness: The guiding vision of the mental health service system in the 1990s. *Psychosocial Rehabilitation Journal, 16*(4), 11–23.

Antonovsky, A. (1979). *Health, stress, and coping*. San Francisco, CA: Jossey-Bass.

Antonovsky, A. (1987). *Unraveling the mystery of health*. San Francisco, CA: Jossey-Bass.

Armstrong, P., & Armstrong, H. (1996). *Wasting away: The undermining of Canadian health care*. Toronto, Canada: Oxford University Press.

Attorney General's Task Force on Family Violence. (1984). *Final report*. Washington, DC: U.S. Department of Justice.

Bard, M. (1972). *Police family crisis intervention and conflict management: An action research analysis*. Washington, DC: U.S. Department of Justice.

Bellah, R. (1985). *Habits of the heart: Individualism and commitment in American life*. New York, NY: Harper & Row.

Berman, L. (1983). *Survey of professional schools: Committee report to AAS board of directors*. Denver, CO: American Association of Suicidology.

Boston Women's Health Book Collective. (1992). *The new our bodies, ourselves*. New York, NY: Simon & Schuster.

Bourget, V. (1993). *Focus group data*. North Bay, ON, Canada: North Psychiatric Hospital, Department of Psychology.

Burgess, A., & Holmstrom, L. L. (1979). *Rape: Crisis and recovery*. Bowie, MD: Brady.

Campbell, J., & Humphreys, J. (1993). *Nursing care of survivors of family violence*. St. Louis, MO: Mosby.

Caplan, G. (1964). *Principles of preventive psychiatry*. New York, NY: Basic Books.

Capponi, P. (1992). *Upstairs in the crazy house*. Toronto, Canada: Penguin.

Cassidy, R. (1995). Supporting the development of a crisis management certificate program: A research project funded by the Calgary community adult learning association and the Canadian mental health association (Alberta division) in conjunction with the suicide prevention training programs. Unpublished manuscript.

Chandler, S. M. (1990). *Competing realities: The contested terrain of mental health advocacy*. New York, NY: Praeger.

Churchill, J. (1995, November). CISD policy development and implementation. *Employee Assistance*, 11–16.

Cloward, R. A., & Piven, F. F. (1979). Hidden protest: The channeling of female innovation and resistance. *Signs, 4*, 651–669.

Coretta, C. M. (2008). Domestic violence: A worldwide exploration. *Journal of Psychosocial Nursing & Mental Health Services, 46*(3), 26–35.

De Jong, K., & Kleber, R. J. (2007). Emergency conflict-related psychosocial interventions in Sierra Leone and Uganda. *Journal of Health Psychology, 12*(3), 485–497.

Dobash, R. P., & Dobash, R. E. (1979). *Violence against women: The case against the patriarchy*. New York, NY: Free Press.

Dorfman, S. (2000). Preventive interventions under managed care: Mental health and substance abuse services. (DHHS Publication No. SMA 00-3437). Rockville, MD: Center for Mental Health Services, Substance Abuse and Mental Health Services Administration.

Dziegielewski, S., & Roberts, A. R. (2004). Health care evidence-based practice: A product of political and cultural times. In A. R. Roberts and K. R. Yeager (Eds.), *Evidence-based practice manual: Research and outcome measures in health and human services*. Oxford, UK: Oxford University Press.

Edleson, J. L., & Eisikovits, Z. C. (Eds.). (1996). *Future interventions with battered women and their families.* Thousand Oaks, CA: Sage.

Ellickson, P., Saner, H., & McGuigan, K. A. (1997). Profiles of violent youth: Substance use and other concurrent problems. *American Journal of Public Health, 87*(6), 985–991.

Elliott, D. E., Bjelajac, P., Fallot, R. D., Markoff, L. S., & Reed, B. G. (2005). Trauma-informed or trauma-denied: Principles and implementation of trauma-informed services for women. *Journal of Community Psychology, 33*(4), 461–477.

Erikson, E. (1963). *Childhood and society* (2nd ed.). New York, NY: Norton.

Felton, B. J., Barr, A., & Clark, G. (2006). ACT team members' responses to training in recovery-oriented practices. *Psychiatric Rehabilitation Journal, 30*(2), 112–119.

Frese, F., Stanley, J., Kress, K., & Vogel-Scibilia, S. (2001). Integrating evidence-based practices and the recovery model. *Psychiatric Services, 52*(11), 1462–1468.

Gerhardt, U. (1979). Coping and social action: Theoretical reconstruction of the life-event approach. *Sociology of Health and Illness, 1*, 195–225.

Golan, N. (1969). When is a client in crisis? *Social Casework, 50*(7), 389–394.

Golan, N. (1978). *Treatment in crisis situations.* New York, NY: Free Press.

Grof, S., & Grof, C. (Eds.). (1989). *Spiritual emergency: When personal transformation becomes a crisis.* New York, NY: St. Martin's Press.

Haddad, M., Plummer, S., Taverner, A., Gray, R., Lee, S., Payne, F., & Knight, D. (2005). District nurses' involvement and attitudes to mental health problems: A three-area cross-sectional study. *Journal of Clinical Nursing, 14*, 976–985.

Hamberger, L. K. (2007). Preparing the next generation of physicians: Medical school and residency-based intimate partner violence curriculum and evaluation. *Trauma, Violence, & Abuse, 8*(2), 214–215.

Hamilton, J. A., Jensvold, M. F., Rothblum, E. D., & Cole, E. (Eds.). (1995). *Psychopharmacology from a feminist perspective.* New York, NY: Haworth Press.

Hansell, N. (1976). *The person in distress.* New York, NY: Human Sciences Press.

Health and Welfare Canada. (1986). *Achieving health for all: A framework for health promotion.* Ottawa, Canada: Author.

Hillman, J., & Ventura, M. (1993). *We've had a hundred years of psychotherapy and the world's getting worse.* San Francisco, CA: HarperSanFrancisco.

Hoff, L. A. (1990). *Battered women as survivors.* New York, NY: Routledge.

Hoff, L. A. (1992). Battered women: Understanding, identification, and assessment—a psychosociocultural perspective. *Journal of American Academy of Nurse Practitioners, 4*(4), 148–155.

Hoff, L. A. (1993a). Battered women: Intervention and prevention—psychosociocultural perspective. *Journal of the American Academy of Nurse Practitioners, 5*(1), 34–39.

Hoff, L. A. (1993b). Review essay: Health policy and the plight of the mentally ill. *Psychiatry, 56*(4), 400–419.

Hoff, L. A. (1995). *Violence issues: An interdisciplinary curriculum guide for health professionals.* Ottawa, Canada: Health Canada, Health Services Directorate (in English and French).

Hoff, L. A. (2010a). *Violence and abuse issues: Cross-cultural perspectives for health and social services.* London, UK: Routledge.

Hoff, L. A. (2010b). Violence issues: Education as prevention and intervention. Poster presentation at the WHO Safety 2010 World Conference, September 21–24, London, UK.

Hoff, L. A., Hallisey, B. J., & Hoff, M. (2009). *People in crisis: Clinical and diversity perspectives* (6th ed.). New York, NY: Routledge.

Hoff, L. A., & Miller, N. (1987). *Programs for people in crisis: A guide for educators, administrators, and clinical trainers.* Boston, MA: Northeastern University Custom Book Program.

Hoff, L. A., & Morgan, B. D. (2011). *Psychiatric and mental health essentials in primary care.* London, UK: Routledge.

Hoff, L. A., & Ross, M. (1993). *Curriculum guide for nursing: Violence against women and children.* Ottawa, Canada: University of Ottawa.

Hoff, L. A., & Wells, J. O. (Eds.). (1989). *Certification standards manual* (4th ed.). Washington, DC: American Association of Suicidology.

Hoover, J. H., & Juul, K. (1993). Bullying in Europe and the United States. *Journal of Emotional and Behavioral Problems, 2*(1), 25–29.

Institute of Medicine Committee on Quality of Health Care in America. (2001). *Crossing the quality chasm: A new health system for the 21st century.* Washington, DC: National Academies Press.

Jacobson, N. (2004). *In recovery: The making of mental health policy.* Nashville, TN: Vanderbilt University Press.

Janoff-Bulman, R. (1992). *Shattered assumptions: Toward a new psychology of trauma.* New York, NY: Free Press/Macmillan.

Johnson, A. B. (1990). *Out of bedlam: The truth about deinstitutionalization.* New York, NY: Basic Books.

Joiner, T., Kalafat, J., Draper, J., Stokes, H., Knudson, M., Berman, A. L., & McKeon, R. (2007). Establishing standards for the assessment of suicide risk among callers to the national suicide prevention lifeline. *Suicide and Life-Threatening Behavior, 37*(3), 353–365.

Joint Commission on Accreditation of Healthcare Organizations. (1993). *Accreditation manual for hospitals* (2 vols.). Oakbrook Terrace, IL: Author.

Joint Commission on Mental Health and Illness. (1961). *Action for mental health.* New York, NY: Basic Books.

Katschnig, H., & Konieczna, T. (1990). Innovative approaches to delivery of emergency services in Europe. In I. Marks & R. Scott (Eds.), *Mental health care delivery: Innovations, impediments and implementation* (pp. 85–103). Cambridge, UK: Cambridge University Press.

Kendall, J., Pelucio, M. T., Casaletto, J., Thompson, K. P., Barnes, S., Pettit, E., & Aldrich, M. (2009). Impact of emergency department intimate partner violence intervention. *Journal of Interpersonal Violence, 24*(2), 280–306.

Koegler, R. R., & Hicks, S. M. (1972). The destruction of a medical center by earthquake. *California Medicine, 116,* 63–67.

Kübler-Ross, E. (1969). *On death and dying.* New York, NY: Macmillan.

Kurz, D., & Stark, E. (1988). Not-so-benign neglect: The medical response to battering. In K. Yllo & M. Bograd (Eds.), *Feminist perspectives on wife abuse* (pp. 249–266). Newbury Park, CA: Sage.

Levine, M. (1981). *The history and politics of community mental health*. New York, NY: Oxford University Press.
Lifton, R. J., & Olson, E. (1976). The human meaning of total disaster: The Buffalo Creek experience. *Psychiatry, 39*, 1–18.
Lindemann, E. (1944). Symptomatology and management of acute grief. *American Journal of Psychiatry, 101*, 101–148.
Lown, B., Woolhandler, S., & Avorn, J. (1997). For our patients, not for profits: A call to action. *Journal of the American Medical Association, 278*, 1733–1738.
Marks, I. M. (1985). Controlled trial of psychiatric nurse therapists in primary care. *British Medical Journal, 290*, 1181–1184.
Marks, I. M., & Scott, R. (Eds.). (1990). *Mental health care delivery: Innovation, impediments and implementation*. Cambridge, UK: Cambridge University Press.
Mawby, R. I., & Walklate, S. (1994). *Critical victimology*. London, UK: Sage.
McCullough, C. J. (1995). *Nobody's victim*. New York, NY: Clarkson/Potter
McFarlane, J., Parker, B., Loeken, K., & Bullock, M. S. (1992). Assessing for abuse during pregnancy. *Journal of American Medical Association, 267*(23), 3176–3178.
McKee, L., Ferlie, E., & Hyde, P. (2008). *Organizing and reorganizing: Power and change in health care organizations*. Houndmills, UK: Palgrave MacMillan.
McKinlay, J. B. (1979). The case for re-focusing upstream: The political economy of illness. In E. G. Jaco (Ed.), *Patients, physicians, and illness* (3rd ed.). New York, NY: Free Press.
Miller, J. B. (1986). *Toward a new psychology of women* (Rev. ed.). Boston, MA: Beacon Press.
Morgan, B. (2010). End of life care for patients with mental illness and personality disorders. In B. Ferrell & N. Coyne (Eds.), *Textbook of palliative care nursing* (3rd ed.). New York, NY: Oxford University Press.
Morgan, S., & Hunte, K. (2008, March). One foot in the door. *Mental Health Today*, 32–35.
Morrison, D. (2004). Real-world use of evidence based treatments in community behavioral health care. *Psychiatric Services, 55*(5), 485–487.
National Institute of Mental Health. (1973). *Suicide prevention in the seventies*. Bethesda, MD: Author.
Office of Applied Studies. (2009). Results from the 2008 National Survey on Drug Use and Health: National findings (DHHS Publication No. SMA-09-4434, NSDUH Series H-36). Rockville, MD: Substance Abuse and Mental Health Services Administration.
Ontario Ministry of Health. (1993). *Putting people first: The reform of mental health services in Ontario*. Toronto, Canada: Author.
Parad, H. (1965). *Crisis intervention: Selected readings*. New York, NY: Family Service Association of America.
Parity: Landmark legislation takes effect: What are the implications for millions of Americans? (2010, January–February). *SAMHSA News*. Retrieved from http://www.samhsa.gov/samhsaNewsletter/Volume_18_Number_1/Parity.aspx
Perry, P. E. (1990). *Beyond context: Uncommon interventions with people in crisis*. Calgary, Canada: Synergy Library.
President's Task Force on Victims of Crime. (1982). *Final report*. Washington, DC: U.S. Government Printing Office.

Quinn, N. (2007). Beliefs and community responses to mental illness in Ghana: The experiences of family carers. *International Journal of Social Psychiatry, 53*(2), 175–188.

Rachlis, M., & Kushner, C. (1994). *Strong medicine: How to save Canada's health care system*. Toronto, Canada: HarperCollins.

Rachman, S. (1990). Learned resourcefulness in the performance of hazardous tasks. In M. Rosenbaum (Ed.), *Learned resourcefulness: On coping skills, self-control and adaptive behavior* (pp. 165–178). New York, NY: Springer.

Ramsay, R. F. (1997). Chaos theory and crisis intervention: Toward a new meaning of equilibrium in understanding and helping people in crisis. *Child and Family, 1*(3), 23–35.

Ramsay, R. F., & Tanney, B. L. (Eds.). (1996). *Global trends in suicide prevention: Toward the development of national strategies for suicide prevention*. Mumbai, India: Tata Institute of Social Sciences.

Regier, D. A., Goldberg, I. D., & Taube, C. A. (1978). The de facto U.S. mental health system: A public health perspective. *Archives of General Psychiatry, 35*, 685–693.

Rieker, P., & Carmen, E. (1986). The victim-to-patient process: The disconfirmation and transformation of abuse. *American Journal of Orthopsychiatry, 56*, 360–371.

Ristock, J. L. (1995). *Discussion papers on health/family violence issues*. Ottawa, Canada: Health Canada.

Roberts, A. R. (1990). Preface. In A. R. Roberts (Ed.), *Crisis intervention handbook*. Belmont, CA: Wadsworth.

Roberts, E., Cumming, J., & Nelson, K. (2005). A review of economic evaluations of community mental health care. *Medical Care Research and Review, 62*(5), 503–543.

Rodgers, K. (1994). Wife assault: The findings of a national survey. In *Juristat Service Bulletin*. Ottawa, Canada: Canadian Centre for Justice Statistics.

Rogers, M. J. (1971). Drug abuse: Just what the doctor ordered. *Psychology Today, 5*, 16–24.

Ross, M., Hoff, L. A., & Coutu-Wakulcyzk, G. (1998). Nursing curricula and violence issues: A study of Canadian schools of nursing. *Journal of Nursing Education, 37*(2), 53–60.

Runyan, C. W. (2001). Moving forward with research on the prevention of violence against workers. *American Journal of Preventive Medicine, 20*(2), 169–172.

Saunders, C. (1978). Hospice care. *American Journal of Medicine, 65*, 726–728.

Shindul-Rothschild, J., Berry, D., & Long-Middleton, E. (1996). Where have all the nurses gone? Final results of our patient care survey. *American Journal of Nursing, 96*(11), 25–39.

Solomon, P., & Stanhope, V. (2004). Recovery: Expanding the vision of evidence-based practice. *Brief Treatment and Crisis Intervention, 4*(4), 311–321.

Stein, L. I., & Test, M. A. (1980). Alternative to mental hospital treatment: I. Conceptual model, treatment program, and clinical evaluation. *Archives of General Psychiatry, 37*, 392–397.

Stephens, B. J. (1985). Suicidal women and their relationships with husbands, boyfriends, and lovers. *Suicide and Life-Threatening Behavior, 15*(2), 77–90.

Sugg, N. K., & Inui, T. (1992). Primary care physicians' response to domestic violence. *Journal of American Medical Association, 267*(23), 3157–3160.

Surgeon General's Workshop on Violence and Public Health. (1986). *Final report.* Washington, DC: Health Resources and Services Administration, U.S. Department of Public Health.

Test, M. A., & Scott, R. (1990). Theoretical and research bases of community care programs. In I. M. Marks & R. Scott (Eds.), *Mental health care delivery: Innovations, impediments and implementation* (pp. 11–16). Cambridge, UK: Cambridge University Press.

Toney, S. (2009). Integrated care, patient coaching show cost-saving promise. *Behavioral Healthcare, 29*(9), 21–23.

United Nations. (1996). *Prevention of suicide: Guidelines for the formulation and implementation of national strategies.* New York, NY: Author.

U.S. Department of Health and Human Services (DHHS). (2003). *New freedom commission on mental health: Achieving the promise: Transforming mental health in America: Final report* (DHHS document no. SMA-03-3832). Rockville, MD: Author.

U.S. Department of Health and Human Services (2000). *Healthy People 2010: Understanding and Improving Health.* Retrieved from http://www.healthypeople.gov/2010/Document/pdf/uih/2010uih.pdf

U.S. Department of Health and Human Services (2010a, September 15). The Affordable Care Act & behavioral health [Video file]. Retrieved from http://www.youtube.com/user/USGOVHHS?feature=mhum#p/a/u/0/plbTLrRXNk8

U.S. Department of Health and Human Services (2010b). *Healthy People 2020.* Retrieved from http://www.healthypeople.gov/hp2020/

U.S. Department of Health and Human Services, Public Health Service. (1992). *Healthy people 2000: National health promotion and disease prevention objective.* Boston, MA: Jones and Bartlett.

U.S. Public Health Service. (1999). *The surgeon general's call to action to prevent suicide.* Washington, DC: Author.

U.S. Public Health Service. (2001). *National strategy for suicide prevention: Goals and objectives for action: Summary.* Rockville, MD: U.S. Department of Health and Human Services.

Ustun, T. B. (1999). The global burden of mental disorders. *American Journal of Public Health, 89*(9), 1315–1318.

Van der Kolk, B. A. (1987). *Psychological trauma.* Washington, DC: American Psychiatric Association.

Van Gennep, A. (1960). *Rites of passage.* Chicago, IL: University of Chicago Press. (Original work published in 1909.)

Walker, H. M. (1993). Anti-social behavior in school. *Journal of Emotional and Behavioral Problems, 2*(1), 20–24.

Watters, E. (2010). *Crazy like us: The globalization of the American psyche.* New York, NY: Free Press.

Whitaker, R. (2010). *Anatomy of an epidemic: Magic bullets, psychiatric drugs, and the astonishing rise of mental illness in America.* New York, NY: Crown.

Woodtli, A., & Breslin, E. (1996). Violence related content in the nursing curriculum: A national study. *Journal of Nursing Education, 35*(8), 367–374.

Woodtli, A., & Breslin, E. (2002). Violence-related content in the nursing curriculum: A follow-up national survey. *Journal of Nursing Education, 41*(4), 340–348.

World Health Organization. (1981). *Global strategy for health for all by the year 2000.* Geneva, Switzerland: Author.

World Health Organization. (2010). UN Millennium Development Goals. Retrieved from http://www.who.int/topics/millennium_development_goals/about/en/index.html

Chapter 2

Illustrations of Education, Training, and Comprehensive Service Needs in Crisis and Psychosocial Care

Chapter Outline

This chapter presents and analyzes situations which require social support and crisis intervention in home care, psychiatric services, and general health facilities. The life studies illustrate the urgency of developing or expanding crisis service and education and training programs and how comprehensive crisis care complements and intersects with other service needs. For each life example, key concepts and training issues that clinicians should understand are cited as a backdrop for planning and developing crisis and other services (including advocacy) on behalf of vulnerable people. The focus here is not on training individual crisis workers around particular situations; that is the function of *clinical* texts in the field (see www.crisisprograms.org). Rather, these examples reveal the important links between violence, victimization, and suicide risk that are central to the *education, training and service program planning* and the *clinical* outcomes of life-threatening and other events.

The five life examples presented here underscore the principle that psychosocial support and timely crisis intervention are *everybody's* business, not just the realm of mental health professionals or hotline workers. They also illustrate a basic principle underlying excellence in crisis care: Knowledgeable, motivated, and skilled crisis workers will be hampered in their clinical performance when agency- and system-wide structural supports are uncoordinated, inadequate, or not grounded in awareness of the complex needs of various people in crisis, including abused health and social service workers caring for clients in crisis. Some of these concepts were introduced in Chapter 1. Here their central importance is elaborated.

A Suicidal Woman Using Several Resources

Example 1: Alice Smith

In Centerville, a city of approximately 60,000 people, federal, state, and local funds support a community mental health center (CMHC). After 5:00 p.m. daily, professional staff are available only by telephone to any clients in crisis. Clients are routinely referred to the local hotline for after-hours needs. Most people in Centerville who are in high-risk crisis states go to hospital emergency departments or seek support through a hotline staffed by volunteers with backup by professional staff. The volunteers and hospital staff receive occasional consultation from crisis specialists, though there are no formal interagency service agreements. Alice Smith, a client of the CMHC, first called her friend and then the local hotline after a heated argument with her husband on Saturday night that left her with suicidal thoughts. Together the Smiths have been under stress from the threat of mortgage foreclosure on their farm. Alice was in therapy for depression and had agreed to a "no-suicide" contract. Alice did not disclose to the telephone worker that she had a regular therapist; nor was she asked, apparently because the telephone counselor was primarily concerned about Alice's suicide risk. After assessment and offering support, the telephone counselor referred Alice to the psychiatric service of the local hospital. While there, Alice received a prescription for an anti-anxiety agent and was advised to see her

CMHC therapist on Monday. The next day Ms. Smith was brought to the hospital emergency department after an overdose with her prescription pills.

Key Concepts and Training Issues

Alice Smith's situation highlights the elements of comprehensive mental health care necessary to avoid life-threatening crisis.

Interagency linkages: When linkages are not formalized by agreement with policy boards responsible for specific services, clients in crisis tend to get lost among loopholes in interagency collaboration. If financial resources are scarce or comprehensive crisis services (24/7 via telephone and face-to-face contact) cannot be provided by a single agency, contractual agreements are even more pivotal in offering smoothly coordinated service which can decrease the probability of suicidal crises like Ms. Smith's.

Service availability: Because the *volume* of acute crisis calls is perceived as small, professional, business, and other leaders may conclude that the community cannot support more than a hotline service. One result is that fiscal constraints will most likely increase rather than decrease because of the greater cost of secondary- and tertiary-level care necessary when primary care and early intervention in life-threatening situations are not readily available. The trend toward proliferating toll-free hotline numbers minus essential linkages to other service elements is not a satisfactory substitute for comprehensive crisis service.

Staffing arrangements: Professional staff of the CMHC appear to have only limited involvement in after-hours delivery of crisis services. Such a staffing pattern suggests the higher status historically assigned to daytime psychotherapy sessions provided by mental health professionals, and the crisis model's contrasting legacy as a mere "band-aid." This staffing arrangement and the informal interagency agreement can result in fragmented services and insufficient professional input to governing body decisions regarding crisis program development. When mental health professionals are trained primarily to deliver psychotherapy services in formal office settings, they may feel inadequate in supervisory and consulting roles to paraprofessionals and others staffing evening and night-time ("off-hours") telephone and outreach services. One psychiatrist assigned to supervise crisis workers acknowledged that she had little to offer before she availed herself to extended in-service training program on community-based high-risk crisis situations. A balanced and cost-effective array of mental health services—especially in the context of managed care and fiscal constraint—includes a tightly orchestrated team arrangement (between professional and paraprofessional staff) covering the entire clock and calendar, because the occurrence of crisis rarely accommodates a psychotherapist's scheduled hours. Such coordinated staffing was central to the original purposes outlined by federal legislation for community mental health services (Levine, 1981), and serves as a powerful buffer against fragmented service delivery. Because of continued fragmentation of services in many instances, this book reaffirms the relevance of ideal service delivery models.

Clinical training: At the clinical level, training of all crisis, health, and mental health providers should include content on gender issues in mental health care, such as the tendency to prescribe more psychotropic medications for women than men. Females are 2–3 times more likely than males to be diagnosed with depression; however, males are four times more likely than females to die by suicide. In addition, females are twice as likely to be prescribed an antidepressant as males (Stagnitti, 2005), which may be indicative of gender bias. It should also be noted that according to the U.S. Department of Health and Human Services (2010), two thirds of antidepressant medications are prescribed in the primary care setting, a trend that underscores the importance of increased training in psychosocial facets of health for the non-psychiatric practitioner (Dupree, Watson, & Schneider, 2005; Goodfriend, Bryant, Livingood, & Goldhagen, 2006; Hoff & Morgan, 2011; Weiss, Haber, Horowitz, Stuart, & Wolfe, 2009; Whitaker, 2010).

Comprehensive Service Needs

Example 1 illustrates that comprehensive crisis services (provided 24/7 and smoothly coordinated in office and community settings) are not routine in many communities, even though emergency mental health and crisis service was declared an "essential element" of community mental health programs decades ago by a congressional task force (Joint Commission on Mental Health and Illness, 1961).

For a client like Alice Smith, the following elements of comprehensive service might have prevented her suicide attempt and its human and financial cost:

- A "no-suicide contract" *in itself* offers no special protection against suicide nor does it provide legal protection for the therapist, crisis worker, or any provider enacting it. The potential value of such a contract lies in the *message that someone cares whether the suicidal person lives or dies*. Thus a no-suicide contract is insufficient and probably useless if not enacted in the context of a *therapeutic relationship* and a client-focused service plan. Such a plan specifies what to do if the client is feeling suicidal—for example, calling the 24-hour hotline, relieving isolation, and having a plan for controlling impulsive self-destructive behavior. In no way should this kind of contract serve as a convenient substitute for the time spent in empathic listening and in planning alternatives to suicide with the despairing person (see Clark & Kerkhof, 1993; Hoff, Hallisey, & Hoff, 2009, ch. 10).

- When professional mental health staff rely on local hotlines for response to after-hours crisis situations like Alice Smith's, hotline staff should be briefed about (a) the likelihood that a suicidal client might call, (b) the suicide or other risk levels already assessed by the therapist, and (c) general directives about how best to maintain continuity of care between agencies. This should always be done with the client's collaboration (permission) within the context of interagency safety planning. Without such interagency collaboration, clients may fall through the cracks, and problems often escalate to full-blown crises. In a situation similar to Alice Smith's, an advocate seeking help for a suicidal person got repeated busy signals from the hotline over a 3-day period. In discussing this with the agency's director, he was told that despite awareness of the problem, no funding was available for installing more phone lines or even to include a referral message directing callers to other resources when all lines are busy.
- Similar collaborative arrangements should be in place between the CMHC and the hospital's psychiatric service. If Alice Smith's psychotherapist had been more available and involved as a person in charge, and a consultant to those with less expertise, the quick-fix drug prescription in the hospital emergency department and the suicide attempt that followed might have been avoided.
- Once such collaborative arrangements are in place, suicidal crises like Alice Smith's may still occur and require a hospital emergency visit. In such instances, following crisis assessment, one option to be considered is a 24- to 72-hour crisis observation stay rather than psychiatric in-patient admission or discharge with only antidepressant medication. Crisis "holding beds" in hospitals are becoming more common. They not only provide a safety measure for high-risk clients but also bypass the stigma still attached to psychiatric hospitalization. Such measures also provide a secure context to conduct intensive crisis counseling, psychiatric stabilization, and follow-up treatment that emphasize client empowerment, community liaison, and psychological growth as goals of crisis resolution. If a crisis overnight stay is indicated, the counseling and treatment planning that ensue should be done in collaboration with the client's regular psychotherapist.
- Similar collaborative arrangements are indicated when the client's therapist is a private practitioner.

Abuse of Caregiver and Risk of Older Adults in Home Care

Example 2: The Cabots (adapted and expanded from Hoff, 2010)

Barbara Cabot, age 64, is a former welfare caseworker and is now the home caregiver for her 69-year-old husband, Walter. Mr. Cabot is cognitively impaired and has been a wheelchair user for the past 10 years. In addition, he has various cardiovascular ailments and sometimes becomes very irritable and physically resistant to care, though he seems to take comfort in his wife's continued presence. Mrs. Cabot is very active as an advocate in a local support group focused on the needs of home caregivers like herself who are increasingly left to pick up the pieces when public services are terminated. She relied on an excellent home-nursing service, which was terminated when the worker "met her goals." The reason for the termination, Mrs. Cabot says, is that the home care program is cost driven and excludes rehabilitation services and psychosocial care. She states that when such professional services are withdrawn, it results in "untold stress, frustration, and fear" for the caregiver and increased risk of abuse for the disabled client.

When asked if she's ever been abusive to her partner, Mrs. Cabot says, "No, no ... you have to be careful of yourself," but she's often miserable, frustrated, and lonely, stating, "I don't think that I can go it alone. I really don't… . I would never hit him. You can be sure of that. My brother had phoned me at Christmas, and it had just been a terrible time and he asked, 'What are you going to do?' And I said, 'I'm looking for two plastic bags, two pieces of rope, and somebody to pull them both.' And then he said 'Well, I'd better come in.' And I said, 'No, don't come near me.' It's just awful. Things like that are very stressful times, Christmas and those things are really bad."

Mrs. Cabot is bitter and feels deeply abused and neglected by "the system," which she says takes unfair advantage of women like herself to fill in for needy older persons such as her husband when money is tight. When asked what kept her from hitting her husband, given the lack of assistance and support, she said, "I guess it goes against everything I believe in."

Key Concepts and Training Issues

The example of the Cabots illustrates the fact that abuse prevention involves more than clinical skills of risk assessment and intervention in actual or potential crisis. It is entwined with several social and public policy issues that should be addressed in training, especially of case managers and administrators.

Health policy: Caretaking at home for ill and needy people—concentrated among older adults—interfaces with the long-standing tradition of assigning such roles primarily to women (wives, daughters, and mothers), although men are increasingly assuming these caretaking roles. Whether inadvertently or as deliberate health care policy, this pattern entails new risks and future societal costs for individual clients, the family unit, and providers alike (Pruschno & Resch, 1989; Sidel, 1986; Sommers & Shields, 1987). The public response of overburdening women with society's caretaking roles provides a temporary "band-aid"—a misplaced "crisis" response—to a larger social and public policy issue arising from the health care needs of a growing population of older people with particular vulnerabilities to abuse (Podneiks, 1990).

Holistic care: The powerful influence of the mind–body dichotomy in devising standards and definitions of what constitutes "care" devalues crisis and psychosocial care as less urgent than physical needs. Very little insight is needed to observe the life-and-death risks for people like the Cabots that result from such outmoded thinking. Palliative care and the advocacy role of nursing, social work, and specialists on aging are central to crisis prevention in this situation (Melillo & Houde, 2011; Morgan, 2010). For example, an astute visiting nurse (grounded in ethics and advocacy principles) would not simply "go along" with short-sighted cost-cutting measures (embedded in the mind–body dichotomy) that are ultimately more costly in both financial and human terms. Rather, in a holistic framework, the nurse would use the documented results of a psychosocial assessment including risk of suicide, danger to others, and homicide (traceable to unrelieved stress on the home caregiver) to authorize the continuation of psychosocial support (as by a social worker or psychiatric nurse) and the prevention of institutionalization or death itself.

Abuse prevention: This example of Mr. and Mrs. Cabot underscores the need for awareness among caregivers about recognizing their own stress levels, knowing which situations are most likely to "push their buttons," and knowing how to talk about a stressful situation before it reaches crisis level. This includes understanding one's own potential for abusing others in stressful care situations without adequate support or crisis consultation.

Comprehensive Service Needs

In a situation like the Cabots', the following elements of comprehensive crisis services could prevent escalation to abuse, suicide, or homicide:

- Assessment of total family needs in the home.
- Assessment of risk of assault and suicide.
- Arranging for respite care for Mrs. Cabot, as a supplement to her support group.

- Teamwork and communication with home health aides, social workers, physical therapists, attorneys, and others whose services are needed by this couple. To the extent that home care services are available only on "doctor's orders," physicians need to assess and authorize nursing services and social workers for crisis and psychosocial care as well as physical health care needs of both the identified client and the caregiver.
- Consultation services (and training in crisis intervention) from mental health and crisis specialists for visiting nurses, social workers, and home health care providers confronted with crises and risk factors such as those presented by the Cabots. It should be noted that in the 1960s and 1970s, community mental health models—which were politically dismantled in the early 1980s (Chandler, 1990; Johnson, 1990; Levine, 1981; Mosher & Burti, 1994, pp. 304–305; Whitaker, 2010)—considered consultation services as central to comprehensive mental health service delivery. In this case, a crisis outreach team might make a home visit to assist in crisis assessment and resolution. One result of such consultation might include the recommendation of possible counseling for Mrs. Cabot to assess more fully her determination to care for her husband at home (at the risk of both homicide and suicide), particularly if advocacy, respite care, and other efforts do not yield the support she needs to continue her home-based caregiver role.
- Community mobilization and political action skills such as lobbying for appropriate funding of home care services.

An Immigrant Woman's System Struggles

Example 3: Fatimah Okoro

Fatimah Okoro is a 32-year-old woman who emigrated from northeast Africa 5 years ago. She left her homeland in an attempt to escape an abusive arranged marriage with a man almost twice her age. After arriving in the United States, she lived in numerous locations and then eventually settled down in the Midwest. She entered into a relationship with a fellow immigrant, Abit, and the abusive cycle started again. Fatimah eventually discovered that she was pregnant and contacted the social service system for assistance with being a single mother. One night, after giving birth to her son, Fatimah, Abit and some close friends were drinking alcohol together. Abit became angry and started to beat her. With the help of friends, she fled the situation and drove off in her vehicle only to be pulled over by police a few blocks away. Because this was not her first alcohol-related driving offense, her license was suspended for a period of 6 months.

With the support of her new family (within the immigrant community where she lived) and social services, she was able to eventually end the relationship with Abit and was now parenting her son alone. Due to legal charges, she was required to receive treatment for substance abuse, which was provided one-on-one due to language barriers. During counseling sessions it became apparent that Fatimah was working with numerous social service providers in an attempt to get all of her needs met but that none of the services were coordinated, despite being assigned a case manager. This left Fatimah running around in an endless attempt to attend necessary appointments and complete all system requirements. This was complicated further by the fact that she was unable to legally drive and public transportation was limited. On occasion, when she could not get a ride from a friend or coworker she would drive, partly because she could not carry her young child in the harsh climate. This resulted in additional driving-related charges which extended her driver's license suspension.

Fatimah would arrive to her counseling sessions emotionally and physically drained. Due to language barriers and not knowing or understanding the proper terminology, she struggled to communicate the steps she was taking to gain support and resolve the various crises she was experiencing. At times she felt hopeless about her future and stuck in a life she could not manage. She was confused about how to navigate the social service system and didn't understand why getting help needed to be so difficult and time consuming. Fatimah had very limited contact with her case manager (whose name she could not remember). Because the system—in which she was drowning—was so disjointed, her substance abuse counselor, whose role did not entail case management, felt unable to help her and after providing the required services discharged her from treatment with hopes that having one less appointment to attend on a weekly basis would lessen Fatimah's burden.

Key Concepts and Training Issues

Fatimah Okoro's immigrant minority and single-parent status renders her doubly vulnerable to crises and the psychological aftermath of violent abuse. This situation illustrates several major issues with training implications.

Social policy: Global politics and economic policies in the postcolonial era result in the inequalities and international tensions associated with mass migration of indigenous populations toward societies which historically have known economic and political privilege—Canada, the United States, and Western European countries (see Desjarlais, Eisenberg, Good, & Kleinman, 1995). Policy makers and the general public need to understand that good mental health is part of human capital that makes it possible for refugees to contribute to society (Beiser, 2009).

Racism: The particular vulnerability stemming from visible immigrant minority status taps into deep-seated racial bias, with exacerbation of the social isolation experienced by most immigrant and ethnic minority groups.

Some battered women from immigrant and minority groups are reluctant to use immigrant and women's organizations for support out of fear that they may come into contact with a member of their community, thus risking possible negative and dangerous ramifications. Refugees who experience discrimination are also more likely to be depressed (Beiser, 2009).

Communication barriers: The ability to communicate is instrumental in successful integration into a new community. There is a tendency for community members representing the majority culture to become frustrated with those who do not speak the way they do. Recent immigrants may need additional support in understanding and navigating the health care system (Wilson, Silberberg, Brown, & Yaggy, 2007). Linguistic fluency compromises employment, impedes access to services, and diminishes the ability to engage in civic life and mainstream entertainment. Women, those who are poorly educated, and the elderly are least likely to learn English—which increases isolation (Beiser, 2009).

Human rights and psychiatry: Though cross-cultural responses to stress vary, such variation should not obscure the basic human right of freedom from violence and abuse (Jang, Lee, & Morello-Frosch, 1991; Walker, 1992). Immigrants need awareness-raising about the seriousness of intimate partner violence, including long-term health effects. They will also need reassurance of safety in a nonjudgmental environment (Wilson et al., 2007). Psychiatric history should not be used to mitigate basic human rights or obscure underlying sociocultural issues frequently associated with mental disorders. Although a psychiatric diagnosis can serve a purpose in treatment plans, it should not become a tool to discredit a person's disclosure of abuse which was not attended to at earlier crisis points. The diagnosis of borderline personality disorder can be particularly hazardous for survivors of abuse when long-repressed issues related to abuse have not been satisfactorily addressed.

Humanity: Despite deeply embedded cultural differences we must not lose sight of what unites us as human beings—the struggle for autonomy and affiliations, the centrality of family and community to everyday life, the need to feel productive and cared for, and the need for continuity as a counterpoint to the search for novelty. Culture often casts a veil over universal longing, discontent, and strengths, and it is our job to uncover that without being offensive (Beiser, 2009).

Comprehensive Service Needs

In a situation like Fatimah Okoro's, the following elements of comprehensive crisis services could prevent escalation to more serious mental health issues:

- Language ability or accessibility to translator services. In some situations it may be safer to use a battered women's advocate as an interpreter rather than an on-call community interpreter.
- Crisis assessment and intervention as a strategy to prevent deterioration of mental health in a case like Fatimah's, which can appear after years of unalleviated stress from spousal abuse, resettlement, and system expectations. Using an interdisciplinary approach can provide nonintrusive emotional support and personal safety that can build resiliency and promote positive mental health for asylum seekers at risk of harming themselves (Procter, 2005). Despite a gruesome history of abuse, most refugees do not become mental health casualties. Although the resettlement process can be difficult, the stressors and protective factors around it are closely tied to mental health. Having a supportive significant other aids in the process.
- Advocacy to protect people like Fatimah from the complicated criminal justice system that is often impossible for immigrants to understand and comprehend.
- For professional follow-up care, referral to a therapist explicitly attuned to cross-cultural and feminist issues in the psychiatric treatment of women with histories of abuse. Through increased collaboration, crisis centers can be a critical link between the client and health care providers working with diverse clientele (Wilson et al., 2007).
- Referral to community groups with expertise in the problems and issues of minority and immigrant groups can lead to decreased isolation. Resettlement is a lifelong process with constantly changing needs and coping strategies (Beiser, 2009), and community groups can serve as a great source of support during this journey. Additionally, when crisis providers network with these same community groups, an increase in culturally sensitive services can result.
- Referral to a women's shelter (if necessary) for culturally appropriate support services, groups, housing, and general service coordination. Training and education for both staff and the shelter guests will strengthen the ability to respond to immigrants' needs. Immigrants will sometimes hide or minimize their mental health needs in order to gain access to a shelter. The time spent in a shelter is a window of opportunity to address barriers, provide information, and successfully link shelter guests to necessary services. Untreated, undertreated, or undiagnosed serious mental illness; mobility-limiting chronic pain; and uncontrolled substance abuse can prevent a successful transition from shelter services (Wilson et al., 2007).
- Most of the issues and risk factors affecting immigrants in general are typically exacerbated among refugees and others seeking escape and asylum from torture and human trafficking for sex and cheap labor. Persons

suffering from these global crimes—mostly women and children—usually require specialty service carefully synchronized between medical, mental health, and legal specialists. See Chapter 9 of Hoff (2010), "Torture and Trafficking Survivors, and Abuse of Immigrants."

The interdisciplinary facets of care include awareness by nurses, physicians, and other health care providers of the special needs of disadvantaged groups, and vigilance to avoid cultural relativism as well as interpreting cross-cultural differences in a narrow psychopathological framework (Hoff, 1992). *Cultural relativism* refers to the interpretation of certain practices as the norm in particular cultures (Lorber, 1997). For example, domestic abuse or female genital mutilation (FGM) may be explained or excused as "relative" to a certain group, as in the case of Fatimah and spousal abuse. In contrast, the World Health Organization has defined these practices as universal human rights violations that apply across cultures (Delport, 2007).

Violence in Learning and Work Environments

Example 4: Juan Lopez

Juan Lopez, age 24, graduated from high school as valedictorian of his class and at age 17 began studies toward an engineering degree at a prestigious technological institute. Both of Juan's parents held graduate degrees and conveyed to him their expectation of high academic performance. His first year of college was successful, but Juan fell short of his high school achievement level. As a result of his perceived academic "failure," Juan suffered bouts of depression, which was exacerbated by his girlfriend breaking up with him. Observing both his down mood interspersed with angry outbursts for no apparent reason, one of his friends urged Juan to seek help at the student counseling service. He refused, and instead took refuge in periodic heavy drinking with his male buddies. Juan's academic performance was in sharp decline by the end of his third semester. In a Social Issues class, which included content about service deficits in the U.S. mental health system, Juan thought the professor was referring specifically to him. Feeling anxious and angry, he confronted the professor, but could not accept the professor's explanation about the factual evidence for including this policy issue in class content. The professor spent about 10 minutes with Juan after class; expressed concern about his problems, late papers, and so on; and suggested that Juan talk with his parents and seek help at the student counseling service, which he reluctantly agreed to do, but followed through with only two sessions. The professor conferred with the department dean about Juan and his failing grades, and, although wary of Juan's angry confrontation, agreed this was all they could do. Meanwhile, Juan dropped hints among his buddies about somehow "getting back at the professor for what he deserves."

Pressures mounted for Juan; he failed three of his four courses and was suspended from college. After crashing with one of his friends for a couple nights, he returned to his parents' home and obtained a low-paying job. Juan continued to experience erratic behaviors and frequent fights with his parents. Following a particularly volatile argument, Juan finally agreed to see a psychiatrist. He was diagnosed with schizoaffective disorder and accepted a prescription for a psychotropic medication and 20-minute follow-up appointments once a month. For a few months Juan calmed down considerably, but complained to his parents, "I just can't stand how those drugs make me feel." After several arguments with his parents about his drinking, he stopped the medication, and dropped hints to his mother that he wanted to go back to the college and "teach that professor a lesson." After a night of heavy drinking and another argument with his father, Juan became physically violent, resulting in a call to the police. Juan was taken by police to the local hospital emergency department (ED). While there he tried to strike the admitting nurse, resulting in physical and chemical restraint. Juan was kept overnight in the "crisis holding" unit and discharged the next day with a recommendation to follow up with his psychiatrist. Juan did not follow discharge recommendations, which resulted in two other ED admissions. Juan and his family were finally connected to an individual therapist with a more holistic orientation. Juan was eventually readmitted to college and maintained his emotional health through ongoing therapy and medication monitoring.

Key Concepts and Training Issues

Juan's life development stage plus his unexpected change from academic excellence to low-wage employment illustrate long-established concepts about crisis prevention and intervention, and one's vulnerability to serious mental disorder often co-occurring with stressful life events.

Early recognition: Vulnerability to crisis stemming from serious transitions, such as moving from high school to college, is present here. During the normally tumultuous developmental stage of adolescence, the additional emotional stress that ensues from leaving the usual comforts of home along with the increased academic, social, and relational demands of college place many young people at risk. Overall, this period in a young person's life coincides with the developmental phase when biological correlates of serious psychiatric disorders may surface under the pressure of major life transitions such as Juan's (Earley, 2006; Hoff & Morgan, 2011, chs. 7 and 8). Early recognition of these struggles is a key component of prevention of more serious illness.

Power and control: Although adolescents and young adults require the support of parents during transitional stages, resentment of overinvolvement often occurs due to its direct conflict with their need to gain independence. When parents need to assert control over their children, as in the case of Juan and his mental health needs, feelings of frustration, shame, and powerlessness can result in defiance, which compounds the already stressful situation. In situations like Juan's, there is a clear need for professional help to gain insight and regain a sense of control over his life. This includes sharing, with him and his family, in lay language, the interrelated psychosocial and biological factors related to his serious symptoms.

Power and control issues are also apparent in service agencies, such as the hospital ED. When patients present as "out-of-control" and threats to physical safety are present, the use of physical and chemical restraint should be administered according to "least restrictive principles" and respect, and it must be remembered that excessive force can exacerbate a patient's anger and sense of helplessness—thus potentially triggering more violence later (see Hoff et al., 2009, ch. 12).

Danger assessment and rights of persons with mental illness: In cases where students exhibit extreme mental health concerns, we must recognize that persons with serious mental illness have a basic right to education. This right, however, hinges on the sensitive point of persuading a seriously disturbed student, who is also potentially dangerous, that he or she must accept help and cooperate with professional mental health providers in a treatment program that would allow for continued studies. Implied here is that all students, faculty, and other college personnel should have access to staff development opportunities that include the basics for recognizing dangerousness and how to respond to stressful and scary situations before they reach life-threatening proportion; for example, walking a student to the student counseling center for immediate assistance, rather than a vague suggestion such as "I think you should see a counselor."

Besides danger to others, on-campus violence prevention should include recognition of clues to suicide, as a student also hinting at suicide presents even greater danger of assault or homicide in that all accountability for violence is lost through suicide. These points underscore the reality that college campuses are not "fortresses," and that seriously ill but poorly treated students may come back to campus seeking revenge, as the tragedies at Virginia Tech and in Tucson, Arizona, attest. These risk assessment concepts also apply to all health providers in hospitals and other worksites, where assaults and even homicides might be prevented with in-service education on violence issues, and workplace safety programs are a regular feature of providing a safe work environment (see Chapter 9's discussion of Vida Health; Runyan, 2001).

Comprehensive Service Needs

The transition to college is one of the most stressful times in a young adult's life. In situations like Juan Lopez's, the following comprehensive services could prevent emotional and behavioral turmoil following adolescents' challenging transitions:

- Well-established orientation and first-year experience (FYE) programs. Staff and student volunteers within these programs should have at least basic understanding of crisis assessment and be well versed in appropriate referral sources. University counseling services can be an excellent source for training and consultation. In addition, taking the time to develop name and face recognition between orientation, FYE, and counseling center personnel will lessen the stigma and confusion associated with the referral process.
- Educating parents on what their child may experience as the realities of college life set in, what is "typical" versus "atypical" adjustment, and how best to support their child's personal growth. Additionally, a child's transition to college is equally stressful for many parents, who now find their usual routine and sense of purpose disrupted. Education and referral to appropriate support services for parents may be necessary.
- Incorporation of the "wellness" concept throughout the university environment. It is important for students to learn about the importance of balance in their lives. The inherent freedom embedded in a student's transition to college can lead to poor health habits (lack of exercise, sleep, and appropriate nutrition along with excessive use of caffeine, tobacco, alcohol, and other mood-altering substances). Students need to hear from multiple sources (faculty, residential housing assistants, academic support services, coaches, advisors, student affairs workers, etc.) about the importance of holistic health.
- Although much has been done to increase mental health services for students in crisis or suffering serious mental illness, the apparent "missing link" in many publicized reports of suicide or assaults on others is that clues to such danger were present, but those hearing "cries for help" did not know how to respond, or there was evidence of serious loopholes in smooth coordination of services. In Juan's case, his suspension from college was the result of academic policy, but there was no explicit referral or coordination of needed service between the student counseling center and a community-based mental health service or private psychotherapist. Also, when Juan finally agreed to seek psychiatric help, the major treatment was

a psychotropic drug—the side effects of which were not closely monitored as an essential facet of treatment. In addition, there was no recognition by either college personnel or emergency department staff of the support needed by Juan's parents on behalf of their seriously disturbed son (see Hoff et al., 2009, ch. 5; McHenry & Price, 2000). Having policies that address risk assessment and response, and continuum of care expectations, may close many of the loopholes that lead to larger crises.

- Juan's situation presents an opportunity for prevention of the vicious cycle or "revolving door" regarding psychiatric patients and workplace violence: (a) *the client*: expulsion from college—inadequate mental health treatment coordination—escalation of violence—hospital admission for deescalation—early discharge with psychotropic drugs—repeated violence—readmission to ED; (b) *the nurse*: short staffing—insufficient time for communication—hasty use of restraint—escalation of client anger—discharge with no firm psychiatric follow-up linkage—repeated violence—admission to ED—repeat threats or attacks on staff; and so on. Together, these revolving-door experiences can be traced to two major sources already discussed in this book: (a) national policy issues regarding deinstitutionalization of seriously mentally ill persons without adequate supports in the community, and (b) the general failure to include more than a smattering of content on crisis and violence issues in the generic curricula of health and social service professionals (see Hoff, 2010, chs. 3 and 13). The human and financial costs of these omissions in service and educational programs are very serious, but can be reduced by building on the premise of *knowledge as prevention and intervention*.

A Young Woman Unable to Escape Bullying

Example 5: Ashley Johnson

Ashley Johnson, age 18, was excited to start classes at the local university. She described her senior year in high school as the "worst time of my life" and was looking forward to a fresh start. Ashley, an attractive, athletic, and intelligent young lady, did not appear to be the likely target of youth bullying; however, she had endured such actions since junior high. As the bullying escalated, she transferred to another school in an attempt to find relief; however, despite living in a large community, her "reputation" followed her. Ashley endured malicious rumors regarding sexual behavior, social isolation, threatening and demeaning texts and chat messages, and physical threats to her safety from both male and female peers. During her sophomore year in high school, she sought services with a local psychologist in an attempt to deal with extreme anxiety and depressive symptoms. She found this helpful but was not always able to see her therapist in moments of crisis. She formed a close relationship with her mother and frequently turned to her for support when feeling alone and suicidal.

Ashley was devastated to learn that one of the bullies from junior high was also living in campus housing. The bullying had followed her to college and was spreading within her new social environment. Despite having a group of supportive friends, she could not escape the torment of new rumors and threatening text and chat messages. When asked if she had thought about moving far away from her hometown to attend college and escape anyone who might know her, she commented, "I don't want to run from my problems."

Key Concepts and Training Issues

An example like Ashley Johnson's, which represents ongoing victimization by youth bullies over multiple years and settings, highlights the need for crisis and psychosocial care that is sensitive to the experience of the bullied victim.

Prevalence and diversity risk factors: The prevalence of bullying was first studied and reported by Dan Olweus in the 1970s. Since that time, research has widely documented the worldwide prevalence and implications of bullying. Bullying is repeated aggressive behavior that causes intentional harm over time within an interpersonal relationship characterized by an actual or perceived imbalance of power (Nansel et al., 2001; Olweus & Limber, 2010). Bullying behaviors typically fall into four categories: physical, verbal, relational, and cyber. Research findings reveal that more than one half of all students experience verbal or relational bullying, such as rumors, excluding, name calling, or teasing, either as the bully or the victim, with cyber and physical bullying occurring less often (Pergolizzi et al., 2009; Wang, Iannotti, & Nansel, 2009). Bullying appears to peak in middle school (Nansel et al., 2001; Pergolizzi et al., 2009).

Gender differences: Although girls and boys tend to be at equal risk of bullying (Pergolizzi et al., 2009), they typically use different methods. Males are more likely to engage in verbal or physical bullying, whereas females are more likely to use social-relational tactics such as spreading rumors and social exclusion (Nansel et al., 2001; Raskauskas, 2010; Wang et al., 2009).

Socioeconomic status (SES): Students from more affluent families may be protected from physical bullying; however, having a higher SES increases risk of involvement with cyber bullying, most likely because of increased access to technology (Wang et al., 2009). Students from lower SES bullied in childhood show an increase in emotional and behavioral problems in adolescence (Bowes, Maughan, Caspi, Moffitt, & Arseneault, 2010) and higher rates of depressive symptoms in adulthood (Due, Damsgaard, Lund, & Holstein, 2009).

Prejudice and dominance: Bullying is an attempt to assert dominance over someone perceived as less than the bully. Homophobic bullying is present in many youth settings, and the use of biased language related to sexual orientation is common, even if the victim does not identify as homosexual. Administrators, teachers, and counselors must counteract the use of biased language by regularly intervening when offensive language is used and creating safe and supportive opportunities for interaction with sexual minority youth (Poteat & DiGiovanni, 2010).

Support system and parental role: Parental support appears to be a protective factor against engaging in bullying behaviors and the risk of, and reaction to, being bullied (Bowes et al., 2010; Wang et al., 2009). Students with conflictual home environments and lack of supervision are more likely to bully other students (Holt, Kantor, & Finkelhor, 2009). Students with more friends were more likely to be the bully and less likely to be bullied (Wang et al., 2009).

Technological advancement: In the past, school bullying was fairly limited to the confines of the school day and home was a safe haven for many. As the use of cell phones (with text and picture messaging options) and computers with internet access increases, so does the window of opportunity for bullies. In recent studies, cyber bullying was reported in one of every four to seven students (Pergolizzi et al., 2009; Raskauskas, 2010; Wang et al., 2009). Victims of text bullying were found to also be victims of other bullying (Raskauskas, 2010).

Psychosocial functioning: Disturbances in psychosocial functioning can be observed in both perpetrators and victims of bullying. Some perpetrators have serious histories of abuse and other negative experiences in childhood. Victims of bullying often experience depression, anxiety, and isolation. Behavioral outbursts and other forms of acting out are also frequently observed. These symptoms may continue into adulthood (Bowes et al., 2010; Due et al., 2009; Nansel et al., 2001; Olweus & Limber, 2010; Raskauskas, 2010).

Comprehensive Service Needs

In cases of youth bullying such as Ashley Johnson's, the following comprehensive service elements could help to prevent bullying and mitigate the effects on its victims:

- Schools, parents, students, and those providing crisis and psychosocial care must be made aware of, and acknowledge the presence of, bullying in their environment.
- Focus on creating and maintaining a safe antibullying environment. Effective prevention and intervention programs require a solid understanding of the social and environmental factors that facilitate or inhibit bullying and peer aggression. Armed with this knowledge, educational and psychosocial staff can create school and social environments that promote healthy peer interactions and intolerance of bullying. This involves making changes within the school and classroom climate to increase awareness of bullying and increase teacher and parent involvement and supervision, forming clear rules and strong social norms against bullying, reducing the opportunities and rewards for bullying, and providing support and protection for those being bullied (Nansel et al., 2001; Olweus & Limber, 2010).
- Adoption and implementation of effective bullying prevention curriculum. Although many states require some form of prevention curriculum to be implemented, there are no specific requirements to use evidence-based tools. In order to implement a prevention curriculum, school administrators need adequate knowledge about the prevalence of bullying, the short- and long-term consequences, and effective prevention and intervention practices. They also need sufficient motivation to implement comprehensive school-based efforts and the resources to do so (Olweus & Limber, 2010).
- Antibullying intervention strategies that involve youth in all stages of discussions and activities related to bullying (Olweus, 1994). Adolescents suggest that having serious talks with the students involved, parental involvement, improving victims' coping strategies, school staff intervention, and teaching antibullying strategies were among those that students felt would be most beneficial (Frisen & Holmqvist, 2009).
- The inclusion of parents in school-based prevention and intervention programs (Bowes et al., 2010; Frisen & Holmqvist, 2009; Holt et al., 2009). Some parents do not believe that they should be part of bullying prevention curricula and see this as the school's responsibility (Holt et al., 2009); however, as stated above, parental support can be a protective factor when it comes to bullying. Providing education to parents through prevention curricula heightens their awareness of bullying behaviors.
- Teaching students, parents, and school staff nonviolent conflict resolution strategies. Holt et al. (2009) found that some parents believe their children should fight back, which underscores the necessity of providing students and parents with other tactics.

- Increasing communication between children and parents regarding bullying behaviors. Holt et al. (2009) found that students were more likely to tell parents about bullying when they were the victims as opposed to when they were the perpetrators. In addition, many students were reluctant to tell parents when they were victims of text bullying due to the fear of having cell phones taken away or their use restricted (Raskauskas, 2010).
- Inclusion of the topic of bullying and effective prevention and intervention measures in university curricula and continuing education offerings for future teachers, administrators, mental health professions, and law enforcement officials (Olweus & Limber, 2010).
- As antibullying curriculum is developed and incorporated, the needs of students with disabilities, who are often targeted due to lack of social skills and low self-confidence, need to be taken into consideration (Briggs, Simpson, & Gaus, 2010).

A Psychosociocultural Crisis Paradigm

The issues, concepts, training implications, and service approaches illustrated in these life examples are familiar to many clinicians. They underscore not only the potential and limitations of the crisis model but also the necessary coordination of crisis care with other service modalities. This is particularly necessary in life-threatening situations arising primarily from cultural attitudes, including racism, and an economically disadvantaged position in the social structure. The categorization of crisis into "transitional" and "situational" types is inadequate to explain the experience of and guide to clinical practice for large numbers of distressed people who do not fall into these definitions (Antonovsky, 1979, 1987; Burgess & Holmstrom, 1979; Herman, 1992; Hoff et al., 2009; Lifton & Olson, 1976). Because violence against women was considered a "private" matter before it was made public by women's advocates in the late 1970s, logically it follows that professional crisis discourse before that time did not generally include violence and related phenomena in theory development.

Though most clinicians today have moved beyond simplistic crisis formulations, the inclusion even of Caplan's (1964) original concept of cultural "supplies" and a broader sociocultural context of crisis is the exception in crisis theory and practice. Although Caplan addressed the crisis response of *individuals* experiencing hazardous life events, he did so with consistent emphasis on the person in the *context* of his or her environment. That is, people in crisis are members of cultural communities and need social networks of support (sociocultural "supplies") to avoid the danger and embrace the opportunities in life crisis situations. Social support includes elements of emotional, cognitive, and material support (Weiss & Lonnquist, 2006).

The secondary status of sociocultural factors even in crisis theory is not surprising, of course, given the individualistic bias and biomedical dominance characterizing entire health care systems. Many practitioners have abandoned the legacy of victim blaming in crisis care around violence and abuse. Yet, we are still prone to consider, for example, the social and personal crisis of teenage parenthood (with all the risks entailed) primarily in individual rather than socioeconomic terms. As the battle over sex education and teen pregnancy rages, it is noteworthy that five generations of (largely ignored) historical data reveal the correlation between women's educational and economic status and their personal control of reproduction.

The theoretical model in Figure 2.1 depicts (a) the experience of individuals in crisis (from origin to resolution), (b) predictors of crisis response and resolution based on that experience, and (c) the aids available (natural and formal crisis management) to facilitate growth and avoid negative crisis outcomes. The model is derived from in-depth field research with battered women and their families (Hoff, 1990). This crisis paradigm incorporates important concepts from life event research and international studies such as those of Lifton (1967), which reveal theoretical links between the experience of Holocaust and atomic bomb survivors and others whose personal crises and despair can be traced primarily to *sociocultural roots* rather than personality factors. It shows the overlap between the emotional, sociopolitical, physical, and material dimensions of particular crisis situations.

Hoff et al. (2009) have applied these concepts to other crisis situations. For example, parents suffering the loss of an infant through sudden infant death syndrome (SIDS) need primarily emotional and social support. Unless prior psychopathology is present, peer support through a SIDS parents' group, and perhaps crisis counseling for the parents, often suffices to avoid negative crisis resolution. In contrast, if the crisis arises from personal injury through malice or neglect (such as youth violence, sexual assault, workplace violence, or contamination by environmental hazards—as in the BP Deepwater Horizon oil spill in the Gulf of Mexico), some kind of social action (for example, implementation of bullying prevention curriculum, or demanding court-ordered victim compensation for suffering from lost income) is indicated in addition to the support the person may need for emotional healing and closure. In another example, receiving a diagnosis of leukemia portends the possibility of emotional crisis. But if that diagnosis originates in one's exposure to hazardous waste and public neglect of safety and cleanup measures, individual crisis counseling most likely will be inadequate without simultaneous attention to the *social origins* of such personal distress and corresponding social responses.

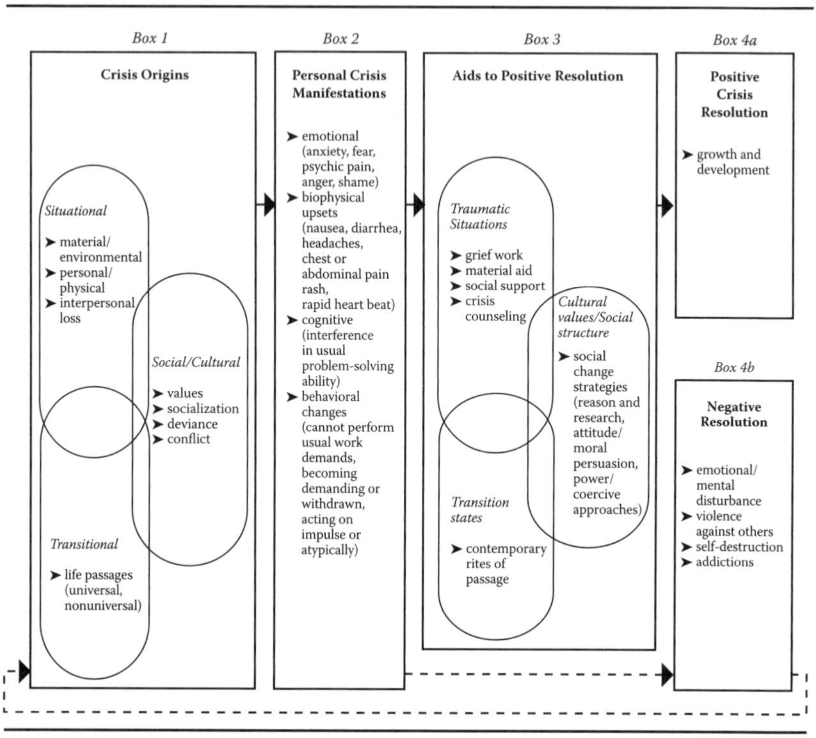

Figure 2.1 Crisis paradigm. Crisis origins, manifestations, and outcomes and the respective functions of crisis care have interactional relationships. The intertwined circles represent the distinct yet interrelated origins of crisis and aids to positive resolution, even though personal manifestations are often similar. The arrows pointing from origins to positive resolution illustrate the *opportunity for growth and development* through crisis. The broken line at the bottom depicts the potential *danger of crisis* in the absence of appropriate aids. The loop between Box 4b and Box 1 denotes the *vulnerability* to future crisis episodes following negative resolution.

Overlapping roles are also relevant in helping people who are homeless because of violence, fire, or flooding. Material aid must be combined with emotional and social support, plus social action if the origin of the crisis is social, as in the case of victimization by crime such as arson. Traumatic stress debriefing alone is not enough. The crisis paradigm, therefore, suggests a tandem approach to crisis care—that is, attending to the immediate problem while not losing sight of the social and public health strategies needed to address the complex sociocultural origins of crisis.

Overall, this crisis paradigm offers a framework for understanding, assessing, and responding to "normal" life crises such as divorce or the death of a loved one, as well as crisis states following horrific traumas (such as sexual assault at gunpoint, or terrorist bombing) that fall outside the range of most people's experience. Applied to the examples we have presented, this theoretical model situates the *origin* (Box 1 in Figure 2.1) of their crises primarily in sociocultural factors such as sex role stereotypes, conflict resolution by violence, disadvantaged social status as immigrants, and cultural values regarding violence. In Alice Smith's situation, social factors are evident in marital conflict that escalated to suicidality, whereas gender bias may have influenced her speedy discharge through psychotropic drug prescription. In Barbara Cabot's circumstances, social factors and health care economics intersect with the personal situation of her husband's precarious health status and the challenge of the aging process (transitional state). In Fatimah Okoro's situation, immigrant status and the cultural acceptance of violence against women collide with the complicated, and sometimes unforgiving, social service and criminal justice systems in the United States. The example of Juan Lopez points to the intersection between policy issues and various providers' expert knowledge and skills in comprehensive service for seriously ill persons. In Ashley Johnson's situation, years of victimization by peers lead to stress in her transition to college. Without systematic incorporation of psychosocial assessment in routine health care, critical elements of treatment will be shortchanged. Regarding youth violence, such as bullying, systematic education for students, school employees, and parents on the dangers of bullying followed by policy-enforced action and advocacy when bullying is present is indicated. In workplace violence and abuse incidents, a combination of individual crisis prevention and intervention skills, institutional policy protections, and professional advocacy for vulnerable workers is necessary.

Assessment (Box 2 in Figure 2.1) reveals extreme distress in each case: Alice's suicide attempt, Barbara's risk for both homicide and suicide, Fatimah's vulnerabilities as an immigrant in an abusive relationship, Juan's breakdown with serious mental illness during a critical life transition point, and Ashley's extreme anxiety, depression, and suicidal ideation. In all instances we observe *natural crisis management* (Box 3 in Figure 2.1): Alice called her friend; Barbara confided her near despair to her brother but resisted his offer of immediate relief, suggesting a need for professional assessment and intervention; Fatimah recruited her community family in assistance with transportation, child care, and personal safety needs; Juan returned home to live with his parents; and Ashley solicited support from her mom during her most difficult periods.

In a mental health system more coordinated and sensitive to crisis and diversity issues, these clients' efforts might have been complemented with various *formal crisis care* strategies (Box 3 in Figure 2.1) toward the *positive health benefits* (Box 4a in Figure 2.1) of all concerned and the prevention of *negative crisis outcomes* (Box 4b in Figure 2.1) such as psychopathology, addictions, posttraumatic stress disorder, suicide, and homicide.

A variation on the concepts depicted in the crisis paradigm is the medicine wheel and the Lakota sacred circle philosophy and the need for attention to the sociocultural and political roots of crisis among indigenous populations. Their personal crises today are connected to their suffering and the oppression of their language, and confinement to reservations after confiscation of original tribal lands (see Hoff, 2010, ch. 8).

To summarize, theoretical models (or paradigms) are not exact depictions of reality. In health care practice, they are merely intended as a guide to understanding distressed people and framing intervention accordingly. The crisis paradigm informing this book builds on earlier work. It especially complements the works of Antonovsky, Caplan, Herman, and Lifton in its holistic emphasis on the inherent connection between personal and sociocultural factors influencing the crisis response of large numbers of people.

References

Antonovsky, A. (1979). *Health, stress, and coping*. San Francisco, CA: Jossey-Bass.

Antonovsky, A. (1987). *Unraveling the mystery of health*. San Francisco, CA: Jossey-Bass.

Beiser, M. (2009). Resettling refugees and safeguarding their mental health: Lessons learned from the Canadian refugee resettlement project. *Transcultural Psychiatry, 46*(4), 539–583.

Bowes, L., Maughan, B., Caspi, A., Moffitt, T. E., & Arseneault, L. (2010). Families promote emotional and behavioural resilience to bullying: Evidence of an environmental effect. *Journal of Child Psychology and Psychiatry, 51*(7), 809–817.

Briggs, M. J. G., Simpson, C., & Gaus, M. D. (2010). Using a team approach to address bullying of students with Asperger's syndrome in activity-based settings. *Children and Schools, 32*(3), 135–142.

Burgess, A., & Holmstrom, L. L. (1979). *Rape: Crisis and recovery*. Bowie, MD: Brady.

Caplan, G. (1964). *Principles of preventive psychiatry*. New York, NY: Basic Books.

Chandler, S. N. (1990). *Competing realities: The contested terrain of mental health advocacy*. New York, NY: Praeger.

Clark, D. C., & Kerkhof, A. J. F. M. (1993). No-suicide decisions and suicide contracts in therapy. *Crisis, 14*(3), 98–99.

Delport, E. (Ed.). (2007). *Gender-based violence in Africa: Perspectives from the continent*. Pretoria: Centre for Human Rights.

Desjarlais, R., Eisenberg, L., Good, B., & Kleinman, A. (1995). *World mental health: Problems and priorities in low-income countries*. New York, NY: Oxford University Press.

Due, P., Damsgaard, M. T., Lund, R., & Holstein, B. E. (2009). Is bullying equally harmful for rich and poor children? A study of bullying and depression from age 15 to 27. *Journal of Public Health, 19*(5), 464–469.

Dupree, L. W., Watson, M. A., & Schneider, M. G. (2005). Preferences for mental health care: A comparison of older African Americans and older Caucasians. *Journal of Applied Gerontology, 24*(3), 196–210.

Earley, P. (2006). *Crazy: A father's search through America's mental health madness.* New York, NY: Berkley Books.

Frisen, A., & Holmqvist, K. (2009). Adolescents' own suggestions for bullying intervention at age 13 and 16. *Scandinavian Journal of Psychology, 51*, 123–131.

Goodfriend, M., Bryant, T., III, Livingood, W., & Goldhagen, J. (2006). A model for training paediatricians to expand mental health services in the community practice setting. *Clinical Pediatrics, 45*, 649–654.

Herman, J. (1992). *Trauma and recovery: The aftermath of violence.* New York, NY: Basic Books.

Hoff, L. A. (1990). *Battered women as survivors.* New York, NY: Routledge.

Hoff, L. A. (1992). Review essay: Wife beating in Micronesia. *Isla: A Journal of Micronesian Studies, 1*(2), 199–221.

Hoff, L. A. (2010). *Violence and abuse issues: Cross-cultural perspectives for health and social services.* London, UK: Routledge.

Hoff, L. A., Hallisey, B. J., & Hoff, M. (2009). *People in crisis: Clinical and diversity perspectives* (6th ed.). New York, NY: Routledge.

Hoff, L. A., & Morgan, B. D. (2011). *Psychiatric and mental health essentials in primary care.* London, UK: Routledge.

Holt, M. K., Kantor, G. K., & Finkelhor, D. (2009). Parent/child concordance about bullying involvement and family characteristics related to bullying and peer victimization. *Journal of School Violence, 8*, 42–63.

Jang, D., Lee, D., & Morello-Frosch, R. (1991). Domestic violence in the immigrant and refugee community: Responding to the needs of immigrant women. *Response, 13*(4), 2–7.

Johnson, A. B. (1990). *Out of bedlam: The truth about deinstitutionalization.* New York, NY: Basic Books.

Joint Commission on Mental Health and Illness. (1961). *Action for mental health.* New York, NY: Basic Books.

Levine, M. (1981). *The history and politics of community mental health.* New York, NY: Oxford University Press.

Lifton, R. J. (1967). *Life in death.* New York. NY: Simon & Schuster.

Lifton, R. J., & Olson, E. (1976). The human meaning of total disaster: The Buffalo Creek experience. *Psychiatry, 39*, 1–18.

Lorber, J. (1997). Female genital mutilation: A women's rights/cultural conflict. *Democratic Left, 2*, 3–5.

McHenry, P. C., & Price, S. J. (Eds.). (2000). *Families and change: Coping with stressful events and transitions* (2nd ed.). Thousand Oaks, CA: Sage.

Melillo, K. D., & Houde, S. C. (2011). *Geropsychiatric and mental health nursing* (2nd ed.). Sudbury, MA: Jones and Bartlett.

Morgan, B. (2010). End of life care for patients with mental illness and personality disorders. In. B. Ferrell & N. Coyne (Eds.), *Textbook of palliative care nursing* (3rd ed.). New York, NY: Oxford University Press.

Mosher, L. R., & Burti, L. (1994). *Community mental health: A practical guide.* New York, NY: Norton.

Nansel, T. R., Overpeck, M., Pilla, R. S., Ruan, W. J., Simons-Morton, B., & Scheidt, P. (2001). Bullying behaviors among U.S. youth: Prevalence and association with psychosocial adjustment. *Journal of the American Medical Association, 285*(16), 2094–2100.

Olweus, D. (1994). Annotation: Bullying at school: Basic facts and effects of a school based intervention program. *Journal of Child Psychology & Psychiatry & Allied Disciplines, 35*(7), 1171–1190.

Olweus, D., & Limber, S. P. (2010). Bullying in school: Evaluation and dissemination of the Olweus bullying prevention program. *American Journal of Orthopsychiatry, 80*(1), 124–134.

O'Sullivan, M. J., Siqueira, C. E., Sperrazza, K., Koren, A., Melillo, K. D., Hoff, L. A., White-O'Sullivan, E. M., & Slatin, C. (2008). It's part of the job: Healthcare restructuring and the health and safety of nursing aids. In L. McKee, E. Ferlie, & P. Hyde (Eds.), *Organizing and reorganizing: Power and change in health care organizations* (pp. 99–111). Houndmills, UK: Palgrave MacMillan.

Pergolizzi, F., Richmond, D., Macario, S., Gan, Z., Richmond, C., & Macario, E. (2009). Bullying in middle schools: Results from a four-school survey. *Journal of School Violence, 8*, 264–279.

Podneiks, E. (1990). *National survey on abuse of the elderly in Canada: The Ryerson study.* Ottawa, Canada: Health and Welfare Canada, National Clearinghouse on Family Violence.

Poteat, V. P., & DiGiovanni, C. D. (2010). When biased language use is associated with bullying and dominance behavior: The moderating effect of prejudice. *Journal of Youth and Adolescence, 39*, 1123– 1133.

Procter, N. G. (2005). Emergency mental health nursing for self-harming refugees and asylum seekers. *International Journal of Mental Health Nursing, 14*, 196–201.

Pruschno, R. A., & Resch, N. (1989). Husbands and wives as caregivers: Antecedents of depression and burden. *The Journal of Gerontology, 29*(2), 159–162.

Raskauskas, J. (2010). Text-bullying: Associations with traditional bullying and depression among New Zealand adolescents. *Journal of School Violence, 9*, 74–97.

Runyan, C. W. (2001). Moving forward with research on the prevention of violence against workers. *American Journal of Preventive Medicine, 20*(2), 169–172.

Sidel, R. (1986). *Women and children last: The plight of poor women in affluent America.* New York, NY: Penguin.

Sommers, R., & Shields, L. (1987). *Women take care: The consequences of caregiving in today's society.* Gainesville, FL: Triad.

Stagnitti, M. (2005). Antidepressant use in the U.S. civilian non-insitutionalized population, 2002 (Statistical Brief #77). Rockville, MD: Medical Expenditure Panel, Agency for Healthcare Research and Quality.

U.S. Department of Health and Human Services. (2010, September 15). The Affordable Care Act & behavioral health [Video file]. Retrieved from http://www.youtube.com/user/USGOVHHS?feature=mhum#p/a/u/0/plbTLrRXNk8

Walker, A. (1992). *Possessing the secret of joy*. New York, NY: Harcourt Brace Jovanovich.

Wang, J., Iannotti, R. J., & Nansel, T. R. (2009). School bullying among adolescents in the United States: Physical, verbal, relational, and cyber. *Journal of Adolescent Health, 45*, 368–375.

Weiss, S. J., Haber, J., Horowitz, J. A., Stuart, G. W., & Wolfe, B. (2009). The inextricable nature of mental and physical health: Implications for integrative care. *Journal of the American Psychiatric Nurses Association, 15*(6), 371–382.

Weiss, G., & Lonnquist, L. (2006). *The sociology of health, healing, and illness* (5th ed.). Upper Saddle River, NJ: Pearson Prentice Hall.

Whitaker, R. (2010). *Anatomy of an epidemic: Magic bullets, psychiatric drugs, and the astonishing rise of mental illness in America*. New York, NY: Crown.

Wilson, K. S., Silberberg, M. R., Brown, A. J., & Yaggy, S. D. (2007). Health needs and barriers to healthcare of women who have experienced intimate partner violence. *Journal of Women's Health, 16*(10), 1485–1498.

II

EDUCATION AND TRAINING PROGRAM DEVELOPMENT AND IMPLEMENTATION

The three chapters in this section elaborate on essential content for presentation and mastery by students in formal degree programs preparing health and social graduates for effective practice. Additionally, this section addresses the qualifications of educators and trainers, some of whom may lack any formal preparation themselves on various crisis topics. These chapters are also relevant for agency-based programs where trainees typically arrive with a diverse array of the *knowledge*, *attitudes*, and *skills* required for either volunteer or paid staff positions in agencies offering a range of crisis services.

Chapter 3

Essentials of Educational and Clinical Training Programs

Chapter Outline

Standards for Crisis Training Programs
Core Content for Education and Training in Crisis Theory and Practice
Qualifications of Educators and Trainers in Crisis and Psychosocial Care
Continuing Education for Educators and Trainers
Certification of Individual Crisis Practitioners

For several decades now, health professions educators—especially in mental health disciplines—have included elements of crisis theory and practice in formal curricula. Trainers in community-based crisis programs—particularly those that are nationally certified—have prepared thousands of volunteers in the basics of crisis intervention. This chapter addresses the essential features that educators and trainers must attend to for achieving excellence in the preparation of crisis workers.

Standards for Crisis Training Programs

Those who do not learn from history are doomed to repeat it.

—**George Santayana**

Crisis training standards flow from the crisis field itself as a formalized body of knowledge and practice. The creation of such standards in the United States can be traced to three interrelated strands in the development of this service area:

- The move during the 1960s to create alternatives to traditional health service delivery systems that would appeal to disaffected members of the community, especially those presenting in crisis states or experiencing other psychosocial problems.
- The beginning of the suicide prevention movement spearheaded by Edwin Shneidman and Norman Farberow (1957), a result of studying suicide notes in greater Los Angeles.
- The results and recommendations of the Joint Commission on Mental Health and Illness (1961) in the United States. A major finding from this commission was that 42% of distressed persons with any problem initially sought help from physicians or clergy, not mental health professionals—a point of obvious relevance to contemporary emphasis on primary care (Hoff & Morgan, 2011).

In spite of the recommendations from the 1961 Joint Commission and massive federal funding to support the development of 24-hour emergency mental health programs as a key feature of comprehensive community mental health centers, it was largely volunteer citizen groups who responded to the need for such emergency services. However, reliance on volunteers' goodwill and intuition as a basis for practice was not enough, nor was a piecemeal approach to training sufficient to prepare volunteers for frontline crisis work. Similarly, professionals such as nurses, physicians, and social workers could no longer rely on their academic degrees alone to qualify them for helping people in crisis. Program administrators, crisis specialists, and licensed mental health professionals became concerned about wide disparities in training requirements and certain questionable practices in some training contexts (e.g., requesting trainees to role-play their own possible suicide without providing follow-up support).

In the early 1970s, these concerns were central to the crisis movement and to the development of training standards for various workers in the crisis field. These standards were originally published in 1976 in Area 2 of the *Certification*

Standards Manual (Hoff & Wells, 1989) sponsored by the American Association of Suicidology (AAS) Committee on Accreditation. The AAS *Organization Accreditation Standards Manual* has gone through several revisions since then, with the 10th edition being published in 2011 (AAS, 2011).

Besides grassroots efforts such as the women's movement drawing attention to victim-survivors of sexual assault and battering, three federal bodies in the United States focused on the neglected area of victims in crisis: the President's Task Force on Victims of Crime (1982), the Attorney General's Task Force on Family Violence (1984), and the Surgeon General's Workshop on Violence and Public Health (1986). All three of these works highlighted the fact that double victimization or secondary trauma can occur when health and criminal justice professionals lack basic knowledge and skills in their work with victim-survivors—knowledge and skills that are common to crisis workers trained according to international standards. If people in crisis, including various victims of crime, are to receive the service they are entitled to, it is imperative that all health and human service workers are trained in the essential components of crisis theory and practice. At the Surgeon General's Workshop, members underscored this point in their final report by recommending that victimology and crisis intervention be included in the curricula and licensing examinations of all health and human service professionals. The eligibility criteria for agencies or programs seeking accreditation reflect these ideals around the preparation of health and social service personnel working with distressed people. This broad array of programs and the persons staffing them are the focus of the core content described here and exemplified in Chapter 9. Our aim here is not to simply repeat history, but to *learn* from it, and to implement the decades-old ideals of crisis care across education and practice arenas.

In this chapter, we outline core content in crisis theory and practice and its placement within the broader arena of psychosocial aspects of health and social service in primary, secondary, and tertiary care settings. We also discuss the qualifications of educators and trainers in the field and suggestions for their own continuing education. Finally, we elaborate on individual crisis worker certification for both volunteers and paid workers in various crisis service programs—whether crisis work is the agency's primary mission or is integrated into other facets of comprehensive health care. In this discussion, we assume the common distinction between education and training. *Education* is associated with formal preservice preparation of professionals in universities or colleges, whereas *training* refers to continuing education (or in-service) programs for those already employed (or anticipating employment—paid or volunteer) in a practice setting. For simplicity, we use *education* and *training* interchangeably.

Core Content for Education and Training in Crisis Theory and Practice

The notion of core content can be used in several different contexts. In formal preservice professional programs, such as nursing, medicine, social work, and psychology, core crisis content would be part of a total curriculum, usually addressed progressively in beginning, intermediate, and advanced clinical courses dealing with the psychosocial aspects of health. The term *curriculum* refers to the complex array of learning activities or a body of courses organized to achieve specific educational goals. *Core curriculum* encompasses those courses required of all students graduating from an educational institution, without which the educational goals would not be met.

Moving to the course level, core crisis content refers to the *knowledge*, *attitudes*, and *skills* essential to any person practicing as a crisis worker, regardless of the setting or framework in which he or she learned this essential content. The concept of core content is important for several reasons. It emphasizes what every worker needs for managing complex crisis situations and avoiding unhelpful approaches, such as inadvertent collusion in victim blaming (for example, manifesting impatience with a woman who doesn't take immediate steps to leave an abusive partner or using excessive force with an angry or unruly patient). It also corrects the assumption that traditional curricula are enough without formal attention to *recently* developed crisis content. Specification of core content also serves as a framework for assessing ad hoc or unexamined additions or deletions of essential content.

This is not to say that traditional curricula have totally ignored crisis content. For example, all nursing, medical, social work, and psychology programs address suicide; yet many nonpsychiatric nurses and physicians have less confidence in basic crisis intervention with a suicidal person than trained lay volunteers staffing suicide prevention hotlines have—overall, a reflection of the mind–body split in health care services. On most university campuses, the dichotomy between physical and mental and emotional health concerns is symbolized by structural arrangements: The "health" service (emphasizing general physical problems) is staffed by nonpsychiatric physicians and nurse practitioners, whereas "counseling" services are staffed by psychologists and social workers. Sometimes this mind–body split is exaggerated further by separation of the medical and counseling services in different buildings (see Hoff & Morgan, 2011, ch. 1). There is, however, a growing trend toward integrating these services under one managing body, but not without the growing pains of altering this deeply engrained traditional mind-set. For instance, at one Midwestern university, this integration will play out over several years before all services will be provided in one location under one unified program. Our intention here is not to suggest complete role blurring or elimination of medical and counseling specialties; rather, we propose increased and complementary familiarity with one another's specialties as an aid to more holistic care and more efficient and effective use of consultation with specialists, as in the following example.

Example: Anxious Student

> At a university's Anxiety Screening Day (part of a national program in the United States), a graduate student, age 30, was screened by a counselor and expressed very high anxiety around maintaining the grade point average required to continue in his major area of study. He had set unrealistic performance standards for himself and confided concerns about conflicts in his marriage of 4 years. He also revealed a two-generation family history of thyroid problems. The counselor, in consultation with the nurse practitioner, referred the student for thyroid testing in addition to a follow-up counseling session.

Recent trends toward primary health care and other developments (such as holistic health care) suggest that disease models are inadequate to address contemporary problems like youth suicide and crises stemming from social problems such as hazardous waste disposal and victimization by crime or abuse. In addition, mastery of core crisis content enhances effective communication between training groups and various practitioners who are on the front lines of crisis service delivery. Such communication avoids duplication of training and augments the trainees' sense of accomplishment around the knowledge and skills already mastered. Thus, if a volunteer in a victim assistance program or other crisis service has successfully completed a four-semester-credit crisis course with a clinical practicum conducted by a qualified instructor or trainer, she or he should not have to repeat the core content in an agency's training requirements (see Chapter 9). Rather, the volunteer could be examined on concepts from the core content, and the remaining time could be focused on application of this content to the unique circumstances of the employing agency. This recommendation also assumes the principles of adult education (interactional and experiential versus hierarchical) (Knowles, 1980).

What, then, is this core content, and how was it identified as core? As with most health and social service curriculum segments, core crisis content falls into three categories: *knowledge*, *attitudes*, and *skills*. These broad categories lay the foundation for objectives defined in terms that demonstrate acceptable knowledge, attitudinal, and skill outcomes. For example, a student can *identify* the steps of the crisis management process (knowledge), *demonstrate* a nonjudgmental attitude in a role play (attitude), and *apply* the techniques of assessing suicide risk or victimization trauma in a real or simulated case situation (skill). These behaviorally defined outcomes or objectives are discussed in detail in Chapter 4.

The elements of core content were derived from the collective knowledge and experience of nationally and internationally recognized crisis specialists and suicidologists during the 1960s and 1970s. The development of crisis content in various professional programs was also stimulated by a proposal from the National Institute of Mental Health (NIMH) in the United States for a basic crisis curriculum and recommended reading lists in the field during this same period. This content was continuously refined through exchanges among experts at professional meetings and through evaluation of training programs by trainees, students, and trainers or educators in crisis settings around the United States and other countries. In the late 1980s, various movements on behalf of victims, including the National Organization for Victim Assistance (NOVA) and advocates for abused women, led to the inclusion of violence issues and the care of victim-survivors of abuse in core crisis content (see Chapter 4 for details regarding implementation of core content).

Knowledge

Essential concepts that crisis workers should master include the following:

- Crisis theory and principles of crisis care:
  - Origins and development of crisis
  - Crisis prevention (through public education and emotional first aid such as traumatic stress debriefing)
  - Manifestations of crisis, including effective and ineffective crisis coping
  - Steps of the crisis management process: assessment, planning, implementation, and evaluation
  - Application of crisis care to special groups at risk for crisis—people addicted to alcohol and other drugs, victims of abuse and sexual assault, the chronically disabled (either physically or mentally), and immigrants or refugees
- Suicidology, including principles and techniques of assessment and suicide prevention
- Victimology, including assessment of assault and homicide potential and victimization trauma, and crisis intervention with victim-survivors and assailants
- Death, dying, and grief work
- Principles of communication
- Ethical and legal issues regarding suicide, crime, and victimization
- Voluntary and involuntary hospitalization criteria regarding high-risk clients
- Identification and use of community resources in crisis intervention and resolution
- Team relationships and self-care in crisis work

- The consultation process and its application in crisis work
- Principles and structures for record keeping

As educators and trainers consider this core content, they must also evaluate the different approaches to it taken by various writers. Serious attention to the theoretical underpinnings of crisis work is sometimes slighted because rapid action is often called for in crisis situations. It can also be short-changed by some students' and trainees' disinterest in theory and history, and their eagerness to get on to more practical concerns. Since the original work of Caplan (1964), Lindemann (1944), and Erikson (1963), very few new theoretical approaches have been proposed to advance the crisis field. Exceptions to this include Taplin's (1971) work, Burgess and Baldwin's (1981) typology of six classes of crises, Ramsay's (1997) discussion of chaos theory, and Hoff's (1990; Hoff, Hallisey, & Hoff, 2009) crisis paradigm based on research with battered women and application of the "life event" and stress literature (such as Antonovsky, 1979, 1987) to the crisis field. The increasing importance of skilled crisis workers in the managed care context suggests the need for more conscious attention by practitioners to the theoretical foundations of their work.

For example, early work on child abuse was labeled as the "battered child syndrome" (Kempe, Silverman, Steele, Droegemueller, & Silver, 1962). Basic to Kempe et al.'s "perpetrator-victim model" of etiology is the "syndrome" or physical examination findings in the child victim, which can be traced to the psychopathology of the parent-perpetrator. This focus flows logically from the history of medicine, which is heavily influenced by the philosophy of Descartes emphasizing mind–body separation, although most physicians today embrace more holistic models. This philosophy supports the idea of "the body as a machine, of disease as a breakdown of the machine, and of the doctor's task as repair of the machine" (Engle, 1977, p. 131). Descartes's dualistic philosophy is at least partially responsible for the general neglect of the social-psychological aspects of health and illness (see Whitaker, 2010).

In another theoretical framework, abusive parents may be viewed primarily as criminal, with the result that punishment, not treatment, is emphasized. The reality is more likely somewhere between these extremes and complexly related to other contextual factors. Some abusive parents may be psychopathologically disturbed, but they are nevertheless influenced by a culture in which many people believe that *some* physical punishment is necessary for children, punishment that many may define as abusive and others as "normal." Also, although child abuse involves more than criminal activity, crisis workers dealing with parents are influenced by the internationally recognized legal mandate (required of health and social service workers, as well as teachers and clergy) to report child abuse and protect the rights of children.

Educators and trainers can contribute to new theory development in the crisis field through thoughtful critique of the concepts proposed by writers and researchers that guide clinical practice. In varying depth, the major clinical texts outline general conceptual frameworks of their authors (see www.crisisprograms.org). Some texts rely heavily on general systems concepts, whereas others are more sociocultural and interactional in orientation (see Hoff et al., 2009, ch. 1, for an overview of theoretical influences on crisis theory). Educators and administrators need to critically examine textbook authors' conceptual frameworks and their implications for practice. Also, more research is needed to examine theory and practice and to build on the early concepts proposed by Caplan, Lindemann, and others.

In general, the *knowledge* component of core crisis content is the easiest for students or trainees to master. Good textbooks, audiovisual resources, training seminars, the abundance of web-based resources—and students' willingness to read and attend training opportunities—will complement classroom interaction and critique of the basic concepts (see www.crisisprograms.org). The *attitudes* and *skills* necessary for effective crisis work are the more challenging elements of core content for students and trainees to master—whether as one's main practice or integrated into other service facets.

Attitudes

Core crisis content includes these attitudinal outcomes for training:

- Acceptance of and nonjudgmental response to persons different from oneself and toward controversial, emotional, or value-laden issues, such as self-injurious behavior (Trepal, Wester, & MacDonald, 2006), substance dependence, crisis pregnancy, or suicidality.
- A balanced, realistic attitude toward oneself in the provider role. An effective crisis worker does not expect to "rescue" or "save" all potentially suicidal people or to solve all the problems of the distressed person, such as expecting a woman to leave her abusive partner in spite of the fact that she may not be ready because of self-identified obstacles she feels she cannot overcome. This issue is particularly challenging for health practitioners in service settings where they may be pressured to limit the time spent with a patient to 10- or 15-minute slots and may feel that there is not enough time to "solve" the patient's problems. Here it is useful to recall the success of trained hotline workers who, when facing a potentially lethal crisis situation, can empathically "tune in" to the distressed person, identify the key issues or problem precipitating the crisis, obtain vital information (place, weapons or drug possession, etc.), maintain

open communication, and effectively link the person to crisis outreach or hospital emergency resources sometimes within less than 10 minutes and without the structural supports accorded by an on-site team. Attitude—the conviction that such crisis work is "everybody's business," not merely the specialty of hotline workers—and knowledge-based confidence are crucial here.

- A realistic and humane approach to death, dying, self-destructive behavior, victimization, and other human issues (for example, not implying to a rape victim that she or he is at fault for having been intoxicated at the time of the assault).
- Coming to terms with one's own feelings about death, dying, and potential for violence, insofar as these feelings might interfere with or deter one from helping others.
- Openness to the varied responses of individuals in crisis.
- Activating with conviction one's advocacy role in client empowerment, and having the general belief that a client can and will usually navigate the crisis situation successfully. When acknowledging interpersonal violence as a human rights issue (Delport, 2007), De Jong and Kleber (2007) urge that human rights violations necessitate speaking out for those who cannot (for example, "What happened to you is not your fault").

Teaching and training around these attitudinal issues require the instructor's and clinical supervisor's continuous attention to his or her own attitudes and role modeling of open-mindedness to these sensitive issues. It also means realizing that helping people in distress is not a value-free endeavor. Attitudes will invariably be revealed in interaction between the health and human service worker and the person in distress. Therefore, if crisis trainers or clinicians discover that personal attitudes and beliefs will present a barrier to impartial and compassionate responses to distressed people regarding controversial issues, it is best to acknowledge the problem and remove themselves from working with trainees or clients. For example, a female provider who has unresolved violence issues in her life may find it very difficult to provide clinical intervention and support to a victimized woman, as these issues may resurface in the helping process. For such providers, counseling or psychotherapy is recommended. Additionally, if clinicians or trainees find themselves struggling to develop a therapeutic relationship with a challenging client, additional training and supervision on fostering a recovery oriented relationship may be warranted (Felton, Barr, & Clark, 2006).

It is important to note that rejection of problematic or challenging clients or value-laden responses to them may arise from insufficient knowledge of the dynamics and ramifications of some psychosocial and crisis situations. Concerning violence issues, people who find it difficult to understand why an abused woman stays with her abuser usually take another view of the issue when presented with the array of problems such a woman faces, problems much more complex than a superficial analysis reveals. For example, some women whose lives are threatened by very possessive and controlling partners sense the increased danger they may face when leaving a man who states, "If I can't have you, nobody can," or who is threatening suicide as well as murder.

People with inflexible views on controversial social issues such as abortion, suicide, and HIV/AIDS are probably not suited for crisis work—or, for that matter, *any* mental health work. For example, a person in crisis living with AIDS has enough issues to face without the additional judgmental attitude of someone who believes that the disease is a deserved punishment for "immoral" behavior. In general, then, whereas the *attitudes* of some practitioners may remain fixed, new *knowledge* often results in the kind of flexibility necessary to assist distressed persons. Studies and general social observation reveal that much bias is based on ignorance rather than malice, and lack of experience with persons different from oneself (see Fadiman, 1997; Hoff et al., 2009, ch. 1). For instance, Penn, Esposito, Stein, Lacher-Katz, and Spirito (2005) found that a single training episode for correctional staff working with incarcerated youth significantly improved their understanding and acceptance of the need for mental health treatment among this population.

Skills

Without certain skills, nonjudgmental attitudes and thorough knowledge of concepts will not suffice. Trainees must be able to use their knowledge and attitudinal stance in a systematic, effective approach to helping distressed people. An effective approach means assisting the person toward problem solving, empowerment, and crisis resolution consistent with the individual client's values and meaning system. Crisis and psychosocial care can help distressed people avoid negative crisis outcomes such as violence (toward themselves or others), alcohol and other drug abuse, or chronic emotional or mental disability. Necessary skills to work effectively with people in crisis include the following:

- Applying the techniques for formal crisis care—*assessment*, *planning*, *implementation*, and *evaluation* (including assessment of victimization trauma and risk of suicide or violence toward others)
- Communicating well—listening actively, questioning discretely, responding empathically and calmly, and providing appropriate information and direction
- Mobilizing community resources efficiently and effectively—for example, engaging the rescue squad within 15 minutes of receiving a suicide attempt

call, collaborating with the police in a violent situation without escalating the crisis and precipitating more violence, and making an appropriate referral for follow-up counseling or therapy

- Implementing agency policy and keeping records accurately and efficiently—for example, recording essential notes in succinct form within the same work shift so they are useful to the next worker, ensuring consistent client care, and satisfying legal requirements (e.g., should legal action be pursued)
- Implementing the procedures for voluntary and involuntary hospitalization when indicated
- Carrying out these crisis care steps while withholding judgment on controversial behaviors and not imposing one's own values on the distressed person and his or her family
- Prioritizing information and action to ensure an organized, systematic intervention process that focuses on the most critical problem first; maximizing clinical support where needed; and minimizing the possibility of escalating a problem to crisis proportions
- Using crisis intervention skills in a culturally relevant and locally accepted manner (see De Jong & Kleber, 2007)

Crisis assessment and intervention assume a definition of most crises as *normal* rather than pathological. Crisis care involves distinguishing between life-threatening and chronic problems, implementing short-term crisis prevention and intervention strategies, offering support and accessible, available follow-up resources, and knowing when to seek the services of a crisis or psychiatric specialist. Crisis specialists must be able to utilize their skills in a highly emotional and quick-paced environment.

The minimum number of hours recommended by the American Association of Suicidology's *Organizational Accreditation Standards Manual* (2011; see also Hoff & Wells, 1989) for achieving the knowledge, attitudinal, and skill outcomes essential to effective crisis work is 40 hours, of which 32 hours are formal training and 8 hours are supervised clinical practice. This is roughly equivalent to a three- or four-semester-credit college course. It is also similar to the training programs conducted by certified crisis programs in the United States and Canada. For professional students in social work, nursing, and psychology, for example, these recommended hours of instruction need to be orchestrated with other curriculum requirements; for example, "communication skills" as essential content would be covered in some depth in a course (or unit within a course) on clinical interviewing. The ability to teach or train in a way that will result in these *knowledge*, *attitudinal*, and *skill* outcomes suggests an array of qualifications for the crisis trainer or educator.

Qualifications of Educators and Trainers in Crisis and Psychosocial Care

"Those who do not know how to do, teach" goes the old saying, "and those who do not know how to teach, consult." Dedicated clinical teachers hope this criticism will never apply to their work. Yet professional educators and trainers for clinical practice have long struggled with the demands of teaching and training in a content area that demands the same work as of any other teacher and further requires keeping their practice skills up-to-date in rapidly developing clinical fields. Unlike education in theoretical disciplines, concepts in practice disciplines must be meaningfully linked to their application in the clinical field to maintain relevance to students and trainees. Not to do so—in effect, teaching practice strategies without knowing how to *do* them—reduces both the students' interest and the teachers' credibility.

The psychosocial and crisis field is no exception in making this demand on clinical educators and trainers. In fact, the stress inherent in frontline crisis work may be even greater than in slower paced practice fields. As noted, crisis educators and trainers must manage to keep up their clinical practice skills in addition to meeting the usual demands of teaching and training: content preparation, timely delivery, support of students and trainees, and evaluation of teaching methods and outcomes. Educators and clinical trainers who manage this dual challenge will do so more easily if they possess appropriate qualifications.

At the other extreme are teachers who lose credibility by assuming that a skilled practitioner is automatically a skilled trainer. Although some expert clinicians, with or without professional degrees, are also excellent trainers, there is no *necessary* equivalence between the skills required of clinicians and of teachers. To assume that there is suggests a devaluation of education as a distinct field requiring knowledge, attitudes, and skills different from those of clinicians. Those individuals who stand out for their clinical expertise *and* their ability to transmit core content in a highly effective manner are the products of formal training in both areas, accompanied by supervised practice by experts. What, then, should constitute the preparation of trainers and educators qualified to teach crisis and psychosocial care?

First, let us consider trainers working in health agencies or crisis programs' staff education and development positions. The *Organizational Accreditation Standards Manual* (AAS, 2011; Hoff & Wells, 1989) states that this person should have a *minimum* of "one year of supervised experience in crisis work … in which the prospective trainer demonstrates at least *above average* performance in the knowledge, attitudinal, and skill areas" discussed here. This evaluation of a prospective trainer is based on an agency's established criteria for satisfactory performance.

In addition, a trainer should have basic instruction in training methodology and techniques, which would support the following:

- Develop a course syllabus (objectives, content, methodology, evaluation, and bibliography).
- Make appropriate bibliographical material available.
- Develop lesson plans.
- Develop or obtain audiovisual and technological materials and other teaching aids.
- Devise tests or other means of evaluating students or trainees.
- Provide student and trainee support and direction.
- Screen out and advise students and trainees who fail.
- Develop systematic course evaluation plans as a basis for revision.

Ideally, an instructor's preparation would include work as a supervised co-trainer with an opportunity to discuss lesson plans and training problems. A properly prepared trainer will also arrange to be observed and evaluated by an experienced trainer.

In educational settings that prepare various health and human service professionals, such as nurses and social workers, the faculty who teach crisis content should make themselves aware of the standards defining preparation of crisis trainers. In addition, they should possess the same clinical performance ability as any clinical agency-based trainer. Such faculty members should have successfully completed at least one formal course in crisis theory and practice, or its equivalent in continuing education courses, in addition to formal qualifications in their particular practice disciplines for university or college teaching. For trainers in service settings who are not required to meet basic faculty qualifications, we recommend at least some post secondary preparation. In addition, instructors and trainers might develop skills in the generic area of human relations through various training experiences emphasizing communication skills, conflict resolution, and similar topics. Faculty should also recognize that a college degree or graduate degrees in mental health disciplines do not necessarily qualify people as crisis trainers.

Because the crisis field's recognition as a distinct body of theory and practice is relatively new, many would-be trainers and educators find themselves pressured to meet these requirements. Those working in areas where resources, especially experienced crisis trainers, are limited can seek creative alternatives that conform to the principles cited here. For example, an aspiring trainer could complete the following exercises for self-instruction:

- Read several crisis textbooks for a thorough grasp of concepts and different theoretical approaches, and connect the content therein with existing knowledge of psychosocial care.
- Take a local college course on educational psychology or teaching methods.
- Arrange for an observation experience in a local emergency facility to broaden firsthand knowledge of crisis situations.
- Arrange for a participant observation experience with high-risk crisis situations (for example, with police officers responding to domestic violence and sexual assault calls) and the realities of community integration for effective crisis work. Such experience also expands the base of knowledge and experience for consultation in complex crisis situations.
- Plan to attend national and regional conferences for gaining up-to-date information about the field and for networking with crisis experts.
- Work as a volunteer or arrange a summer internship in an established, publicly approved crisis service, preferably when a training course is being conducted (see Chapter 9).

Continuing Education for Educators and Trainers

Once crisis trainers or educators have met the basic requirements, the need to broaden and update their base of knowledge and refine their training skills continues. Many programs exist to meet this demand, as the necessity for continuing education in all health and human service professions is now widely mandated. In fact, licensed professionals (for example, nurses, physicians, counselors, and social workers) in most states and provinces are required to participate in a minimum number of continuing education hours to maintain their certification, college membership, or license to practice. Although such legal requirements do not bind trainers, international training standards constitute a professional mandate to enhance their training skills through continuing education programs.

Educators preparing professionals in university programs have easy access to information about the many available programs. A wide array of service agencies are on the electronic and traditional mailing lists of university continuing education departments and private continuing education organizations. However, individuals who need to attend these programs may not always see the program announcements because they are usually sent to department heads or agency directors. In addition, the organization or agency may not provide the necessary time and financial support for staff trainers to attend continuing education programs. If either is the case, enterprising trainers need to seek out these sources on their own.

In addition to universities' continuing education programs and private continuing education providers, a number of excellent curricula are offered by the staff education divisions of well-established service agencies such as hospitals and certified crisis centers (see Chapter 9). Most in-service programs include at least 4–6 hours of instruction, with some courses extending several days to a week. National meetings provide another valuable avenue for continuing education. Each year, the American Association of Suicidology, for example, offers preconvention workshops on various topics in the crisis field. Also, *Newslink*, the quarterly newsletter of the AAS, announces continuing education curricula nationwide. The Centre for Suicide Prevention (CSP) in Canada hosts the Suicide Information and Education Centre (SIEC) database, a comprehensive collection of information on suicide, crisis, and related topics. It also produces the SIEC Alert, a quarterly quick reference guide to some of the newest resources in the field of suicide prevention. See www.suicideinfo.ca/csp for additional information.

Additionally, trainers can plan more individualized experiences for themselves such as those suggested for basic qualifications. For example, a trainer needing more background in high-risk situations might arrange to observe some police training sessions along with a patrol ride-along experience. A trainer working in a hospital staff development program might attend the training sessions at a local crisis center with telephone hotline observation. Conversely, the crisis center trainer could attend staff development sessions with hospital emergency department observation.

Networking exchanges like these provide shared information about training techniques and crises, and may help to bridge the gaps and ease the natural tensions between indigenous crisis services and traditional providers such as hospitals or police. For example, police officers may feel that their frontline crisis work is not valued by "professionals," but when they share a training experience the message is clear that no one has all the answers and everyone has something to teach and to learn. Teamwork in crisis intervention not only is recommended but also can be a *matter of life and death*. Though some people may fear the police patrol experience for safety reasons, it should be remembered that police officers take extraordinary precautions to protect civilians in these circumstances even though a release-from-responsibility signature is often required.

Trainers might also spend some time in one of the many shelters for homeless individuals, where a majority of the clientele are deinstitutionalized psychiatric patients, a high-risk group for crisis, and many are victims of domestic violence. Other training sources include riding with ambulance officers (emergency medical technicians), working with specialized police crisis teams, and accompanying street workers for youth, for example Operation Come Home in Canada and Bridge Over Troubled Waters in Boston. Another option is combining crisis worker training sessions that encourage interagency information and resource sharing, foster familiarity among diverse workers, and facilitate consultation and collaboration.

Finally, trainers can keep updated on training opportunities through the internet and libraries of local colleges and universities—where updated information on innovative technological resources such as distance learning, web-based tutorials, webinars, and streaming video and audio options are available. These resources are particularly useful for those in rural areas or who lack travel funds for on-site training sessions.

Certification of Individual Crisis Practitioners

Underpinning the certification of individual crisis practitioners are concerns similar to those that led to certification standards for agencies delivering crisis services. Because volunteers with no formal preparation in human service practice traditionally have staffed many of the community-based crisis and distress centers, quality control by employing agencies emerged as a basic issue. Thus, a certified crisis center reassures the public that volunteers who staff these programs have met the minimum training requirements for crisis workers as defined by international standards. This includes a process to screen out training applicants who do not qualify. Regarding providers with professional credentials, we have already noted that a graduate degree in one of the mental health disciplines is no guarantee of having mastered core crisis content needed to meet agency standards.

Individual certification goes a few steps beyond these agency training program standards. Thus, in 1989, the Individual Certification Committee of the AAS launched a program to examine and certify crisis workers. In 1996, following an increase in Canadian crisis workers seeking certification, the AAS entered into formal collaboration with Canadian sponsors of individual certification. Canadian crisis experts served as face validity panelists for the first examination, and the panel of experts reviewing the 1996 edition of the examination consisted of seven Canadian and nine U.S. members, thus assuring a broader cross-cultural base than earlier editions.

In addition to AAS, several other organizations provide individual credentialing of crisis workers: the National Organization for Victim Assistance (NOVA) provides a National Crisis Responder Credentialing Program (NCRCP), the American Institute of Health Care Professionals (AIHCP) offers a Certified

Crisis Intervention Consultant option, and the Alliance of Information and Referral Systems (AIRS) has individual certification available. All of these individual crisis worker certification options evaluate education, training, and work experience (refer to the organizations' individual websites for specific information on each option).

Certification as a crisis worker is part of the broad field of credentialing various providers such as substance abuse counselors, physicians, nurses, social workers, and psychologists. In these instances, certification signifies, for example, that a registered nurse with a master's degree (in addition to a general license, regulated by state or provincial authorities, to practice nursing) has met the special requirements of a "certified psychiatric nurse," controlled by professional organizations such as the American Nurses Association or Canadian Nurses Association. Certification as a crisis worker signifies that an individual has met or exceeded minimum standards in the crisis field on a test of knowledge, experience, and ability to perform. Although certification attests to some basic ability on the part of the certificate holder, it does not guarantee high-quality performance, nor does it mean that the certified individual will be all things to all distressed people. Rather, certification offers consumers and employing agencies a vehicle to better gauge a person's *probable* performance potential.

Other advantages for the certified worker are status and prestige, particularly for those who, though very knowledgeable and skilled from years of training and experience, do not have other formal credentials such as an MSW or PhD degree. These benefits are especially prestigious in a culture where credentialing has taken on so much importance and consumers in distress are vulnerable to questionable entrepreneurs whose major motivation is profit and not the provision of service. At a time when crisis services are being recognized as a needed form of clinical intervention, many practitioners presume to practice this specialty without the benefit of essential training and knowledge. The demand for crisis services creates the opportunity to "cash in," sometimes at the expense of the client. Individual certification also offers protection to people when there are pressures from certain political or health-financing sources to develop services without the careful preparation demanded by international standards.

Although quality assurance to clients is the major incentive for certification, those certified may also enjoy powerful market advantages. In organizations, administrators may find that certified individuals are less costly to employ than uncertified volunteers or paid staff. Primarily, the certified person may require considerably less training, as there will obviously be some overlap between agency programs and the training required of individuals who qualify for certification.

References

American Association of Suicidology. (2011). *Organization accreditation standards manual* (10th ed.). Retrieved from http://www.suicidology.org/c/document_library/get_file?folderId=234&name=DLFE-306.pdf

Antonovsky, A. (1979). *Health, stress, and coping.* San Francisco, CA: Jossey-Bass.

Antonovsky, A. (1987). *Unraveling the mystery of health.* San Francisco, CA: Jossey-Bass.

Attorney General's Task Force on Family Violence. (1984). *Final report.* Washington, DC: U.S. Department of Justice.

Burgess, A. W., & Baldwin, B. A. (1981). *Crisis theory and practice.* Englewood Cliffs, NJ: Prentice Hall.

Caplan, G. (1964). *Principles of preventive psychiatry.* New York, NY: Basic Books.

De Jong, K., & Kleber, R. J. (2007). Emergency conflict-related psychosocial interventions in Sierra Leone and Uganda. *Journal of Health Psychology, 12*(3), 485–497.

Delport, E. (Ed.). (2007). *Gender-based violence in Africa: Perspectives from the continent.* Pretoria, South Africa: Centre for Human Rights.

Engle, G. L. (1977). The need for a new medical model: A challenge for biomedicine. *Science, 196*, 129–136.

Erikson, E. (1963). *Childhood and society* (2nd ed.). New York, NY: Norton.

Fadiman, A. (1997). *The spirit catches you and you fall down.* New York, NY: Noonday Press, Farrar, Straus and Giroux.

Felton, B. J., Barr, A., & Clark, G. (2006). ACT team members' responses to training in recovery-oriented practices. *Psychiatric Rehabilitation Journal, 30*(2), 112–119.

Hoff, L. A. (1990). *Battered women as survivors.* New York, NY: Routledge.

Hoff, L. A., Hallisey, B. J., & Hoff, M. (2009). *People in crisis: Clinical and diversity perspectives* (6th ed.). New York, NY: Routledge.

Hoff, L. A., & Morgan, B. D. (2011). *Psychiatric and mental health essentials in primary care.* London, UK: Routledge.

Hoff, L. A., & Wells, J. O. (Eds). (1989). *Certification standards manual* (4th ed.). Washington, DC: American Association of Suicidology.

Joint Commission on Mental Health and Illness. (1961). *Action for mental health.* New York, NY: Basic Books.

Kempe, C. H., Silverman, F. N., Steele, B. F., Droegemueller, W., & Silver, H. K. (1962). The battered child syndrome. *Journal of American Medical Association, 181*, 17–24.

Knowles, M. S. (1980). *The modern practice of adult education: From pedagogy to andragogy.* Chicago, IL: Association Press/Follett.

Lindemann, E. (1944). The symptomatology and management of acute grief. *American Journal of Psychiatry, 101*, 101–148.

Penn, J. V., Esposito, C., Stein, L. A. R., Lacher-Katz, M., & Spirito, A., (2005). Juvenile correctional workers' perceptions of suicide risk factors and mental health issues of incarcerated juveniles. *Journal of Correctional Health Care, 11*(4), 333–346.

President's Task Force on Victims of Crime. (1982). *Final report.* Washington, DC: U.S. Government Printing Office.

Ramsay, R. F. (1997). Chaos theory and crisis intervention: Toward a new meaning of equilibrium in understanding and helping people in crisis. *Child and Family*, *1*(3), 23–35.

Shneidman, E. S., & Farberow, N. L. (Eds.). (1957). *Clues to suicide*. New York, NY: McGraw-Hill.

Surgeon General's Workshop on Violence and Public Health. (1986). *Final report*. Washington, DC: Health Resources and Services Administration, U.S. Department of Public Health.

Taplin, J. R. (1971). Crisis theory: Critique and reformation. *Community Mental Health Journal*, *3*, 13–23.

Trepal, H. C., Wester, K. L., & MacDonald, C. A. (2006). Self-injury and postvention: Responding to the family in crisis. *The Family Journal: Counseling and Therapy for Couples and Families*, *14*(4), 342–348.

Whitaker, R. (2010). *Anatomy of an epidemic: Magic bullets, psychiatric drugs, and the astonishing rise of mental illness in America*. New York, NY: Crown.

Chapter 4

Implementing Core Crisis Content

Chapter Outline

It is one thing to know essential core content and who is qualified to teach it. But even more challenging is the task of creatively applying this knowledge with a diverse audience in clinical settings, and evaluating its outcomes. This chapter addresses these teaching and training challenges.

The Diversity of Training Goals

The principles and methodologies discussed in this chapter apply to the education and clinical training of both specialists and generalists who will be providing crisis care. We emphasize preparation for the *clinical* expertise needed by *all* crisis workers. Crisis *specialists* utilize their preparation as crisis workers routinely in everyday practice. Though such practitioners are always on alert for crisis situations, records from certified crisis centers reveal that at most only about 20% of total clients served are in acute crisis. These data show that crisis specialists spend the majority of their time on *crisis prevention* around the myriad psychosocial issues and hazardous events presented by their clients.

Generalists, by contrast, integrate their crisis preparation into another specialty area. As primary care and emergency practitioners know—given the inherent connection between mind, body, emotional, and spiritual issues—their everyday normal work inevitably includes crisis prevention and intervention, even though these health care providers may not define themselves as crisis workers.

Example: Medical and Psychosocial Care

Gerry Black comes to the emergency department (ED) via ambulance on Saturday afternoon with very labored breathing and a diagnosis of end-stage AIDS. The trauma team is called, blood levels are drawn, and intravenous lines are inserted into both arms, with immediate preparation to intubate the patient if necessary. There is no information from the emergency medical team except that a friend was at the house, a half block away, and is en route to the ED. The psychiatric nurse requests delay of intubation until the patient's DNR (do not resuscitate) status can be verified by the HIV/AIDS clinic where Mr. Black is followed. His friend Lily Wong arrives, meets with the psychiatric nurse, and verifies that a plan is in place. She has brought her friend's living will, which specifies no intubation and no cardio resuscitation. Ms. Wong is part of a supportive group of friends who have agreed to be with Mr. Black in his dying, but today she was alone with him when his condition deteriorated. She had not known what to expect and panicked when things started happening so quickly. Once in the ED, the living will was presented to the trauma team and heroic intervention was averted. Mr. Black and Ms. Wong spent a short time longer in the ED, while the rest of his support team was mobilized. He died at home a few hours later, with the arms, the voices, and the love of friends surrounding him. And that day, the entire staff in the ED felt better about their work, their mission, and their humanity.

Crisis training is conducted by a university or college-based educator, a mental health professional, various topical specialists, or a lay person specifically chosen for the task. Implicit in this discussion is recognition of the crossover between training categories and goals. For example, educators preparing students for eventual practice in any of the health and human service professions (nursing, social work, medicine, clinical psychology, and counseling) will conduct formal classroom sessions in the university or college setting, supervise the students' clinical experience in agencies providing crisis service (such as a crisis center or hospital), and hold seminars on clinical topics and experience in either the *academic* or *agency setting*, whichever is available or more convenient to the students and instructors. Trainees from various practice disciplines are those who did not have crisis content in their preservice programs, may wish to update their knowledge and skills, or specialize in one of the crisis field topics, such as sexual assault, child abuse, or programs for perpetrators (see Chapter 9). These programs vary widely in focus and extent, depending on the recipients' needs. Some of the most common formats are one- or two-day workshops or a seminar series over several weeks.

In general, these trainees do not function full-time as crisis workers. Rather, their knowledge and skill in the crisis field are incorporated into their regular practice as nurses, physicians, psychotherapists, or other human service practitioners. Although psychotherapists are by definition comfortable with the psychosocial aspects of care, the same comfort level does not necessarily apply to crisis situations (especially those in community outreach settings) without special training. A psychotherapist trained in crisis management will feel confident, for example, in assisting an individual or family through hazardous events such as abuse and threats of suicide or assault, and secure in his or her ability to put psychodynamic issues temporarily on hold while dealing with such acute crisis episodes.

Among nonpsychiatric primary care health practitioners, some are highly skilled at recognizing and appropriately responding to psychosocial parameters of general health care; others may be prone to deal with nonmedical problems by prescribing psychotropic medication too quickly or making a premature referral to psychiatry (Hoff & Morgan, 2011; Whitaker, 2010). *Primary care practitioners* here refer to physicians and advanced practice nurses (nurse practitioners) who function in the role of the traditional GP (general medical physician or "family doctor"). These health care providers are also the main gatekeepers with the crucial role of making astute assessments of presenting clients and ensuring appropriate referrals of those needing specialty services, including crisis counseling and in-depth psychosocial or psychiatric care.

In hospitals and home settings, where crises associated with illness, accidents, surgical loss, victimization, or death are commonplace, nurses and physicians untrained in crisis management may feel uncomfortable in assisting such clients in crisis. For example, because at least 25% of pregnant women in Canada and the United States have current or past experience of abuse by their partners, the importance of crisis assessment, empathic support, safety planning, and referral of these women to support groups by primary care practitioners, midwives, and obstetricians cannot be overemphasized (Hoff & Morgan, 2011; McFarlane, Parker, Loeken, & Bullock, 1992; Sugg & Inui, 1992). A study by Haddad et al. (2005) involving over 200 nurses in the United Kingdom found that in the past 5 years, three fourths of the nurses had not received any training in the area of psychosocial care despite their participation in a wide range of psychosocial activities. The nurses expressed a desire to increase their understanding and skills in the areas of mental disorders, anxiety management, crisis intervention, and pharmacological treatments for depression. As mental health becomes further integrated into primary care, staff will need to play a more active role in helping to manage their patients' mental health concerns; workplace training will certainly play an important role in future development in the field (Haddad et al., 2005).

We are not suggesting here that these nonpsychiatric practitioners take on major counseling or psychotherapy roles. We clearly recognize that if these practitioners' major interest were mental health work, they would have chosen another specialty. But just as mental health professionals must recognize and take seriously the medical problems of their clients, so must non–mental health professionals recognize crises and offer timely response. Basically, this means implementing the first steps of the crisis resolution process (emotional first aid, safety planning, and referral) for those seeking help in the general medical arena around normal and extraordinary life events.

In contrast, the preservice preparation of volunteer or paid staff in a designated crisis service (for the general population or distinct groups such as abused women or other victims of crime) usually occurs in the agency where the trainee will eventually work. Such training is conducted by an agency staff member with special preparation for this job or by outsiders with expertise in psychosocial aspects of health, preparation as a crisis trainer, and sensitivity to the unique needs of the particular setting. Similarly, continuing education or in-service training of these groups also takes place in the agency setting, though these workers may also take advantage of continuing education programs offered by a university or health agency (see Chapter 9).

In working with the special population of children and adolescents, ongoing training and supervision are imperative to ensure the safety of these young and vulnerable clients. Mandated reporting, including thorough documentation, is particularly relevant in this population. Developing a preventive partnership with parents, schools, and law enforcement is useful. Training specific to the parent's right to know needs to be given careful consideration in delicate crisis situations such as suicidal intent, substance abuse, and sexual health issues. Being present with the youth when parents are informed or telling the youth before you tell parents is indicated (Van Pelt & Hancock, 2007). Age of consent for substance abuse and sexual health intervention varies from state to state.

Regardless of the focus (preservice or in-service) or setting (educational or service delivery), those facets of the education and training process that apply to all who encounter psychosocial issues and life crisis situations need to be highlighted. Training is not the same as teaching, and the design of crisis training programs is a highly specialized area of practice, involving small-group skills, effective communication style, and other strategies that are not easily mastered in didactic (classroom-based) instruction. The crisis trainer must be willing to take risks and to model the integration of *knowledge*, *attitudes*, and *skills* required of a crisis worker.

The remainder of this chapter focuses on strategies dealing with the most challenging aspect of preparing practitioners in crisis and psychosocial care: The attitudes and skills required for dealing with sensitive issues and managing very stressful and sometimes life-threatening situations. This book emphasizes approaches to necessary knowledge acquisition that are more successful than the commonly used lecture method or "banking concept" of education—which consists of imparting large numbers of facts to trainees without integrating these facts with appropriate attitudes and skills. It is assumed that professional students, who are degree candidates in a health or other human service profession, will meet regular college and licensure requirements and pursue more theoretical and research underpinnings of crisis work than other trainees might.

Defining Objectives in Behavioral Terms

The first step in a training program design is the development of clearly written learning objectives. These are most meaningfully stated in behavioral or outcome terms, rather than in vague theoretical constructs. Objectives stated behaviorally provide both the trainee and the trainer with a clear understanding of what is to be accomplished. They define a task-oriented experience that provides for attitudinal exploration, change, and growth. Framing the objectives in measurable terms provides both trainer and trainee with clarity of expected achievement. Too often, broad statements like "This class will provide the trainee with information about suicide risk assessment, crisis theory, and intervention strategies" function as objectives for crisis intervention training programs. Such a generalized description does not help the trainee to understand what is to be mastered; nor does it help the trainer define a way of measuring the content, if, in fact, it has been absorbed and integrated. An objective stated behaviorally might include statements like the following:

- At the end of the third session, trainees will be able to identify five major factors to be considered in conducting a suicide risk assessment.
- At the conclusion of the fourth session, the trainee will be able to define the agency's criteria for mobilizing the crisis outreach team in a life-threatening situation.

In effect, clearly stated objectives outline the content of the training program. With a precise outline of the training format, the trainer can determine the total amount of time to spend on the program. This way, any time normally spent on focusing and refocusing the objective can be devoted to constructive training instead. Next, the trainer defines the skeleton of the training program's basic framework, the core content. Also, any content specific to the agency or organization in its cultural and socioeconomic setting needs to be identified. Finally, the trainer determines the balance of time and approach for adequate coverage of the material.

Appropriate textbooks or carefully compiled lists of selected reading material are vital to the educational experience. Much of the didactic material can be mastered through reading done on the learner's own time, organized so that each unit of assigned reading is completed prior to the relevant session. Thus, classroom time can be used to review the material, address special issues and concerns, and practice assessment and intervention strategies through role-play, modeled intervention, and other training exercises. It is also important to allow time for discussion of personal biases and attitudes as well as to process with trainees any feelings of distress that may emerge from specific subject areas like suicide, HIV/AIDS, or sexual assault.

Basically, the time assigned to different content areas should flow from the behaviorally defined course objectives. Instructors can facilitate course planning by administering a pretraining questionnaire that identifies a participant's educational, training, and experiential background. Such information should guide the proportion of time allocated to the knowledge, attitudinal, and skills aspects of core content. It also contributes to the participatory instructional process that is so important in training around sensitive topics in crisis and psychosocial care. In the hybrid instructional model combining classroom and online formats, chat-room exercises with fellow trainees on their own time can be critiqued and enriched with the instructor in the in-person seminar sessions.

The training curriculum is clearest when objectives, content, and methodology are stated in relationship to each other. From such examples, we can observe the logical flow from stated objectives to content to methodology. Evaluation strategies for both trainees and the training program seem to construct themselves. It may also be possible to develop a test for measuring the attainment of behavioral objectives, administered prior to training and on its completion. Such a test allows an evaluation of the trainee's mastery of the material and the impact of the training program as a whole. This becomes particularly important when the crisis program utilizes the skills of several different trainers at different times. It allows a measure of intertrainer reliability by comparing the outcomes of one group with another and determining patterns of strengths and weaknesses. Careful attention to these elements of training will bode well for agencies seeking accreditation of its crisis programs. It also lays a solid foundation for those seeking individual certification as crisis workers, as discussed in Chapter 3. See www.crisisprograms.org for sample courses and workshops.

Creating a Climate for Training

Training workers in crisis and psychosocial care is unlike most teaching experiences because a didactic approach alone cannot achieve the learning objectives set forth. The major instrument that trainers use is an educated, secure self, which includes a high level of personal awareness, sensitivity, and objectivity; all are essential. Trainers must have a clear understanding of crisis theory, intervention strategies, and awareness of adult learning principles (Hoff, Hallisey, & Hoff, 2009; Knowles, 1980).

A successful crisis training curriculum requires some initial time to create a climate of trust. This is true no matter who the trainees are: police, nursing students, hotline counselors, or any other group. Once trust is established, trainees will be willing to take learning risks, to examine their own biases, and to assist one another. The trainer must be willing to take the same risks as the trainees—for example, to model role-plays illustrating concepts addressed in lectures and readings. Learning occurs most effectively when the student participates actively in the learning experience. This is especially true when one is dealing with material that has potential emotional impact. The classroom and online formats become laboratories for practice.

It is useful to communicate training policies at the beginning. These should be stated in terms of clear expectations regarding attendance, participation, assignments, and other details. The structure of the training program may be described briefly. During this initial session (and in subsequent sessions), it is important to include opportunities for interaction between trainers and trainees because the emotional strength of the group collectively provides an encouraging atmosphere for trainees to take learning risks. There are numerous exercises to facilitate the building of an appropriate climate. One of the most effective is to ask the group to divide into pairs who do not know each other well and have them spend 15 minutes interviewing each other. The trainers should participate, if possible. When the time has elapsed, each person will introduce his or her partner to the group. This exercise has numerous benefits. It usually generates one supportive relationship in what may be a group of strangers. It can be utilized as an introductory exercise on the importance of listening and as a demonstration of how cautiously we open up to strangers, even when not in crisis.

The importance of well-timed refreshment breaks should not be underestimated. The ideal time in this first session is after the paired introductions.

This allows people to pursue informally any conversations that were interrupted because of time constraints on the exercise. It also gives trainees a chance to converse about things they learned about each other in the introductions, which contributes to group formation. Finally, appropriate refreshment breaks and a comfortable setting reduce evaluation outcomes that focus on the "bad food" and "too cold room" and enhance the probability of obtaining evaluations of the curriculum's substance.

Other areas to include in the first session are an exploration of the particular service setting for which workers are being trained; ethical considerations in crisis work, with special emphasis on confidentiality concerns and complex issues like informing potential victims of the danger of assault (see Hoff et al., 2009, ch. 12; Van de Creek & Knapp, 1993); and a discussion of the use of role-plays and appropriate feedback in the training program.

Each of these issues should be discussed in a participatory manner. One might examine the particular setting by asking the group what they think the agency's mission is about, what kinds of crises they anticipate working with, and what their experience has been. This approach helps to reveal the myths and realities of a given program and approach. It is vital that the controlling philosophy of the community, the specific agency setting, and the personal models brought to crisis work be acknowledged, understood, and, if necessary, modified.

Throughout training, the trainer should utilize every opportunity to model basic attitudes desirable in work with distressed people. A trainer who is shy, has poor communication skills, or lacks respect for people's abilities to cope or their capacity for new learning will not work successfully to help trainees develop as effective workers. A skilled trainer allows trainees to anticipate certain experiences during each session through a clear statement in the written training objectives, content, and methodology.

Trainees should also be informed that they will be evaluated as fairly and objectively as possible and will be invited to evaluate the presentation and effectiveness of the program. Although the trainer becomes personally invested in the success of the group, it is vital to maintain awareness that the well-being of the client is always the bottom line. Trainees who demonstrate unsuitability for crisis work should be given opportunities to address and change problem behavior or attitudes. But, if skills, knowledge, and desirable attitudes cannot be integrated, they should be asked to participate in some other area of work or to leave the program.

The introduction of ethical and legal considerations is important at this early phase. In particular, a discussion regarding client confidentiality and the confidentiality of trainees-colleagues in the training group is imperative, as inevitably some trainees will introduce highly personal material or have unexpectedly intense reactions to particular content (such as suicide or sexual assault) in the presence of other trainees. Also, throughout training, the instructor should cite actual or simulated case material to illustrate and animate theoretical constructs. This is appropriate only after a clear and thorough discussion of confidentiality and in full awareness of the delicate and complex issues involved. Similarly, the legal concerns and stances of a group in particular jurisdictions must be acknowledged. For example, instructors must explain the legal mandates regarding the reporting of child abuse. Ethical and legal issues will arise repeatedly, especially about interventions in high-risk situations. In some crisis situations (for example, warning a potential murder victim of danger based on assessment of high risk for assault or homicide), a crisis worker may be mandated to share information without the would-be assailant's consent. Thus, trainers must be particularly sensitive to the anxiety these issues may generate.

Role-playing serves as a major training vehicle, so it is important to help trainees understand how to role-play, what kind of content is appropriate, and what their responsibilities are to each other for providing useful feedback. It is very helpful at this point for the trainers to model a brief role-play that contains both strengths and weaknesses so that helpful feedback can be provided for the group. Trainees should be instructed to avoid using current personal problems that border on crises in their own lives. Their "counselor" is most likely to be another novice crisis trainee, so there will probably be no capacity for follow-up. For example, Applied Suicide Intervention Skills Training (ASIST) program trainers ask trainees to avoid using personal experiences in their role-play examples and at the end of each scenario ask trainees to "shake off" the role by listing two reasons why they are not the person they portrayed, thereby allowing them to distance themselves from a somewhat emotional role-play. To illustrate the theoretical constructs, it may be useful to prepare a number of suggested script outlines for use in each session, relating to the session content (for example, a complex description of a current life situation for purposes of demonstrating risk assessment). However, the scripts must be skeletal enough to demand from the trainees some emotional energy investment so that the role has meaning as a training strategy. See www.crisisprograms.org for role-play examples.

The group should be encouraged to ask questions freely and express concerns as they surface. However, it is vital to have a reality check for the group because initial levels of anxiety may be high (what we have come to refer to as the "what-if" phenomenon, which can occupy endless amounts of class or training time with hypothetical discussions). Trainers need a good grasp of service program realities or should have a co-facilitator who works with day-to-day aspects of program operations to contain these "what-ifs" within a reality-based context.

Another vital issue in crisis intervention training is the trainer's sensitivity to the experience of trainees. Ideally, a careful screening process should have occurred and should include trainers in interviewing and decisions about applicant acceptance into training (see Chapter 8). This is certainly true for crisis intervention centers and suicide prevention programs. It is probably less true of classroom situations (for example, nursing and social work students or police), where one is less certain of the background and emotional stability that trainees bring. As noted earlier, even with careful screening, certain content areas can bring up uncomfortable issues that trainees thought they had fully resolved. Examples might be sessions focusing on alcoholic parents or violence toward women, issues that may have been carefully repressed. The trainer, therefore, must be alert to the responses of the group. Trainees who seem withdrawn, manifest signs of distress, are disruptive, or disclose a personal experience in the presence of other trainees should be approached at the break or at the end of the session. Also, it is important to let people know at the beginning that they may find themselves upset by a particular concern or aspect of training and to inform them of the immediate resources available to share these concerns. The Canadian Training Institute, for example, inserts the following cautionary note in their pre-workshop screening material: "CAUTION: The program may be evocative to some individuals, particularly those who are survivors of abuse, violence, or other forms of trauma. Participants must take the responsibility of self-screening if stressful situations are a concern. Participation should be discussed with one's therapist if the participant is currently in therapy." Many places now have co-facilitators, one doing the training and the other on standby for dealing with disclosures or other personal issues raised by trainees. In university or college courses, faculty are urged to have well-established linkages for mental health referrals for distressed students.

In our experience, even in a straightforward lecture on suicide prevention, for example, there are usually people in the audience for whom the material raises serious concerns, reminders of past losses, or current issues. Similarly, if students or trainees have histories of child abuse or other traumatic events that have never been addressed, discussion of violence issues can trigger uncovering of repressed memories, precipitating possible crisis (see Hoff et al., 2009, ch. 11). To accommodate these realities, it is always important to allow time for such concerns to be addressed. After-class discussions also reveal that crisis work does not fit neatly into the traditional therapy hour, and that crisis workers must bring to their endeavors a high degree of flexibility and accessibility.

Linked to all these issues are the many reasons why people are drawn into the helping professions. Of concern is the individual who "needs" to help others, and so nurtures many unresolved personal concerns. These trainees become counterproductive to the process of crisis and psychosocial care and its ultimate goal of empowering the client. Trainers must quickly identify such trainees or students and determine the most appropriate measures that need to be taken, including counseling into alternative career paths.

Implementing the Course Content: Methodologies

Education and training in crisis and psychosocial care use a number of modalities for instruction. These may include lecture, readings, modeled role-play (including the use of previously taped role-plays), and role-play practice. It is helpful to include guest lecturers (for example, a 911 operator) and survivor stories, when possible. A well-designed training program will probably involve some of each. The pretraining questionnaire discussed earlier can alert an instructor to the methods and teaching styles that trainers find most conducive to learning. In this section, we suggest some of the ways each method might be most useful. But whatever modalities are planned, the educator or trainer should periodically assess with trainees their appropriateness for maximum achievement of learning objectives. Educators and trainers desiring sample crisis course syllabi and workshop designs may consult the Life Crisis Institute at www.crisisprograms.org.

Lecture

This is perhaps the most overused teaching approach found in formal education and training programs. Trainees and students should be able to absorb written concepts—content communicated through written work in a training manual or textbook. The trainer may wish to lecture about complex and vital areas such as lethality assessment, legal and ethical considerations in rescue, or warning potential victims of an impending lethal assault. We recommend that lecturing be considered the method of last resort. But, when interactive learning is not possible through other means and there is essential content to be communicated, lecture may be the most efficient route.

Readings

Many books dealing with crisis and psychosocial care are available. In addition, many certified crisis centers have developed their own training manuals, which typically include readings from a broad range of sources. Some are generic; others include information about specific areas of focus for the particular organization. Information about available training manuals can be obtained from certified crisis or distress centers as well as from the American Association of Suicidology in the United States and the Center for Suicide Prevention (CSP) in Canada (see Chapter 9 and www.crisisprograms.org).

Modeled Role-Play

This technique demonstrates concepts and approaches. It is very helpful, for example, to model a role-play in which risk assessment is conducted. Trainees with little or no crisis experience find it helpful to hear a skilled person ask directly about the client's self-destructive thoughts and behaviors or emotional pain from abuse, and possible danger to others. Trainers should be sensitive to any thematic difficulties that arise in the class and use demonstration role-plays to clarify problem issues. However, inexperienced trainees may be overwhelmed by the ease and competence with which trainers perform in role-plays. Their anxiety and need to identify special meanings and forms of self-expression should be addressed. They need to know that the trainers do not expect that upon completion of learning everyone will achieve the same training results. Even though discussion time is important, trainers should be wary of allowing it to continue for long periods of time. Role-playing often generates performance anxiety, and trainees may sabotage this part of training by diverting the trainer with questions and discussion.

Training DVDs and videos should be utilized as supplements to classroom training, rather than as substitutes for experiential learning. Limited use of these tools will allow for class time to be concentrated on refinement of skills through actual role-playing assignments. However, taped role-plays may be very useful when it is important to demonstrate the client part of the scenario, for example when modeling a response to a sexually exploitive caller to a crisis service. Taped role-plays or scenarios can also provide students with the opportunity to identify signs of distress in the client and qualities or techniques of the counselor. Viewing a video clip and then processing what was observed can be a precursor to actual role-playing or can be used to refine assessment and intervention skills.

Modeled role-play techniques are also highly recommended for the development of communication skills. All crisis workers need to learn basic communication skills—active listening, the use of open-ended questions except when there is the clear need for immediate and concise information, clarification, gentle confrontation, and so on. Students or trainees in formal mental health programs usually have had basic instruction in communication through other required courses. Undergraduate nursing students, for example, typically are required to do process recordings as an aid to understanding interpersonal dynamics and mastering basic interviewing skills. There are numerous articles and books useful in designing a communication skills unit. In addition, many crisis centers include communication skills material in their training manuals. Finally, every crisis educator and trainer should take advantage of the rich, up-to-date training resources available through the Center for Suicide Prevention (CSP), which hosts the Suicide Information and Education Collection (SIEC), a resource library containing written and audiovisual materials specific to the topic of suicide and related topics.

Role-Play

Some of the concerns raised by role-playing have already been described. Every certified crisis or distress center puts considerable emphasis on role-play as a central aspect of training. Whenever possible, it is helpful to have several trainers available to assist small groups in processing role-plays. It is also useful to interrupt role-plays that are clearly going in the wrong direction and unlikely to straighten out. The role-playing "counselor" can be helped to see where the counseling contact derailed and what was overlooked (such as missed suicidal clues), and be given the opportunity to try again.

Feedback should be specific, immediate, and in small doses. Role-playing teams might contract to give each other honest feedback. Some role-players may adopt an unspoken contract to state essentially the following: "I am the client and I can feel you struggling in your role as the counselor. I feel uncomfortable to see you in such distress, so I will 'get well quickly' and tell you how helpful you have been to me." Implicit in this message is the expectation that when roles are reversed the other person, in the role of client, will be equally generous. Trainees must be helped to see how vital honest feedback and consistency in role-playing are to their learning experience. It is useful in these sensitive and sometimes painful training situations to remember the principle of constructive criticism: Unlike general criticism or mere fault-finding, constructive criticism provides a rationale for the correction or disagreement offered, and *always* offers an *alternative* to the approach being critiqued. The trainer should model such constructive feedback while eliciting group response to role-play scenarios.

Group role-playing can serve as a method to ease trainees into role-playing exercises. In this method, the trainer plays the role of the client. The group of trainees sits in seating arranged in a "U" shape. As the "client" plays their part, the trainees are asked to volunteer to respond as the counselor. All trainees are encouraged to participate even if their response duplicates another response. This multiple response pattern allows trainees the opportunity to hear different ways to respond to the client.

Clinical Practice for Crisis Trainees

An apprentice period (also known as a *practicum*, *clinical placement*, *internship*, or *shadowing*) is a significant phase of training. Trainees should not be expected to apply the principles and techniques of the classroom in real life situations without the support and supervision of a skilled crisis practitioner, either the trainer or someone designated for that function. Such apprenticeship periods must be *formally* planned, lest the trainee's need for supervision be left to chance. National surveys of accredited schools of nursing in the United States and Canada reveal that planned experience for students around the care of victim-survivors of abuse, for example, is *incidental* rather than systematic (see Ross, Hoff, & Coutu-Wakulczyk, 1998; Woodtli & Breslin, 1996, 2002). Thus, the pairing of trainees with experienced crisis workers—especially for complex situations—plays a vital role in the trainees' education.

Experienced crisis workers (or preceptors) help trainees and students process actual practice situations they have observed, explain why certain decisions were made, analyze the process of the contact, and answer any questions trainees have. This, however, puts considerable pressure on the experienced worker because trainees emerge from their classroom learning experience with the material fresh in their minds and clear notions of the "right" way to do things. It may also be threatening to a preceptor who is slightly out of touch with the *formal* aspects of his or her own training. In short, the worker may also feel microscopically observed and needs to have a clear understanding of her or his preceptor role in helping people through apprentice periods (see Chapter 9 for further discussion of classroom and on-site learning).

All of these points can be addressed with the establishment of a learning contract whereby the goals, objectives, and evaluation process of the apprenticeship are clearly defined. The contract assures that specific roles and expectations of both the trainee and the experienced supervisor are understood, an outcome enhanced when the contract is mutually developed and agreed on (see Hoff et al., 2009, ch. 4).

As trainers select various methodologies to use in crisis training, they may find it useful to consider the principles of self-directed learning that apply especially to adult learners. The term *andragogy* has come to be associated with the needs of adult learners. It originates from the Greek prefix *andr-* ("[adult] male") on the pattern of *pedagogy*. *Andragogy* describes the body of theory and practice on which *self-directed* learning is based. It is thus defined as the art and science of helping adults (or maturing human beings) learn. In contrast, *pedagogy* from the Greek *paid* (meaning "boy, child") and *agogos* ("leader") is the body of theory and practice on which *teacher-directed* learning is based, defining it as the art and science of teaching children (Knowles, 1975, 1978, 1980).

These two models do not represent good–bad or adult–child dichotomies, but rather a continuum of assumptions to be evaluated in terms of their appropriateness for learners in particular situations. If a pedagogical assumption is realistic for particular circumstances, then pedagogical strategies are appropriate.

For example, if certain crisis content areas are entirely new and strange to a learner, that person will be dependent on a teacher until enough content has been acquired to enable self-directed inquiry to begin. However, even in essential content areas such as assessment for risk of suicide or danger to others, which entails evidence-based knowledge and particular techniques, a learner-centered or problem-based process is recommended. For example, because everyone has ideas about why people commit suicide or abuse others—some accurate and some misguided—these ideas can be elicited from trainees as a way to activate them in the learning process and help dislodge common myths such as "Talking directly with people about suicide puts the idea into their heads." To avoid gender bias in language, we suggest the term *interactive* as a substitute for Knowles's "andragogical" model of learning. As noted earlier, an interactive approach is more effective than other training methods for sensitive topics in the crisis field because of the learner's increased involvement. These ideas are summarized in Figures 4.1 and 4.2.

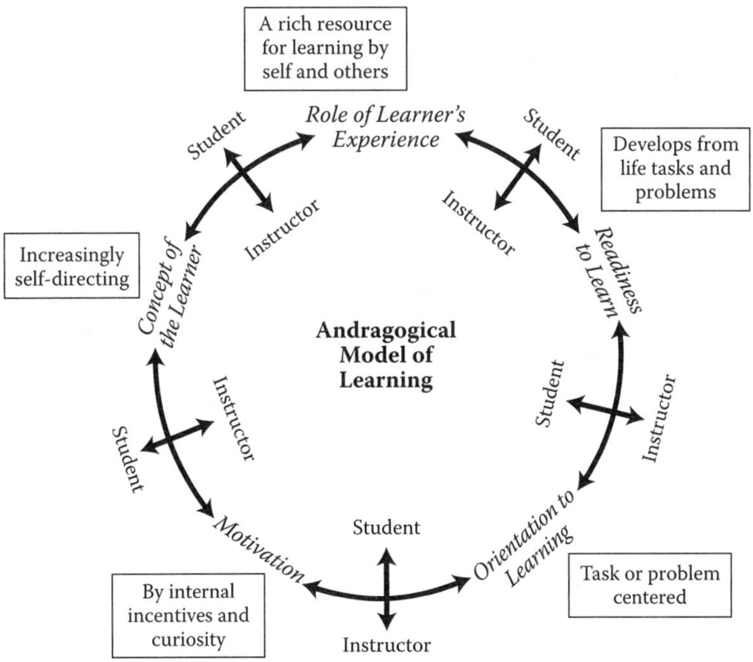

Figure 4.1 Interactive learning: Assumptions about learning and the learner. Adapted from Knowles (1980, p. 51); reprinted by permission of Hoff and Miller (1987).

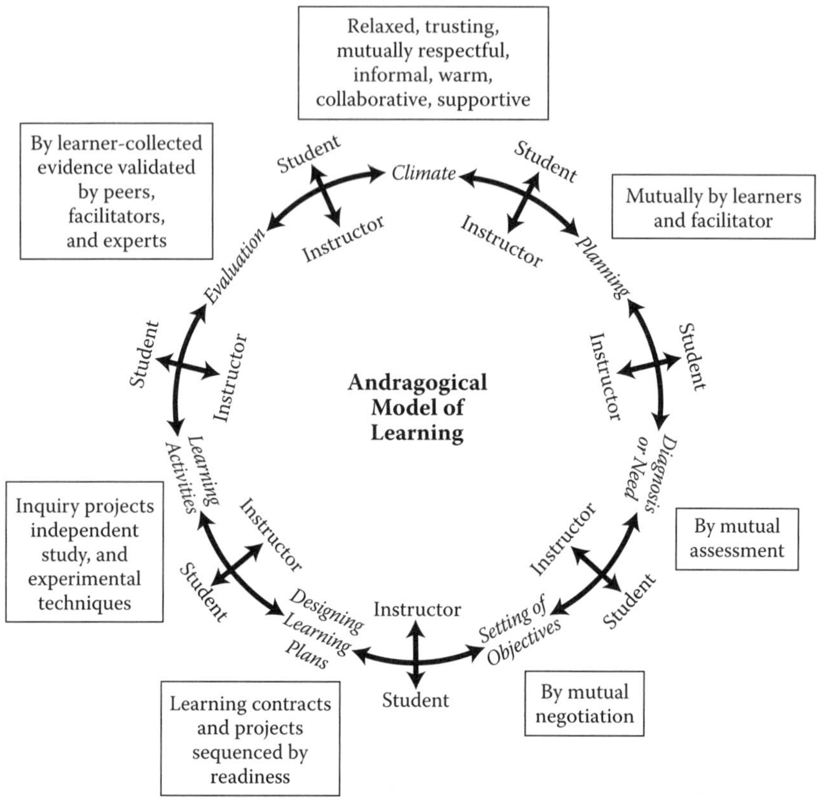

Figure 4.2 Interactive learning: Elements of the teaching–learning process. Adapted from Knowles (1980, p. 53); reprinted by permission of Hoff and Miller (1987).

Evaluating the Training Process and Outcomes

Crisis programs use a number of strategies for evaluating the impact of training. As noted above, one particularly effective approach is the administration of a test before and after training. Such a test can measure, through objective questions, the trainee's or student's knowledge of crucial areas such as risk assessment, legal and ethical considerations, and basic counseling approaches. In the *Final Report* of the U.S. Surgeon General's Workshop on Violence and Public Health (1986), a recommendation included examining all professionals on violence-related content as a condition of licensure. Decades later, such evaluation is by no means standardized in most health professions education programs, although considerable progress has been made. Subjective evaluation of trainee performance is a valid part of the evaluation process; however, it is vital to have clear criteria for evaluation. This may be done by a final role-play with the trainee observed for the integration of knowledge, attitudes, and skills. Alternatively, some computer-assisted training tools contain options for testing learner outcomes. Formal evaluation of training also serves to prepare those who apply for certification as crisis workers.

Trainees should be given the opportunity to evaluate their training experience, either after each session or at the completion of the course, and again a few months later when they have been working in a crisis service setting. Furthermore, it is important for the agency to communicate the seriousness with which such evaluations are viewed. These evaluations should be used to revise and redesign training approaches when thematic difficulties or areas for improvement emerge from the trainee's experience and suggestions. In addition to trainees' evaluations, it is highly desirable to assess the effectiveness of training based on its impact on the clients served by those trained. Such assessments, however, need to be complemented by independent judges of the client's functioning. This type of evaluation usually requires formal assistance from professionals trained in evaluation research methods. Graduate students at local universities might be recruited to assist with such evaluation projects. Agencies should seek out such sources to supplement the in-house evaluation methods that are an ideal of every training program.

References

Haddad, M., Plummer, S., Taverner, A., Gray, R., Lee, S., Payne, F., & Knight, D. (2005). District nurses' involvement and attitudes to mental health problems: A three-area cross-sectional study. *Journal of Clinical Nursing, 14*, 976–985.

Hoff, L. A., Hallisey, B. J., & Hoff, M. (2009). *People in crisis: Clinical and diversity perspectives* (6th ed.). New York, NY: Routledge.

Hoff, L. A. & Miller, N. (1987). *Programs for people in crisis: A guide for educators, administrators, and clinical trainers.* Boston, MA: Northeastern University Custom Book Program.

Hoff, L. A., & Morgan, B. D. (2011). *Psychiatric and mental health essentials in primary care.* London, UK: Routledge.

Knowles, M. S. (1975). *Self-directed learning: A guide for learners and teachers.* Chicago, IL: Association Press/Follett.

Knowles, M. S. (1978). *The adult learner: A neglected species* (2nd ed.). Houston, TX: Gulf.

Knowles, M. S. (1980). *The modern practice of adult education: From pedagogy to andragogy.* Chicago, IL: Association Press/Follett.

McFarlane, J., Parker, B., Loeken, K., & Bullock, M. S. (1992). Assessing for abuse during pregnancy. *Journal of American Medical Association, 267*(23), 3176–3178.

Ross, M., Hoff, L. A., & Coutu-Wakulcyzk, G. (1998). Nursing curricula and violence issues: A study of Canadian schools of nursing. *Journal of Nursing Education, 37*(2), 53–60.

Sugg, N. K., & Inui, T. (1992). Primary care physicians' response to domestic violence. *Journal of American Medical Association, 267*(23), 3157–3160.

Surgeon General's Workshop on Violence and Public Health. (1986). *Final report.* Washington, DC: Health Resources and Services Administration, U.S. Department of Public Health.

Van de Creek, L., & Knapp, S. (1993). *Tarasoff and beyond: Legal and clinical considerations in the treatment of life-endangering patients* (Rev. ed.). Sarasota, FL: Professional Resource Press.

Van Pelt, R., & Hancock, J. (2007). *The youth worker's guide to helping teenagers in crisis.* Grand Rapids, MI: Zondervan.

Whitaker, R. (2010). *Anatomy of an epidemic: Magic bullets, psychiatric drugs, and the astonishing rise of mental illness in America.* New York, NY: Crown.

Woodtli, A., & Breslin, E. (1996). Violence related content in the nursing curriculum: A national study. *Journal of Nursing Education, 35*(8), 367–374.

Woodtli, A., & Breslin, E. (2002). Violence-related content in the nursing curriculum: A follow-up national survey. *Journal of Nursing Education, 41*(4), 340–348.

Chapter 5

Differential Application of Core Crisis Content

Chapter Outline

The Diversity of Training Recipients
Community and Cultural Context of Crisis Training
Assessing Attitudes, Background, and Needs of Trainees and Students
Tailoring a Training Program in Interaction With Trainees
In-Service Training and Continuing Education Programs
Community Gatekeeper Training

We espouse the ideal that crisis prevention and intervention are everybody's business, not the specialty of a particular discipline. This chapter explores some of the differential training implications for various community groups. Emphasis is placed on general principles that might guide professional educators and agency-based crisis trainers in designing programs that fit the needs of particular students and trainees. Implicit in this discussion is the core content, which will vary in focus depending on the needs of trainees and the theoretical framework of the individual educator or trainer.

As highlighted in this book's framework, crisis content is embedded in the broader context of psychosocial aspects of health care. Thus, for example, the psychosomatic complaints or chronic pain of a person presenting to a physician or nurse practitioner may be related to long-repressed psychological trauma from abuse (Hoff & Morgan, 2011). Likewise, the increasing number of children identified with behavioral problems and mental health disorders, in combination with a shortage of child psychiatrists, has created the acute need for pediatricians to play a more active role in assisting children and families (Goodfriend, Bryant, Livingood, & Goldhagen, 2006). Of course, such primary care providers are not expected to deliver in-depth counseling for these individuals, but they *are* expected to make essential mind–body connections and do all they can to link such persons to mental health or psychological trauma specialists rather than relying primarily on psychotropic medications (see Whitaker, 2010).

The Diversity of Training Recipients

The range of people for whom crisis education and training is relevant and crucial includes a broad spectrum of health and human service workers—firefighters, child protection workers, clergy, physicians, nurses, allied health workers, funeral home directors, law enforcement officers (including security guards in hospitals, clinics, and college campuses), mental health professionals, and others. In addition, crisis training is important for gatekeepers—teachers (for example, to recognize themes of death or violence in essays and make appropriate referrals), bartenders, urban outreach workers, campus residential housing advisors, telephone operators, disc jockeys, hair stylists, Traveler's Aid workers, neighborhood watch programs, and anyone else who encounters distressed people on the front lines, who may be in a life-or-death situation or in a deteriorating state of mental health.

Many distressed persons divulge their despair first to various "natural network" members, not mental health professionals. Thus, because of the broad spectrum of "natural" and "formal" crisis responders, trainers must consider the contextual factors and unique needs of various groups to master and integrate the knowledge, attitudes, and skills for an effective response to distraught or mentally disabled people. Too often one hears of tragedies that might have been prevented if more people were familiar with the signs of suicidal despair or dangerous assault. In one small community, for example, *after* a teenager brutally murdered his girlfriend, family members and others recalled the number of times this young man talked about killing the girl, but no one took him seriously (see Hoff, 2010).

Community and Cultural Context of Crisis Training

The content and shape of the training material will be somewhat controlled by the setting and community in which training is offered and the individuals for whom it is provided. Although core content is always included, working with home health aides in a rural community, for example, involves a different psychosocial milieu and probable concerns than training police officers in a large metropolitan area. This may seem absurdly self-evident, yet some small-town police officers are trained as if they are being prepared for intervention in urban gang warfare, when in reality their work will focus primarily on social service and the intersection between the criminal justice and mental health arenas (see Hoff, Hallisey, & Hoff, 2009, ch. 12). Police in small or suburban communities are likely to work with 10 times as many suicidal people, adolescents in crisis, and domestic violence situations as armed robberies; yet, officers may be provided with only skeletal training in working with suicidal and emotionally distressed individuals and making effective linkages to mental health and victim or survivor care services. Criminal justice personnel on reservations face the additional complexities of working with federal, state, and tribal laws across multicultural jurisdictions (Hobson, 2006).

The provision of crisis and psychosocial care in rural and reservation settings is often complicated. For instance, when domestic violence is present, those living in rural areas are often faced with increased isolation, limited resources, and unique cultural barriers. The Rural Assistance Center (RAC), a product of the U.S. Department of Health and Human Services Rural Initiative, was developed as a health and human services information portal for those living and working in rural areas. RAC's purpose is to provide information about available programs, funding, and research to aid in the improvement of services available in these areas.

Another distinction to keep in mind is the community's general access to resources and technological development. For example, training in core crisis content for health aides on a Native American reservation or for community health workers in Inuit villages will be strongly influenced by crises in these settings that stem from poverty and the lack of resources that most people in industrialized societies take for granted. The ability to meet certain needs—housing, personal safety, leisure activities, finances, and transportation—is crucial for individuals with chronic mental illness and who are deeply influenced by poverty (Perese, 2007).

In addition, there are cultural factors to consider when designing any training program. These may include linguistic barriers and different cultural values regarding issues like personal privacy, gender expectations, extended family networks, differential living situations, and other culturally defined patterns. An example would be teaching suicide risk assessment skills to First Nations tribal leaders, knowing that many Native people might not be inclined to call mainstream crisis lines. Native Friendship Centres, located throughout Canada, are more acceptable sources for distressed First Nations people (see Hoff, 2010, ch. 8). The First Nations Information Project (www.johnco.com/firstnat/) can also serve as an information resource on Aboriginal communities.

Likewise, utilizing the Black Church in developing interventions for depression and suicide in the African American community is indicated due to its broad acceptance and strong history of helping community members. This may also help to overcome the barrier of distrust toward other community institutions and reduce the stigma associated with help seeking (Morlock, Matlin, Barksdale, Puri, & Lyles, 2008).

Example: The HAVEN Program

Helping Alleviate Valley Experiences Now (HAVEN) is a suicide prevention program within the Black Church. It was developed with four key components: lay helpers, gatekeeper training, a mental health resource directory (MHRD), and a community education program. The hallmark of this program is its aim to strengthen network ties of all church members, not just those seen as high risk.

These cultural factors are central in designing training programs relevant to their constituencies. The community and cultural definition of *good health* must be taken into consideration. According to the Athabasca Tribal Council, healthy living is "*feeling vital; having a good social relationship and feeling in control of one's life; being able to do the things which one enjoys; having a sense of connection to a community and its members*" (http://atc97.org/health-social-programs). In other words, being healthy depends on determinates of health, and it encompasses the total environment of good education, housing, justice, and level of income and health services. This definition moves beyond the typical separation between mind and body aspects of health.

Working against deeply held cultural values may condemn crisis intervention efforts to failure. For instance, it has been found that migrant families will not discuss traditional, religious, or political meanings in their initial encounter with health services, even when invited to do so by a culturally sensitive professional. In light of this reality, the element of "time" will need to be incorporated into training for providers. In some instances, it may be appropriate for workers to directly address the explicit and implicit discrimination that these families may have experienced in order to demonstrate a respect for the differences in therapeutic space that they may need to feel safe (Rousseau, Key, & Measham, 2005). On the other hand, one must not make assumptions based on cultural myths. An example is the belief that female genital mutilation is "just part of that group's culture," and that women expect it and accept it. This example of a human rights violation illustrates the dangers of "cultural relativism" as discussed in Chapter 2.

There has been a recent shift toward reinstituting many aboriginal helping practices in an attempt to reconstitute the robust tribal societies of the past. Traditional healing is difficult to merge with the Western mentality of most helping professionals and clinical settings of today (Gone, 2008). The accepted standard of today's society often makes it difficult for professionals to acknowledge the usefulness of alternative treatments without being ostracized. Those clinicians who value cultural resources can open up room for negotiation that allows families to share doubts about Western diagnosis and treatment, thereby paving the way for a therapeutic relationship that is beneficial for the client. Western-trained clinicians need to be cautious not to appropriate knowledge and practices which they have not mastered and should not substitute themselves for traditional healers (Rousseau et al., 2005). For additional discussion on this topic, see Hoff and Morgan (2011, ch. 13) and Watters (2010).

In the early stages of a generic crisis intervention program's development, it is vital to conduct a community needs assessment to determine the nature of the psychosocial problems likely to surface. These will probably always include violence toward women and others (including sexual assault), suicide, sexual identity concerns, addictions, developmental disabilities, and HIV/AIDS. However, the setting also determines the type of problems that arise. A particular city or region may suffer from the stressors of periodic unemployment because a major employer shuts down for periods of time or permanent unemployment because a major industry leaves the community. Similarly, a region subject to periodic flooding, drought, or earthquake has needs determined by the hazardous environment.

Example: Rural Stress Resource

A farmer learns about farm stress resources available through the 2-1-1 resource line. He decides to call the number to get more information. During the course of the conversation, the call specialist tunes in to warning signs of depression in the caller. The call specialist asks about depression, and the farmer discloses that there are financial problems on the horizon and he has thought about suicide as a solution to the problem. The call specialist is able to gain the caller's trust, discuss the topic of depression, and make the appropriate referral to a public agency that will provide a depression screening.

In addition, an area with substantial minority and immigrant populations may struggle more overtly with issues of racism. In other words, program planners need a working knowledge of the types of stressful and crisis-provoking situations to which workers may be called on to respond. A variety of strategies for assessing the needs of the community in relation to overall crisis program planning are discussed in Chapter 6. These needs should be reflected in training.

Assessing Attitudes, Background, and Needs of Trainees and Students

Not only is the *content* of the program framed by its community *context*, but also the nature of the training is shaped by the needs and background of the participants. In teaching the basics of crisis and psychosocial care—assessment, planning, implementation, and follow-up—there will be contextual differences specific to the trainees or students who may be police officers, nurses in a psychiatric or family care master's degree program, or lay volunteers in programs such as a crisis hotline, victim assistance program, or abused women's shelter. Therefore, general principles and various examples should be presented, while avoiding a single overarching model. For example, in a baccalaureate nursing program, crisis content might be taught around these key concepts in the nursing curriculum: person or family, environment, health, and nursing. That is, *a person* may experience an emotional crisis state as a result of being raped in a cultural *environment* generally not safe for women alone at night. Depending on the *help* received by the rape victim (from *nurses* or others), her *health* status may be negatively affected by this experience. Figure 5.1, an adaptation of nursing's paradigm, illustrates the broader context and graduated approach to essential content on violence and abuse (Hoff, 2010).

Both undergraduate and graduate students will need more theoretical underpinnings if their study of crisis care is part of academic coursework, including critical analysis of existing theories. However, because graduate students in the mental health professions have generally mastered the basics of communication skills central to all human service work, they usually need less emphasis on this content area than police officers or paramedics, for example. Similarly, the level of psychological complexity in the content will be different in the preparation of psychiatry residents, nurses, and social workers than emergency medical technicians (EMTs; in Canada, ambulance officers). The program should be tailored to the participants' abilities and requirements, to knowledge and skills already mastered, and to the realities of potential clients. It is also important to make the content substantive enough to provide sufficient intellectual and emotional challenge, especially to graduate or advanced students.

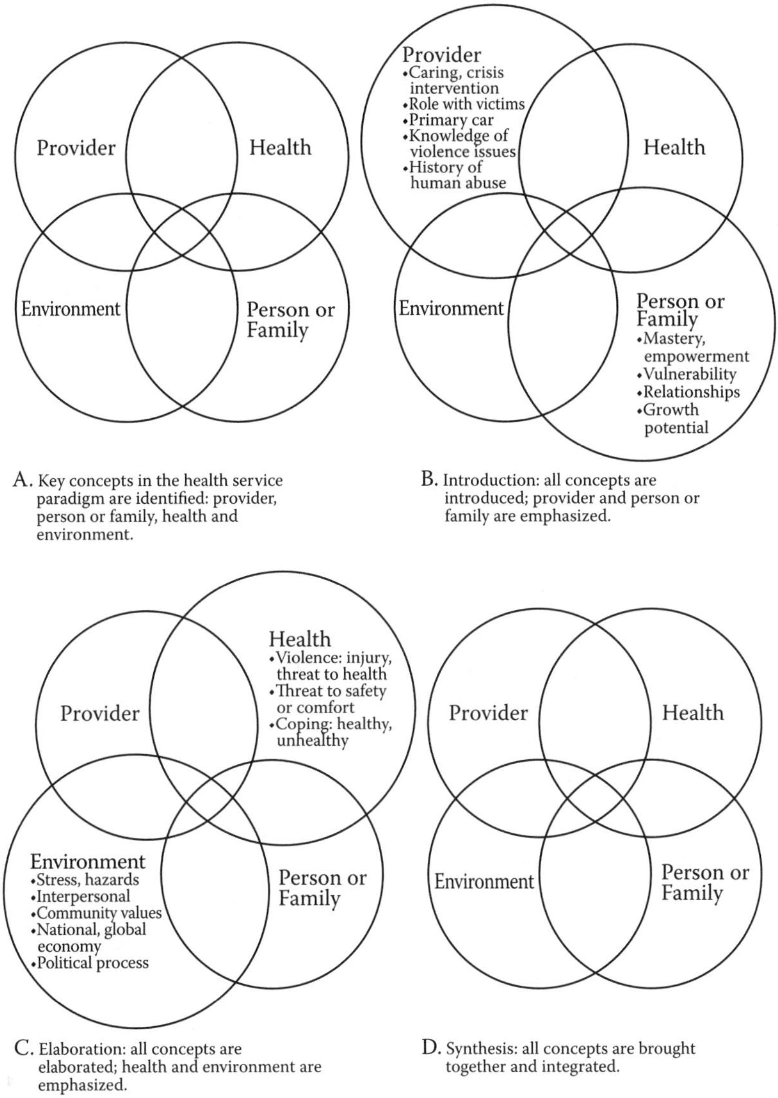

Figure 5.1 Health service paradigm. This model illustrates the centrality of the four key concepts in the health service paradigm: provider, person or family, health, and environment. A few supporting concepts (especially those pertaining to victimization) are illustrated as well. The model also shows the emphasis on these concepts at three levels of the curriculum: introduction, elaboration, and synthesis. Adapted from Hoff (1995, p. 66). Used by permission of Health Canada.

Trainers must also consider the biases they might encounter with a particular training group. Medical students traditionally have brought deep commitment to in-office or in-hospital care and a treatment model focusing on illness and cure, although primary care is now increasingly embraced across disciplines. In addition, it is important to emphasize the differences between crisis intervention and substantially different approaches in mental health care (see Hoff et al., 2009, ch. 1; Hoff & Morgan, 2011).

An example of clarifying different service models is the growing area of mediation and conflict resolution. Often clients served by these professionals are in a crisis situation (such as undergoing separation or divorce, or dealing with violence issues). The mediation process is based on both persons being present, each person having a side to the story, and both having a chance to present their side of the story. However, in the case of domestic violence, this process does not deal with the typical *power imbalance* between masculine and feminine roles. In this general systems process, conciliation is occurring, not crisis intervention (see Edleson & Eisikovits, 1996, for an empowerment approach to domestic conflict).

In general, biases and entrenched ideas based more on myth than fact must be openly addressed and challenged during training sessions in a nonhostile manner, emphasizing that various biases can have a negative impact on clinical outcomes, especially around sensitive social issues. Adequate information is the best response to most biases. The trainer should also have a thorough and communicable knowledge of crisis theory with a deeply held conviction about the benefits of providing assistance in the *least restrictive setting possible* in any given situation (this often translates to a community setting or the person's home). If the agency's focus is on violence toward women, trainers must ascertain whether participants carry some of the traditional attitudes toward abused women, for example, holding the victim rather than assailant accountable for violence. Despite ongoing public education campaigns, some people may still believe that if an abused woman really wanted to get out, she would.

The type of training manual or text used will be framed by the context of the training program, the instructor's theoretical framework, and the educational level of the participants. Assessment information, crisis theory, intervention strategies, operational and procedural guidelines, a code of ethics, and sample forms should be part of any training manual. A manual that reinforces basic concepts of crisis intervention and management, whatever the special focus of the program, is of the utmost importance. However, if one is training advocates to work with abused women, for example, one might assign additional material such as excerpts from various self-help books on the subject, whereas if one is training police officers, sources on community policing (emphasizing bridge building in neighborhoods) might be assigned.

In other words, the application of crisis theory and intervention to a specific population group enlivens what might otherwise seem too general for crisis workers who are in a focused setting. For example, sharing information about the realities faced by abused women helps trainees realize that many, if not most, abused women have, at times, some suicidal feelings. Also, a substantial number of such women have acted on these feelings because a suicide attempt may seem like an easier way to escape a violent relationship than their other options (Stephens, 1985). This kind of example dramatically emphasizes the need for training in risk assessment (danger to self and others) within the context of an experience to which trainees can relate.

Tailoring a Training Program in Interaction With Trainees

If crisis training is provided for staff of a program already in operation, it is important to develop a data collection mechanism that tailors the training program to the real demands placed on workers. The training designer should involve workers through interviews and questionnaires that indicate the nature of their experience, areas in which they feel the need for crisis training, and other relevant issues. This will provide a sense of ownership by those participating in the training and will reduce resistance and skepticism by people who feel that they already "know it all." An example might be providing training for case managers who work with persons discharged from mental health facilities. These are frontline workers, subject to a great deal of stress from a high-risk population, a typically overwhelming caseload, frequent inability to summon support from the psychiatric community when needed, and often too little pay. To be effective, a crisis training program must relate directly and concretely to the types of stressors these case managers experience and must recognize what they already know. Training can be offered as a way of helping them to be more effective, be less dependent on outside "experts" to get a client through a period of crisis, and feel more confident in their ability to make assessments.

At Some Other Solutions Society for Crisis Prevention (SOS) in Fort McMurray, Alberta, volunteer files are kept to catalogue training and skill enhancement needs, as well as gaps in training programs. With the availability of technology such as iCarol, a web-based program designed for crisis centers like SOS, they are able to provide up-to-date reports to funders and the community served—a means of accountability, but also utilize data gathered to determine training needs.

Similarly, training programs must be tailored to consider the stresses inherent in the high-risk work of police officers and other crisis workers. The trainer must acknowledge that some police officers are killed intervening in domestic violence situations—sometimes because they lack the crisis intervention skills needed to deal with these dangerous encounters in a more safe and effective manner. This underscores the importance of crisis training and the 24/7 availability of expert consultation for police in interpersonal violence situations (Hoff, 2010, ch 13; see Sully, 2002, and Sully, Greenway, & Reeves, 2005, for such programs in London, UK). This approach forges an alliance between the trainer and the trainees. When possible, engage an indigenous trainer—a trained police officer to work with law enforcement personnel, a physician trained in crisis intervention to work with medical students, a social worker to work with social work students, and so on. Conversely, interdisciplinary approaches to generic crisis content are increasingly valued by many educators. But too often, implementing ideal training models is not possible; therefore, it may be useful to forge an alliance with an indigenous staff member who can serve as a cofacilitator in doing demonstration role-plays and other parts of the training. Interdisciplinary approaches are best taught in carefully planned practicum experiences with exemplary role models (for further discussion, see Chapter 9).

The trainer needs to be sensitive to particular forms of resistance in some aspects of training by certain groups. Some mental health professionals may be reluctant to participate in role-plays. Police officers may be uneasy about guided fantasy exercises. Sometimes modeling by the trainer will help to overcome resistance; however, one needs to be alert to the reactions of the group and not get locked into a combative position. Trainer flexibility is required to shift from one mode of learning to another when resistance is extreme.

In-Service Training and Continuing Education Programs

The continuing education needs of mainstream health workers (for example, nurses and physicians) is determined by (a) the extent and depth of core crisis content in their generic program or formal preparation; (b) new developments in the field such as workplace violence and the emphasis on victimology content for all licensed health workers in the United States (Surgeon General's Workshop on Violence and Public Health, 1986); and (c) changes in the definition of violence as a public health problem. At the conclusion of preservice training for all groups, it should be made clear to trainees that they have only begun their learning experience. Ongoing training is essential for the continued growth of the health worker confronting crisis situations and other thorny aspects of comprehensive health care. In addition, in-service education reinforces skills and concepts marginally mastered during the initial training. At certified crisis or distress centers, in-service training for staff (volunteer or paid) is mandatory. Many agencies offer excellent in-service programs; however, some are not sufficiently rigorous about requiring attendance, particularly of their volunteers. Yet volunteers have the same obligations and expectations as paid workers; they are simply paid in a different currency.

In general, in-service training requirements are determined by program context in the same way as preservice training designs. One of the most useful ways to assess in-service training needs is with a questionnaire after the trainee has completed 3 to 6 months of posttraining service. The worker is then in a position to comment on how well training equipped her or him for the actual work, areas of training that need reinforcement or were not covered at all, concerns raised by clinical fieldwork, new client populations that have been identified, and other issues that emerge. This evaluation can be used to plan in-service training sessions.

Example: Emergency Department Training

A Canadian hospital's emergency department staff discussed their reluctance to deal with victims of sexual assault. The social work crisis team developed an in-service training package on sexual assault, focusing on knowledge, attitudes, and skill enhancement. This ongoing training program provided emergency staff with the necessary information, resources, and confidence to more appropriately and effectively intervene with survivors of sexual violence.

We have found that the most effective program balances *informational* sessions (speakers from outside agencies who describe the work and functions of their programs or who address special concerns, such as for refugees or victims of human trafficking) with *experiential*, skill-oriented sessions (for example, reviewing lethality assessment through role-plays and developing advanced counseling techniques).

Continuing education programs are often in-house, but there are other options, depending on the locale and the resources of the agency. Many of these are similar to those suggested for trainers in Chapter 3. It may be possible for people to attend regional, state-wide, provincial, or national meetings to update knowledge of crisis theory and practice. Before their national conventions, for example, the American Association of Suicidology and Canadian Association of Suicide Prevention conduct continuing education programs on some aspect of crisis work. In addition, web-based tutorials, webinars, streaming video and audio, e-books, and DVDs now serve as valuable training supplements. Some agencies may wish to make their own video or audio recordings for in-service training. The Boston Medical Center for Refugee Health and Human Rights, for example, developed a video and training guide for Congolese and Somali women who suffered rape as a weapon of war (see www.bcrhhr.org for more information).

Periodic refresher courses are also recommended. One agency conducts what has affectionately come to be known as "retread training," a 12-hour mandatory refresher course given to volunteer staff every second year. And, the aforementioned Canadian hospital emergency department mandates attendance of all new staff (including medical students, interns, and residents) to monthly in-service training sessions regarding crisis intervention and prevention, and hospital protocols dealing with the identification and treatment of victims of violence, perpetrators, and sudden unexpected death.

Agency personnel may also wish to look elsewhere in the community for ongoing training. There are many national training companies that offer self-study courses. It may be useful for some of the staff to take emergency medical technician training sponsored by the local Red Cross. Others who are preparing to move to a supervisory level can participate in a course on supervision at a local institute or social work program. A cooperative relationship with other mental health services will facilitate co-sponsorship of in-service programs and notification when other agencies are providing workshops. Notices should be prominently displayed for agency staff—volunteer and paid. Some of these programs are available at reduced rates for students and low-income applicants (it always pays to ask!). In a climate of fiscal constraint, this option is becoming increasingly necessary, if not the only one available.

Most crisis programs offer opportunities for workers to increase their responsibility. This professional development is important for both paid staff and volunteers. Line workers may move to a supervisory position, join crisis outreach teams, become trainers, or assist by conducting interviews of job applicants (volunteer or paid). The agency must provide adequate training for these new responsibilities.

Community Gatekeeper Training

Community gatekeepers are persons who frequently encounter people in crisis, but whose primary role is not crisis intervention or other health or social services. These gatekeepers include bartenders, disc jockeys, teachers, hair stylists, campus resident housing advisors, telephone operators, and 4-H and Scout leaders.

Training for these community groups is based on two premises. First, most people accept the slogan that "Suicide prevention is everybody's business" and that everyone is obliged on humanitarian grounds to assist fellow human beings in acute distress—in essence, people have a sense of community. We all have a *social* responsibility to assist our fellow human beings in trouble, and some of us also have a *professional* ethic obliging us to learn all we can about contemporary approaches to helping acutely distressed people.

Example: Community Gatekeeper Training

> A Seattle program encourages every resident to learn cardiopulmonary resuscitation (CPR) and the Heimlich maneuver. The assumption is that it is everyone's business to care for one another and everyone is provided with the knowledge and skills to act. The focus is on detection, empathic response, and appropriate referral to crisis specialists—in this case, EMTs, police, or firefighters. This program has resulted in decreased mortality rates. Acknowledging the crisis responders' actions contributes to community building.

Similar results are reported in communities with crime watch programs developed collaboratively with local police departments, including widely distributed information about self-protection and alertness to common danger signals.

Second, the work of gatekeepers or other residents will be less stressful and scary if their skill as "natural crisis managers" is enhanced by the basics of how to recognize risk of suicide or violence, how to use resources, and how to make an appropriate referral. For example, in many cases of suicide or murder, tragedy might have been avoided if family members were more aware of the common indicators of life-threatening behavior. The goal, then, is not to remake these gatekeepers into regular crisis counselors, but to reduce their stress by providing them the knowledge (including resources and skills) necessary to link distressed people to professional crisis services.

In short, the training needs of gatekeepers and the general public in the basics of crisis intervention can be compared to public health campaigns regarding cancer detection, abuse of health care workers, and the dangers of substance abuse, obesity, and smoking. The focus is on detection, empathic response, and appropriate referral to crisis specialists. This kind of training is also referred to as *community education*, an integral aspect of community mental health work (for further discussion see Chapter 10).

References

Edleson, J. L., & Eisikovits, Z. C. (Eds.). (1996). *Future interventions with battered women and their families.* Thousand Oaks, CA: Sage.

Gone, J. P. (2008). "So I can be like a whiteman": The cultural psychology of space and place in American Indian mental health. *Culture & Psychology, 14*(3), 369–399.

Goodfriend, M., Bryant, T., III, Livingood, W., & Goldhagen, J. (2006). A model for training paediatricians to expand mental health services in the community practice setting. *Clinical Pediatrics, 45*, 649–654.

Hobson, T. L. (2006). Criminal jurisdiction in United States Indian country: A practical guide. *Practicing Anthropology, 28*(1), 28–31.

Hoff, L. A. (1995). *Violence issues: An interdisciplinary curriculum guide for health professionals* (in English and French). Ottawa, Canada: Health Canada, Health Services Directorate.

Hoff, L. A. (2010). *Violence and abuse issues: Cross-cultural perspectives for health and social services*. London, UK: Routledge.

Hoff, L. A., Hallisey, B. J., & Hoff, M. (2009). *People in crisis: Clinical and diversity perspectives* (6th ed.). New York, NY: Routledge.

Hoff, L. A., & Morgan, B. D. (2011). *Psychiatric and mental health essentials in primary care*. London, UK: Routledge.

Morlock, S. D., Matlin, S., Barksdale, C., Puri, R., & Lyles, J. (2008). Developing suicide prevention programs for African American youth in African American churches. *Suicide and Life-Threatening Behavior, 38*(3), 323–333.

Perese, E. F. (2007). Stigma, poverty, and victimization: Roadblocks to recovery for individuals with severe mental illness. *Journal of the American Psychiatric Nurses Association, 13*(5), 285–295.

Rousseau, C., Key, F., & Measham, T. (2005). The work of culture in the treatment of psychosis in migrant adolescents. *Clinical Child Psychology and Psychiatry, 10*(3), 305–317.

Stephens, B. J. (1985). Suicidal women and their relationships with husbands, boyfriends, and lovers. *Suicide and Life-Threatening Behavior, 15*(2), 77–90.

Sully, P. (2002). Commitment to partnership: Interdisciplinary initiatives in developing expert practice in the care of survivors of violence. *Nursing Education in Practice, 2*, 92–98.

Sully, P., Greenway, K., & Reeves, S. (2005). Domestic violence, policing and health care: Collaboration and practice. *Primary Health Care Research and Development, 2005*(6), 31–36.

Surgeon General's Workshop on Violence and Public Health. (1986). *Final report*. Washington, DC: Health Resources and Services Administration, U.S. Department of Public Health.

Watters, E. (2010). *Crazy like us: The globalization of the American psyche*. New York, NY: Free Press.

Whitaker, R. (2010). *Anatomy of an epidemic: Magic bullets, psychiatric drugs, and the astonishing rise of mental illness in America*. New York, NY: Crown.

III

CRISIS SERVICE ORGANIZATION, MANAGEMENT, AND DELIVERY

The three chapters in this section provide an overview of essentials in the development, management, delivery, and evaluation of crisis services that apply across a variety of institutional service delivery models—from a comprehensive community mental health center, to hospital-based emergency medical and crisis services, to free-standing crisis hotline and walk-in crisis programs. Given the urgency of the topic and complexity of crisis service delivery formats, a central theme in this section is the key role of inter-agency and interdisciplinary collaboration to avoid system problems that can compromise clinical outcomes for people in crisis—and in some instances, prevent unnecessary deaths.

Chapter 6

Service Program Planning and Development

Chapter Outline

Diversity of Service Needs
Governing Body
Institutional and System-Related Barriers
Funding
Assessment of Needs and Resources
Political Considerations
Community Visibility and Public Relations

Crisis programs have proliferated over the past few decades. There are rape crisis programs, crisis centers for abused women, distress centers, homeless shelters, hospital-based emergency psychiatric services or crisis intervention teams, issue-specific hotlines (for example, sexual assault or runaway youth), and suicide prevention programs that often expand into crisis intervention services. In fact, studies reveal that many of the callers to suicide prevention centers are *not* suicidal, but call to discuss a crisis or a personal problem. It is not appropriate to apply the term *crisis service* to a program operating within traditional constraints—open from 8:00 a.m. to 5:00 p.m. and office bound. Whether provided by a single agency or several in collaboration, *crisis services must be available 24 hours a day, every day of the year; must be immediately accessible and coordinated with other services; and must be well publicized and clearly understood by the community the program serves.* Thus, it is crucial that the planners, developers, and implementers of a crisis program understand fully the nature of the service they undertake to provide (see Figure 1.1).

Diversity of Service Needs

The establishment of a crisis program may be the result of an identified need or gap within the community. This process is reflected in the growth of rape crisis centers and abused women's shelters. The work of a crisis program may reflect the community's pulse by rendering an early reading of its special stresses, fears, social problems, and needs. For example, in Ottawa, Ontario, one hospital emergency department expanded its crisis services to include a social work crisis intervention team as the increasing number of persons presenting to the emergency department with nonmedical needs was identified. The team was able to provide immediate crisis and psychosocial care including appropriate referral to community resources. This resulted in a more efficient use of hospital services and staff, reduced patient waiting times and recidivism rates, and promoted effective community linkages, thus minimizing duplication of services. A similar program at Boston Medical Center is staffed by a team of psychiatric nurses (see Chapter 9 for other examples).

Crisis program staff should take a proactive position in community planning for services. In Ithaca, New York, a community-based crisis center became acutely aware of the lack of emergency shelter because crisis workers spent many hours attempting to locate resources to house clients. Careful records were maintained, and the center played a central role in community planning meetings that resulted in a task force to develop an emergency community shelter.

Years ago, Fort McMurray, Alberta, recognized a similar need for extended emergency shelter when many families from the Atlantic provinces (suffering high unemployment rates in the fisheries industry) moved West in search of greater economic security. Despite a thriving economy based on the oil industry in Fort McMurray, the actual jobs available did not meet the expectations of arriving families from the East. Such migration patterns put tremendous additional stress on children, with one result being increasing suicidal behavior among youth, while simultaneously placing new demands on all service providers.

In Fargo, North Dakota, a large number of homeless men and women were turned away from traditional shelters each night due to substance abuse and mental health issues. In the process of writing the local 10-year plan (Going Home) to end homelessness, it was found that many of the long-term homeless people had not experienced much success with the traditional homeless shelter model. The planning committee recognized that in order for real change to happen, a new model had to emerge, and the concept of the "Fargo Emergency Shelter" was born with the guiding principle of developing relationships with the "hardest to serve" in order to provide them with a predictable and respectful environment and connect them to services different from what they had experienced in the past. The Fargo Emergency Shelter, now known as the Gladys Ray Shelter, assists this very high-risk population that was greatly underserved.

Responding to a community's need for new services requires a sensitive and farsighted governing body that sees the role of the crisis program in the community as not only working with clients in crisis, but also treating the entire community as a client with potentially crisis-inducing social problems. Therefore, a governing body plays a central role in the direction and impact of any crisis program.

Governing Body

We recognize the various forms of decision-making and governing bodies—a steering committee, board of trustees, collectives, board of directors, advisory committee, and so on. Here, our reference point is the policy board, who in conjunction with senior staff, hold final responsibility for the program itself and its financial viability. The agency's program, however, is implemented by the staff, *not* the board.

Many crisis intervention programs exist as free standing agencies managed by a policy board. Some are programs of a larger organization, like the crisis intervention team of a hospital emergency department. Still others may be a component of a mental health clinic. Whatever the arrangement, the board plays a vital role in the policy making and financial oversight of the crisis program.

Some agencies that utilize volunteer crisis workers do not permit them to serve on the board. Others may have boards composed entirely of crisis workers. Many have settled on a compromise position. Some Other Solutions Society for Crisis Prevention (SOS) in Fort McMurray, Alberta, has a volunteer board with representation from a variety of professional areas of expertise, with some of those professionals having been past consumers or volunteers at SOS. SOS believes that representation by past consumers or volunteers brings great empathy and a passion for the work to the board. Regardless of composition, the governing body is *legally accountable* for the conduct, services, and financial stability of the agency. Therefore, most boards avail themselves of legal services by purchasing malpractice insurance to protect staff and the agency in their service role to the public.

The governing body sets policy, has vision, defines the agency's mission, and ensures that the organization functions in keeping with its mission. A policy board does not get involved with the agency's administration or day-to-day operation. That is the function of the executive director and key staff, who implement procedures consistent with policies set by the board. When these complementary but necessarily different roles and relationships are not well defined and adhered to, internal strife is a common result.

Careful selection of members is vital to the smooth and effective operation of the board. It is important to maintain a balance between people knowledgeable in the areas of financial management and resources, personnel management, and mental health service providers, volunteers, and consumers. Though many boards like to involve prominent members of the community (such as bank presidents and corporation directors), these individuals are usually so overcommitted that they are able to contribute little more than their names to the board. A working board might better be composed of individuals who have the time, energy, and commitment that programs need for active participation from their directors. If the program wishes to involve the community's prominent people, invite them to join an ad hoc advisory committee or to function as consultants in the area of their expertise. In general, board members should include effective fundraisers and persons knowledgeable about marketing, public relations, and the political process. For example, politically savvy members will know how to act on the agency's behalf in a community where public monies are allocated in a way that routinely shortchanges human services in favor of other contenders.

In addition to these factors, the focus of the program and the community's special nature should influence board selection. For example, if a program is targeting adolescents, a representative of the school system will be a useful board member. For crisis programs, because a working relationship with the police or other law enforcement agency is essential, it will probably be helpful to have a respected member of such an agency on the board. If the community has a substantial subpopulation, such as the academic population of a college town, then someone from that population will be an important board connection. For a domestic violence shelter, having a formerly abused woman (not someone currently in crisis) on the board can aid the other board members in understanding the importance of crisis services from a consumer perspective. Politically, it may be advisable to nominate for board membership a representative from an agency or organization that plays a key role in the smooth functioning of the crisis program, such as an administrator from the Department of Social Services or a representative from a major mental health agency. In addition, if relations have been problematic with an agency that is vital to the program's smooth operation, encouraging a representative from that agency will help to work through difficulties.

Example: Stepping Stones Resource Center (SSRC)

The Stepping Stones Resource Center in Fargo, North Dakota, serves as an adolescent and young adult drop-in center for area youth dealing with homelessness. In initial planning it was recognized that many of these youth maintain normal day-to-day functions, such as attending school and working, but "crash" on the couches of friends or other family members at night. The adult advisory committee was intentionally composed of representation from the area public schools, the department of social services, juvenile court, law enforcement, substance abuse and mental health agencies, the domestic violence shelter, the United Way, the area homeless coalition, and other youth advocates in both Cass County (ND) and Clay County (MN) to assure the broadest support for the first service of this kind in the area.

Whenever there is board turnover, if at regular election time or when filling an empty slot, an orientation to the program is vital. This should be conducted by the crisis program's executive director as well as by the board president, and it should include the following:

- An overview of the crisis program, including staffing patterns and an explanation of the organizational chart
- A brief history of the program
- An explanation of the annual budget—income sources and expenditures as well as an explanation of how the board monitors the program's fiscal position
- A description of the board's committee structure
- A tour of the facility
- An explanation of responsibilities and expectations of board members
- The provision of copies of the constitution, charter, bylaws, code of ethics, and policy and procedures manual, where applicable
- An explanation of the board's decision-making process (consensus, majority rule, etc.)
- An explanation of the program's staff grievance procedure

In addition, new board members should receive information packets with the most recent annual report, financial statements, board minutes, list of the full governing body and staff names and positions, brochures, and other material describing the crisis program's work. An organization like BoardSource, which is recommended by United Way, provides guidance on internal standards of excellence for nonprofit boards through training, consultation, and a variety of publications and other resources (see www.boardsource.org for more information).

Board business is often conducted in committees—with the full board receiving reports from the committees and allowing ample time for discussion of committee recommendations. A working board membership is a substantial time commitment. It is only fair to both the crisis program and the potential board member to outline clearly what the commitment comprises. For most governing bodies, this involves at least two meetings a month—the regular monthly board meeting and a committee meeting. It is also useful to enforce the board's policy of requiring members who miss a certain number of meetings to resign. Too many governing bodies carry members in name only from year to year. One solution to these problems is to institute regular elections and term limits for board members. The seat of the absent member might well be succeeded by a highly involved and energetic successor.

Institutional and System-Related Barriers

The unmet need for mental health and substance abuse services has been widely documented. There are many barriers to providing quality crisis and psychosocial care that is accessible to those most in need. Feedback from both service providers and consumers regarding barriers is valuable and should be taken into consideration when planning, developing, and implementing crisis programming and subsequent training.

Barriers to providing quality crisis care, as identified by service providers at rape crisis centers, include lack of funding and agencies' inefficient use of funds among the greatest concerns. Service providers have also identified environmental stressors such as lack of supervision, unresponsiveness to employee's needs, inflexibility within agencies, and excessive paperwork required by funders as major staff barriers (Ullman & Townsend, 2007). Reimbursement of mental health services within primary care has been identified as a major barrier contributing to the unmet mental health needs of many Americans. A U.S. government Expert Forum identified barriers to reimbursement and proposed increased collaboration, policy and procedure dissemination, provision of technical assistance, flexibility in State Medicaid benefits, expanded coverage for nonphysicians, reimbursement of telemedicine, and reimbursement for mental health prevention and screening services as practical and achievable goals (Kautz, Mauch, & Smith, 2008).

Among American consumers with identified unmet mental health needs, the cost of services, lack of insurance, or inadequate insurance are the main concerns. Some consumers are reluctant to seek out services because they are not sure that it is necessary. In addition, the perceived stigma of receiving services keeps many from seeking treatment even when appropriate options are available. Other barriers include not knowing where to go, inconvenient geographical location, and inadequate availability of services. Some of the accessibility components include cultural barriers and need for bilingual services. Additional barriers are negative or victimizing reactions (such as blaming or being disbelieved when telling their story) and secondary victimization from police and the legal system (Substance Abuse and Mental Health Services Administration, 2006; Ullman & Townsend, 2007).

Funding

In an era of limited public money, funding for crisis programs is almost always problematic. In the United States, almost every state mental health department has experienced significant budget reductions, resulting in hiring freezes, employee reduction, required employee furloughs to reduce payroll, cuts to community programs, closure of state hospitals, and restrictions on the number of consumers served. Unfortunately, the same economic forces that decrease state budgets have created an increase in the demand for mental and behavioral health services (Albright, 2009).

Local situations tend to dictate the availability of resources. Rural groups continue to struggle for equitable access to monies, whereas specific populations (immigrants and refugees, Native Americans, First Nations people, Inuit, victims of violence, and those who are mentally disabled) spend considerable time educating potential funders to the uniqueness of their issues. In the Municipality of Wood Buffalo in Alberta, Canada, the five First Nations Bands, which represent over 5,000 Cree and Dene people, receive treaty money from the federal government to support some of their own initiatives in the area of health and wellness. For instance, the Athabasca Tribal Council provides managerial and technical expertise and services to all First Nations People within the northeast Alberta region. The First Nations Bands also use other services already established in the municipality.

Funding includes both public and private models, as well as combinations of the two. One probable resource includes contractual arrangements with state, provincial, or municipal governments. Another option is special funding for targeted programs within a specific agency, such as for young people or the crisis and psychosocial care component of a hospital's trauma program.

A variety of grant opportunities in both the United States and Canada represent a major portion of funding for nonprofit organizations. These include local, state or provincial, and federal government grants; other sources, such as the United Way, private donors, and service clubs; and foundation grants (private, community, and corporate). The U.S. Department of Health and Human Services, for instance, provides research grants, career development awards, research training and fellowships, program project or center grants, and resource grants. The Robert Wood Johnson Foundation, whose mission is to improve the health and health care for all Americans, provides grants through calls for proposals (CFPs) and unsolicited proposals for innovative projects in the areas of service demonstration, gathering and monitoring of health-related statistics, public education, training and fellowship programs, policy analysis, health services research, technical assistance, communications activities, and evaluations. The Dakota Medical Foundation, serving the areas of North Dakota and Minnesota in the United States, provides funding opportunities through initiative grants, responsive grants, matching grants, and donor-advised grants.

Example: United Way

United Way is a worldwide system of nearly 1,800 community-based United Ways in 45 countries and territories. With over 1,300 autonomous locations in the United States, United Way works to advance the common good, by creating opportunities for a better life for all. United Way does this by focusing on education (helping children and youth achieve their potential), income (promoting financial stability and independence), and health (improving people's health).

United Way of Cass-Clay (UWCC) in Fargo, North Dakota, provides funding for local nonprofit agencies and programs in two human service areas: Basic Needs and Prevention and Development. Programs in the Basic Needs category provide essentials for a good life (food, shelter, child care, safety, and emergency services). Programs in the Prevention and Development Category provide services that foster positive behaviors, knowledge, and skills as the building blocks to a good life. In collaboration with other organizations, UWCC is also working to create long-term, community-level change in the area of education through (a) investing in early childhood development and education programs that ensure children have the positive and enriching experiences to succeed in school and in life, and (b) developing long-term strategies to increase on-time high school graduation rates. This collaborative work requires identification of priorities, agreement on how the problems will be addressed, and ultimately agreement on how the community can align resources around these problems and strategies.

Foundation Center, a web-based directory of private philanthropic and grant-making foundations, can be a great place to start when looking for funding opportunities. Nonprofit grant seekers can subscribe to *The Foundation Directory Online* for access to the Foundation Center's complete database of grant makers. The complete online directory can also be accessed for free through many local libraries. See http://foundationcenter.org for more information.

Some funding sources provide matching funds in which an agency can receive up to a certain funding ceiling, provided it can match the dollars from other sources. This presents an effective argument for seeking donations because each contributed dollar generates another dollar of funding. In addition, it may be possible to enter into a partnership with other agencies and organizations, thus maximizing funding opportunities as well as garnering vital support and public profile.

Start-up funds may be obtained through a local foundation or grant process, but it is vital to have a plan for sustainability funding at the time of application. Local funding resources can be identified through an organization such as the United Way, through human service planning departments, by searching the library's reference section, or by an internet web search. If there is a university nearby, personnel from the development or alumni offices may be helpful in identifying local funders interested in human services. Overall, it is important to spend time researching funding possibilities as money is limited and criteria are stringent. Certain funding sources are more lucrative and stable to pursue but extremely competitive and time consuming.

Most agencies will need to conduct some form of fundraising. Possibilities include membership campaigns, charitable gaming, and events like garage sales, book sales, fun fairs, raffles, silent auctions, or entertainment evenings. These events heighten the crisis program's visibility in the community and strengthen the sense of commitment and involvement among those planning and implementing them. But, they may also generate burnout by placing too many demands on people whose skill and time are needed to provide service or monitor the event. A careful balance must be struck. Direct appeals to the public are also possible. Other sources are organizations that raise funds for charitable purposes. Fraternities and sororities often "adopt" an agency and engage in a number of small fundraising activities throughout the year. A membership drive may yield substantial community support, and memorial or endowment funds may be established.

One source of revenue too few agencies explore is the publication and sale of material they have developed for use in-house. Often, with minor modification, this material has utility and relevance in other communities. Examples include brochures that focus on young people and the prevention of suicide and violence among adolescents and college students. Training manuals may be another source of revenue. Training itself may generate income through a well-designed training program offered to other agencies and groups on a fee-for-service basis. An active speaker's bureau staffed by trained volunteers might develop a fee schedule for its services, which can generate considerable income for an agency.

It is also possible to develop after-hours coverage contracts with agencies closing at the end of the traditional work day because crisis programs offer their services 24 hours a day. Telephone crisis line workers have particular expertise in their ability to listen and assess a caller's situation. Because of their skills and availability around the clock, marketing crisis telephone services can generate alternate funding streams. Because this service is provided largely by unpaid volunteers, or because administrators may fail to compute the dollar value of unpaid work into budget reports and cost–benefit analyses, this vital service often remains invisible and undervalued by policy and funding bodies—much as the unpaid work of home caretakers is taken for granted (see Waring, 1988). Contracts for telephone support and crisis stabilization service, trauma and aftermath debriefing opportunities, and employee and family assistance programs are three such examples. If such services are marketed, however, it is crucial that there be sufficient staff available to handle the extra calls and ensure a smooth linkage to comprehensive mental health services. Rape crisis service providers have reported concerns over agencies taking on additional services, sometimes outside of the scope of what the agency could handle, to appease funders in a competitive market (Ullman & Townsend, 2007). The proliferation of toll-free floating hotline numbers is not the answer to crisis services that must be tightly coordinated with other facets of mental health care.

Most crisis and psychosocial programs in the United States and Canada function as the result of diversified funding resources. For instance, SOS in Fort McMurray, Alberta, is funded through a municipal grant, three provincial grants, United Way funding, and several corporate funders. Note that many funding sources require separate budget and reporting forms, resulting in considerable administrative time being spent in developing and responding to these. However, diversification of funding sources strengthens the agency. It is never totally dependent on the vicissitudes of the public sector, and it is protected from grave harm if political opinions shift. However, regardless of funding constraints, crisis workers should not be expected to put in extra hours without appropriate compensation.

Example: Shelter for Homeless Women

Rosie's Place, Boston's oldest shelter for homeless women, relies solely on the generosity of individual, foundation, and corporate sponsors. They do not accept city, state, or federal funding so that they can maintain independence. They work hard to keep administrative and fundraising costs low and proudly report that 89% of all donations go directly into services. Many supporters of Rosie's Place consider it a prize to volunteer their time there and attend fundraising events hosted by various celebrities.

Ideally, residents should be able to take crisis services for granted, just as they expect police and fire protection in a community. If comprehensive crisis services are in place, then, when a new crisis such as a job loss epidemic emerges, the foundation exists for rapid response and refinement of existing programs to meet new stresses.

Once a program is well established, there is the possibility of building an endowment fund. The money raised for this capital fund is invested, and the interest is made available to the agency for ongoing support. Endowment funds may, of necessity, become central in the future of human services. Establishing and managing such funds are time-consuming governing body functions.

Assessment of Needs and Resources

Approximately one full and intensive year of planning is essential before a program begins to function. If a crisis program is in the planning stage, it is important not to repeat past work. Planners—whether from central planning agencies such as a human services coalition, district health councils (Canada), a grassroots coalition, consumer group, or other assemblage—should focus on the unique efforts required by the program envisioned. On the other hand, as new needs and awareness of underserved populations surface, it is important to address them explicitly.

Other possible sources of needs assessment information are the local department of social services, the county or regional planning agency, university social science departments, and other groups with established data collection mechanisms and plans. Community questionnaires may be disseminated. The local newspaper can assist in helping to publicize and perhaps even distribute such a planning document. Certain information may be particularly useful:

- Population of catchment area, including age, sex, education, socioeconomic distribution, and other demographic factors
- Profiles of available services—their target populations, hours of service, rate of utilization, fee structure, etc.
- Primary community problems (for example, a substantial number of discharged patients with serious mental health problems, homeless teenagers and others, pending job loss, and lack of victim assistance programs)
- Population projections

A necessary part of the planning process further includes an assessment of the community's resources. In days of dwindling funds for human services, the most delicate concerns are duplication of services and smooth coordination of existing services. It is vital to ascertain what the community already has established and to what extent it might be possible to integrate the crisis program with existing services, insisting on high standards and specific training. The watchword is *collaboration*, not *competition*.

In addition, the feasibility of designing a particular kind of program must be clarified. A service dependent on trained volunteers suggests a large community or one with some turnover in population, as volunteer crisis workers tend to invest themselves heavily and then, after a period of time, move on. A service designed to be operated by mental health professionals will obviously be more costly. Where will this money come from? What is the availability of emergency service at the local hospital or the local mental health center? Is there a shelter for victims of domestic violence? Frequent staff turnover is costly. How can the rates be reduced? The certification program for crisis workers can provide an incentive for volunteer staff to invest a longer time with an agency and meet the challenge of supervisory and training roles (see Chapter 3). Closer team relationships between volunteer staffers and mental health professionals can also reduce burnout and rapid staff turnover.

Any planning process needs to take into consideration the particular context of the program's location. As noted in the planning of training programs, context also plays a vital role in setting up service programs. For example, the ethnic and racial composition of the community is a crucial planning factor. Will more than one language be important to the agency's functioning? In general, the staffing pattern should replicate the community at large. In Boston, Casa Myra Vazquez, a program for abused women in crisis, offers services in three languages: English, Spanish, and Portuguese.

Similarly, the economic status of the population to be served should be considered in the planning process. Where people struggle with survival issues, adequate food, and affordable shelter, the crisis program will confront harsh realities in trying to assist clients to obtain these essentials. Conversely, it is important not to assume the absence of problems with serious substance abuse, domestic violence, rape, and other traumatic events in middle- or upper-middle-class areas. However, the community infrastructure of these neighborhoods and the personal and social resources of their residents contribute to meeting the basic needs of people in crisis.

No crisis program exists in a vacuum. Most communities already have basic services such as emergency transportation and inpatient hospitalization. Coordination of new services with existing ones provides an efficient and effective method for helping people in crisis. Agreements should be carefully drawn up between those agencies most essential to the delivery of emergency services before any crisis intervention program opens. These would include the police, the telephone company for tracing procedures, ambulance services, immediate treatment settings if the program is not itself staffed or equipped to provide walk-in service, medical and social services, and emergency food and shelter providers. When a family or individual is in the midst of a crisis, the situation will only be exacerbated if the crisis worker must start shopping around to negotiate services, and the delay could seriously jeopardize the desired outcome of the crisis.

The importance of coordination and collaboration to maximize service is illustrated in the following example: A local mental health agency receives a grant to conduct violence prevention work in schools. The local women's program is already facilitating teen dating violence seminars in the schools. These two efforts should be coordinated into one strong presentation. Without such coordination, school staff may shorten each seminar, trying to fit everything in without cutting the regular curriculum.

Because one or more elements of crisis service (for example, 24-hour hotline and rescue capacity) already exist in many communities, future efforts should focus on the following:

- Community examination to learn what services do and do not exist. This can be done by a survey of social service and mental health agencies to determine the extent of an agency's involvement in delivering crisis services. The examination should also include resident surveys. One rural community in Vermont found that people in crisis usually called on registered nurses working part-time in the community. The nurses were then enlisted, on a voluntary basis, to receive training to increase their skills as crisis workers (Marshall & Finan, 1971).
- Development of crisis service elements that do not exist (for example, round-the-clock mobile capacity, outreach, and trained crisis workers to accompany police), and evaluating and improving the effectiveness of those elements that already exist.
- Development of a system for *maintaining* a high-quality crisis service and revising it according to the changing needs of consumers.

In the United States, millions of people have had no health insurance (which will change under the recently passed Affordable Care Act); in Canada, socialized health insurance plans are threatened by debate over inefficiencies; in both countries, a trend toward privatization and for-profit health care organization has threatened to fragment even further some delivery systems that leave more and more people to fall through the cracks. Providing still another freestanding hotline for the most vulnerable populations is like applying a "band-aid" to the gaping wound of health care systems in which the for-profit market replaces service as the driving force. Most ironic about this dangerous trend is its cost in both human and financial terms.

Psychiatric recidivism rates have increased because comprehensive crisis care has been insufficiently practiced or misused as a cover for the broad array of services needed by seriously disabled and disadvantaged populations (see Whitaker, 2010). As noted in Chapter 1, crisis service is an *essential element, not a panacea* for all problems; nor is it a substitute for other facets of comprehensive mental health care. The hazard of unequal insurance coverage for mental health care applies across the array of U.S. service delivery modes—public and private clinics, private practice offices, and hospital settings.

When considering the development or enhancement of a community crisis service, planners must remember that crisis workers can possess all the knowledge and skills necessary for effective crisis and psychosocial care, yet if individual workers feel forced to function in isolation, without the support and help of a well-coordinated human service system, the worker's best efforts can be undermined. Individual efforts are also frustrated when administrators in some agencies are unconvinced of crisis work's importance.

For several decades, volunteers and paraprofessionals have held a historic role in staffing hotline programs, but in some mental health arenas these workers are still regarded as second class. Because volunteers continue to cover most after-hours crisis calls, administrators should routinely factor their contribution into agency budgets. In the broader context of psychosocial care, volunteers engaged in group work are pivotal in such issues as breast cancer, addictions, and hospice care (see Chapter 8).

Commitment to crisis service probably does not exist if it is the last area to be adequately funded and staffed or the first to be eliminated during fiscal constraint, or if workers are not provided the training, supervision, and physical environment they need to help people in distress. Communities considering the development or enhancement of a crisis program should arrange at least one site visit (and possibly program consultation—see Chapters 9 and 10) to a crisis program that has met minimum standards and is certified by the American Association of Suicidology or an organization such as Distress Centres Ontario.

Political Considerations

Although crisis workers scrupulously maintain clients' confidentiality, the program itself must be highly visible to be viable. This entails some political sensitivities and awareness from the staff, board, and volunteers. The service may, for example, wish to reach out to pregnant teenagers. The issue of confidentiality may, in and of itself, become a politicized issue, as when a police officer calls demanding information, or a physician asks for unauthorized information about his or her patient. In addition, the service may receive demands it cannot meet or that might violate ethical standards, such as if someone asks the crisis worker to telephone or intervene on a distressed but nonsuicidal person who refuses to seek help. This issue is particularly sensitive when the request comes from another agency or a prominent member of the community. The best position is reliance on clearly stated policy and to be sure that the administrator fully understands that policy and is comfortable articulating it.

Politically, there are both advantages and disadvantages to running a crisis program. Service users may be reluctant to give public statements of support when the agency is threatened with a budget cut or reduction of funding. The constituency tends to be silent. Carefully chosen board members can be most helpful in these sensitive situations. Generally, though, families may not have the courage to name a suicide prevention center as the recipient of memorial fund donations when a death has occurred (even if the death is not a suicide). As a result, the agency needs to develop vocal support from other resources—community leaders, professionals, grassroots organizations, and other agencies.

Furthermore, the agency's failures tend to be fairly public. The completed suicide is visible; the prevented suicide is almost always invisible. On the other hand, crisis work is dramatic and vitally interesting, and the concern for life is one that attracts people from all parts of the political spectrum. In the hands of skilled staff (paid and volunteer) and an astute governing body, this interest and concern can reap substantial benefits for the program. In addition, a program that relies on trained volunteers has not only a broad-based group of community activists but also an argument for financial support from those who are unable or unwilling to give their time.

Community Visibility and Public Relations

As already noted, the planning phase of the crisis program must include the careful establishment of good community relations. This means taking the time to meet with agency directors, community leaders, potential funding sources, grassroots organizations, advisors, and others important to the program's success. They will have visible as well as hidden agendas; the latter may include concerns about jurisdiction and other territorial anxieties. Professionals may feel challenged by a different approach to helping people and may distrust the use of volunteers as entry-point workers. Police may be cynical about the crisis program responding when needed if no alliance currently exists. Religious leaders may be concerned about the program's stance on reproductive health issues. Social service administrators may worry that crisis workers will become demanding advocates for clients who are not truly eligible for assistance or for those who are.

An effective organization addresses these problems not only through the composition of its governing body but also through a commitment to a public relations program that includes regular meetings with community groups who have concerns about or interaction with the agency. The executive director must be prepared to respond to complaints about the program in an open and nondefensive manner, to assure the implementation of the agency's grievance procedure, and to negotiate a mutually satisfactory resolution. In addition, efforts should be made to establish a working relationship with the press. The agency will depend on the press for publicity regarding its programs, fundraising efforts, community relations, and support during a possible funding crisis.

Finally, the crisis program must find ways to be visible in the community. Numerous strategies accomplish this—a wide distribution of brochures describing agency services, cards listing the agency number (and other emergency numbers in the community, which reduces resistance to their distribution), articles in local newspapers, a user-friendly website, and radio and television interviews and advertisements. The agency may persuade the telephone company to include a listing of the crisis number in the telephone directory's inside cover and in as many ways as possible and affordable (for example, under the directory's "Crisis," "Suicide Prevention," "Rape Crisis," "Mental Health," and "Emergency Counseling" headings).

Example: Media Outreach

> Following the 9/11 attacks on the World Trade Center, the New York State Office of Mental Health (NYOMH) and the New York City Department of Health and Mental Hygiene (DOHMH) alerted the public to LifeNet, a preexisting counseling and referral service. Project Liberty, a federally funded program that provided free, anonymous crisis counseling and public education services, followed. NYOMH viewed the media outreach campaign as critical and found electronic (especially television) and print media along with radio to reach the most consumers (Frank et al., 2006).

An effective speaker's bureau is another method of maintaining good public relations and increasing community visibility. Initially, the program may wish to target certain groups—senior citizens, parent–teacher associations, university or agency staff development, professional associations, and others. It is highly likely that if the speakers are effective, requests will soon exceed the bureau's capacity to respond. It is always useful to bring program material to speaking engagements, both for recruiting volunteers and for informing potential clients and professionals of the range of program services. Program staff should also join community planning committees, serve on relevant boards, and become as integrated in the community as possible. It is no more appropriate for a program director and some of the other staff to be strictly office based than it is for a program to offer its services only in the office from 8:00 a.m. to 5:00 p.m. In general, the public relations program will be more effective if coordinated by a person with marketing skills and sufficient time than if it is conducted on a piecemeal basis by persons unconvinced of the importance of this vital program function.

References

Albright, B. (2009). States of despair: Mental health agencies face deep cuts as state governments slash their budgets. *Behavioral Healthcare, 29*(9), 17–20.

Frank, R. G., Pindyck, T., Donahue, S. A., Pease, E. A., Foster, M. J., Felton, C. J., & Essock, S. M. (2006). Impact of a media campaign for disaster mental health counseling in post–September 11 New York. *Psychiatric Services, 57*(9), 1304–1308.

Kautz, C., Mauch, D., & Smith, S. A. (2008). Reimbursement of mental health services in primary care settings (HHS Pub. No. SMA 08 4324). Rockville, MD: Center for Mental Health Services, Substance Abuse and Mental Health Services Administration.

Marshall, C., & Finan, J. L. (1971). The indigenous nurse as a crisis counselor. *Bulletin of Suicidology*.

Substance Abuse and Mental Health Services Administration. (2006, September). Results from the 2005 national Survey on Drug Use and Health: National Findings (Office of Applied Studies, NSDUH Series H-30, DHHS Publication No. SMA 064194). Rockville, MD: Author. Retrieved from http://oas.samhsa.gov/nsduh/2k5nsduh/2k5results.pdf.

Ullman, S. E., & Townsend, S. M. (2007). Barriers to working with sexual assault survivors: A qualitative study of rape crisis center workers. *Violence Against Women, 13*(4), 412–443.

Waring, M. (1988). *If women counted: A new feminist economics*. San Francisco, CA: HarperSanFrancisco.

Whitaker, R. (2010). *Anatomy of an epidemic: Magic bullets, psychiatric drugs, and the astonishing rise of mental illness in America*. New York, NY: Crown.

Chapter 7

Essential Program Elements and Organizational Structure

Chapter Outline

Overview of Essential Elements
Telephone Service
Online Crisis Service
Face-to-Face Service: Walk-in and Outreach
Emergency Medical and Psychiatric Service
Special Populations
Community Linkage and Coordination Network

This book promotes the vision that every community assures its members in crisis that help is available *when* they need it and *where* it will do the most good—in their real-life, natural community setting. Ideally, the existence of a crisis program in a community should be as routine as the presence of police and fire protection, postal service, and schools. Unfortunately, this concept is less than realistic for many people and communities.

Overview of Essential Elements

Much has been written concerning various crises and how best to handle them. Much less has been written about the structures and organizational factors that influence crisis workers and their effectiveness with distressed people. How do these factors all come together in a practical and workable design? What are the principles and guidelines for achieving excellence in all crisis programs regardless of individual differences specific to certain settings?

Crisis specialists, suicidologists, victim advocates, as well as the National Institute of Mental Health in the United States, Health Canada, Public Health Agency of Canada, departments of mental health, mental health associations, The Joint Commission (formerly JCAHO), Joint Commission International (TJI), the American Association of Suicidology, Distress Centres Ontario, and the National Organization of Victim Assistance (NOVA) have set guidelines for the organization and delivery of crisis services. These guidelines provide practical assistance to governing bodies and program administrators who wish to implement a service or evaluate and refine an existing crisis program. A comprehensive crisis program should include several basic elements, regardless of organizational model:

- Twenty-four-hour-a-day telephone service staffed by trained crisis workers.
- Face-to-face crisis service—walk-in access to crisis centers in local neighborhoods and round-the-clock crisis outreach to homes and other community settings. This includes immediate and systematic follow-up to persons affected by highly traumatic and publicized events or catastrophes such as a rash of youth suicide attempts or completed suicides, school or workplace shootings, natural and other disasters, and abductions of children.
- Emergency medical and psychiatric service—emergency assessment of suicide or other risk to life, availability of emergency medication (preferably from a physician with thorough knowledge of psychotropic drugs), assessment and treatment of persons with acute psychiatric disturbances, and linkage to a psychiatric inpatient service.
- Linkage network with established community emergency services—police, fire and rescue workers, Traveler's Aid network, and other community resources. The network should include standing agreements and a procedure for convening emergency planning conferences when necessary to resolve a crisis or psychiatric emergency constructively.

It is unnecessary and not even possible in most communities to administer these services through one agency. The important requirement is *coordination* to ensure that one element of service does not operate in isolation from the others and that time is not wasted in life-and-death situations due to linkage loopholes.

Rosenfeld, Caye, Ayalon, and Lahad (2005) affirmed our service vision with their PIE model—proximity, immediacy, and expectancy.

Telephone Service

Twenty-four-hour telephone emergency service has had a major impact on launching the suicide prevention and crisis intervention movement, thanks to Norman Farberow and Edwin Shneidman (1961; Shneidman & Farberow, 1957) in North America and Chad Varah and the Samaritans in Great Britain. The crisis telephone service comprises for many the major entry point to the formal mental health system. Telephone services, *the backbone of the crisis movement*, were operated predominantly by lay volunteers with consultation and supervision from professional crisis workers.

The ability to provide round-the-clock prevention and intervention services through the use of telephone crisis lines allows callers to take advantage of the service when they are most ready to try new coping mechanisms. There is an element of control that is maintained by the caller's ability to remain anonymous and end the call when they wish. The downside of this anonymity is when a suicidal caller accesses services via a cell phone. The option to trace calls becomes very difficult, as the cell phone provider may originate out of another city, state, or province. Crisis service providers with the ability to trace emergency calls will need to give consideration to this matter and revise appropriate policy.

Telephone systems must have multiple incoming lines and at least one unpublished outgoing line with the ability to make long-distance calls. Crisis lines should be toll-free. Other helpful elements of the telephone system include cordless headsets (or a long cord), speed dialing for high-frequency numbers, and caller ID. Workers should not use the "hold" option due to the negative psychological impact and the possibility of getting disconnected.

Historically, volunteers have been introduced to a wide range of subject matter prior to answering a crisis hotline. The topics typically include mental illness, suicide, chemical dependency, intimate partner violence, and sexual assault. In addition to knowledge, it is imperative that volunteers learn communication skills and recognize that there is a structured process through which the telephone worker guides the call. The specific tasks required in each phase of a call are summarized as follows:

1. Phase 1 begins the moment the telephone rings. In this phase, the telephone worker *establishes rapport* with the caller and *communicates acceptance.* A telephone worker knows that a workable relationship has been established when the caller is able to *identify the issue or feeling* to be discussed.

2. Phase 2 is the body of the call. It is the telephone worker's task to help the caller *clarify the presenting issue* and to *examine alternatives* and *establish priorities*. During this phase, the telephone worker concentrates on the current situation. Crisis intervention is not designed to be intensive therapy involving a detailed history and examination of the past. A telephone worker must assist the caller to deal with the here and now.
3. In the final phase of the call, the telephone worker *summarizes* the concerns and feelings that have been identified and clarified, and the caller *establishes and implements a plan of action*—essentially the basic steps of problem solving.

Self-disclosure (giving the caller personal information about oneself) is not effective; nor are *should* statements, which can be judgmental and therefore not helpful to a person already dealing with emotional pain. Advice giving to a person in crisis is rarely appropriate, even when requested. An exception is in life-threatening situations or when a person is so acutely anxious that he or she cannot focus on life-saving decisions. Telephone crisis intervention—like crisis work in general—is focused on what the *other person* feels, thinks, believes, hopes, has already tried, and is willing to try.

These elements of telephone crisis work can be found in interactions of 5 or 10 minutes, a half hour, or an hour—depending on the acuteness of the situation—and correspond to the basic steps of face-to-face crisis care. Thus, for example, it usually takes longer to develop and implement an action plan with a caller who has a regular therapist, is chronically depressed and lonely, and thinks often about suicide but is not in an immediate high-risk state. Mental health professionals and other trained counselors will recognize that these key features of telephone crisis work correspond to the general principles of communication and crisis counseling: assessment, planning, implementation of plan, and evaluation. In other words, the essentials of crisis work apply, whether implemented in telephone or face-to-face modes (office or outreach settings).

With changes emerging from "managed" mental health care models, call specialists on crisis hotlines are speaking more frequently with individuals who have serious and persistent mental health problems. These calls are often difficult for volunteers or employees, as the presenting behaviors are disturbing and workers feel frustrated about not being helpful. These frustrations are exacerbated in systems where it appears that mental health professionals are "dumping" their most complex and demanding clients on after-hours crisis telephone staff without the benefit of consultation, supervision, and careful interagency service planning warranted by the serious needs of these clients. Crisis workers often come to crisis hotline work with the intention of "saving lives" and intervening with those in acute crisis. Recruitment of volunteers and employees and their training programs need to incorporate the knowledge and skills necessary in responding to callers who are mentally ill. Administrators must assure that these same volunteers and employees have the required supports they need and linkages to mental health professionals with the special expertise demanded to serve people with serious and persistent mental illness (see Hoff & Morgan, 2011).

Important as the telephone service is, it is not adequate by itself. Volunteer telephone counselors must be able to link a caller with a face-to-face counselor or mobilize an outreach team when needed. Indeed, for some groups—frail older people and Native Americans in the United States, First Nations and Inuit people in Canada, and others living in isolated rural outposts worldwide—telephones are at times not accessible or functional to be useful during a crisis, despite the current worldwide use of cell phones. Another limitation of 24-hour telephone service, if not linked with other elements of service, is that some people at greatest risk are the least likely to use this service. If a telephone service is run largely to meet the needs of an affluent middle-class population, the service will not help many high-risk groups. Homeless individuals, many of whom have been discharged from a psychiatric facility, are a current example of such a high-risk group with little or no inclination to use telephones during periods of crisis, even if toll-free lines are available.

Some psychiatric patients who are discharged prematurely because insurance coverage has lapsed may not be homeless but still lack sufficient community supports and follow-up service. This is a common occurrence in the United States, which lacks a universal health insurance system in general, and in any system which does not grant equal insurance coverage for those with mental illness (as compared with general medical care). These patients may quickly learn that a threat of suicide is the easiest way to gain readmission for psychiatric care. Adapting themselves to these constraints on mental health services, some providers have even advised clients to disclose suicidal or homicidal ideation as a means of assuring a quick response from mental health providers. Such occurrences reveal a lack of coordination between various agencies serving those in need of mental health service, regressive policy decisions, and the resulting general disarray. They clearly indicate the need to unravel the underlying meaning, policy, and program planning implications of these "cries for help." Generally, they do not signify serious suicidal danger (at least not immediately) so much as the need for comprehensive service planning (including prevention) for vulnerable populations (see Hoff, Hallisey, & Hoff, 2009, chs. 9–12). Similar circumstances exist among the poor in many developing countries.

Nevertheless, the telephone service has been expanded in many communities to include services to special groups. Some communities now have teen hotlines, drug hotlines, parents-in-crisis lines, rape crisis lines, and specialized services for abused women, the hearing impaired, and persons living with AIDS.

Example: Rural Telephone Services

An example of a rural crisis line with coordinated services is provided by Some Other Solutions Society for Crisis Prevention (SOS) in Fort McMurray, Alberta. The SOS Crisis Line covers the entire regional municipality of Wood Buffalo (more than 63,000 km^2) and all communities in northern Alberta (708 area code). Trained SOS listeners have access to resource lists for each community and refer callers to the best available resource in their particular region. Follow-up with callers may happen but is not always an option due to the confidential and anonymous nature of the service.

Example: 2-1-1 Resource Line

In the United States, 2-1-1 serves to connect people to a variety of human services including basic human needs resources; physical and mental health resources; employment support; support for older Americans and persons with disabilities; support for children, youth and families; and volunteer opportunities and donation collection. Callers simply dial 2-1-1 to connect to a wealth of information in their area. Call specialists are trained in crisis intervention, including suicide and assault prevention.

First started in Atlanta in 1997, by 2009 2-1-1 services in the U.S. answered 16.2 million calls. Implementation of 2-1-1 was spearheaded by United Way and information and referral agencies in state and local communities. United Way Worldwide (UWW) and the Alliance for Information and Referral Systems (AIRS) strongly supported federal funding so that every American had access to this essential service. As of March 2011, 2-1-1 served over 250 million Americans (83% of the entire population) covering all or part of 49 states, the District of Columbia, and Puerto Rico, with coverage continuously increasing. In addition, as of May 2011, more than 19 million Canadians (more than 56% of the population) had access to 2-1-1 services.

In Fargo, North Dakota, the 2-1-1 or 701-235-SEEK telephone service is linked with other elements of the publicly funded mental health system. One function of this telephone service is a "warm line" which serves persons with chronic mental illness or other concerns who lack sufficient "natural" supports. These individuals have traditionally called crisis center hotlines for supportive care or conversation rather than for assistance in a specific crisis. Mental health departments that do not yet offer this service need to incorporate this important service element in their planning and funding process. The continued invisibility of this essential mental health service in many communities symbolizes the devaluation of crisis workers, as well as the mentally ill clients they serve. These same call specialists shoulder the burden of handling the crank, abusive, inappropriate, and chronic calls that are the bane of hotlines all over the world—a reality demanding training and ongoing support to prevent burnout.

Online Crisis Service

The use of technical applications, such as texting or instant messaging (chatting), in crisis intervention is gaining relevance. One benefit of the technical applications of instant messaging and chatting is the ability to share internet URLs during the chatting session (France, 2007). One example of this type of service is IMAlive, powered by the HopeLine Network. IMAlive is the first online crisis network with 100% of its volunteers trained and certified in crisis intervention. The Kristin Brooks Hope Center has partnered with To Write Love on Her Arms, the QPR Institute, and PostSecret, to launch IMAlive. Volunteers must be at least sixteen years of age, commit to 2 volunteer hours per week for a period of 12 months, have reliable internet access, and a genuine desire and willingness to help those in need. More information can be found at https://www.imalive.org/index.php.

Example: National Sexual Assault Online Hotline

The Rape, Abuse, and Incest National Network (RAINN) is the nation's largest anti–sexual assault organization. They are the host to the National Sexual Assault Online Hotline, which provides a free, confidential, secure service over the RAINN network. This service can be utilized by victims of sexual assault (current or past) or spouses, partners, family members, or friends of victims. The online hotline provides crisis intervention and support, answers questions about recovering from sexual assault, provides information about medical issues, gives explanations of the criminal justice system and what to expect when reporting the crime to police, offers referrals to resources in the chatter's home area, and provides information for family and friends of victims. The service is anonymous instant messaging (communication by typing back and forth) in a private session with a trained volunteer. Trained volunteers receive state-mandated training and ongoing supervision.

Face-to-Face Service: Walk-In and Outreach

In this book, *face-to-face crisis service* refers to the work of mental health crisis clinics (or centers) designed specifically to offer assistance to distressed people by specially trained crisis counselors. The term does not imply, however, that face-to-face crisis services exist *only* in such agencies. For example, medical and nursing personnel in hospital emergency settings, police officers, and other community caretakers such as victim advocates routinely do face-to-face crisis work. But as discussed in earlier chapters, programs preparing such workers do not usually include more than a smattering of content to prepare them for confident and skilled functioning with people in crisis. However, community and mainstream health care workers can provide this kind of face-to-face crisis assistance when trained in accordance with international standards.

Face-to-face crisis service can be offered as an adjunct to 24/7 telephone service, as an integral part of a community mental health center, or as a facet of a hospital-based emergency service. People can "walk in" to such centers or be referred by others. Walk-in services are beneficial to the consumer because they can be seen immediately, especially when they cannot speak confidentially over the phone or are in danger of physical harm in their current environment. Walk-in service, however, can be more hazardous to crisis workers when working with out-of-control clients. The rash of abuse and violence toward health and social service workers has emerged as a serious public health issue (see Chapter 9 for a multifaceted response to this burgeoning problem). These centers are the primary backup service for teachers, police, nurses, physicians, pastoral workers, and all others who often have the *first* face-to-face contact with people in crisis. For client-centered service, and an example of formal documentation, see Hoff et al. (2009, ch. 3), and affiliated website, including a record system that incorporates triage questions, risk assessment protocols, and other factors such as job loss that affect crisis vulnerability.

Ideally, face-to-face crisis service should be organized for mobile capacity. If a person or family in crisis is unable, for whatever reason, to come to a crisis center, experienced counselors must be ready and able to quickly go, as necessary, to the home or other community setting to intervene in acute crisis situations. Over the past few decades, the experience of crisis centers and specialists reveals that crisis outreach work, when carefully planned and supervised, is not often necessary. However, when mobile capacity *is* called for and is not available, the consequences can be drastic in terms of time spent on reconstructive work and, sometimes, lost lives. For example, if crisis outreach for psychiatric emergencies is left largely for police to handle and those officers have inadequate training in the intersection between psychiatry and the criminal justice system, officers may resort to unnecessary lethal force when skilled crisis intervention is required. If mobile outreach teams are not available, police officers should have 24/7 access to telephone consultation regarding psychiatric patients or other crisis situations (Hoff, 1993).

In response to this reality, many police departments throughout the United States are developing crisis intervention teams (CIT). CIT programs can improve officer's abilities to effectively, respectfully, and safely interact with persons with mental illness and subsequently divert more of these individuals away from the criminal justice system and into mental health services. CIT has been widely implemented in medium to large cities across the United States as a policy initiative to improve responsiveness to mental illness (Watson, Morabito, Draine, & Ottati, 2008).

Example: Akron Police Department

The Akron Police Department implemented a crisis intervention team (CIT) in 2000, in collaboration with Summit County Alcohol, Drug Addiction and Mental Health Services Board and its provider agencies, the National Alliance for the Mentally Ill (NAMI) of Summit County, the Summit County Recovery Project, and the Northeastern Ohio University College of Medicine. Implementation has resulted in family members being more comfortable calling police to request help for their loved one and an increase in consumers of mental health services calling the police to request help for themselves or their peers.

Trained officers were more likely to transport a person for treatment than they were before the program was implemented, understand that timely intervention in treatment systems could prevent future emergencies, use their training to deescalate and counsel individuals so that no further emergency intervention is needed, and learn when referral to the mental health system is most effective and when arrest may be preferable. The police and mental health systems developed outreach programs so that those people who didn't need emergency mental health intervention received appropriate mental health follow-up. In addition, the Akron Mental Health Court, for misdemeanors committed by those with severe and persistent mental illness, handles and allows for participants to receive intensive community-based treatment in lieu of incarceration (Teller, Munetz, Gil, & Ritter, 2006).

Crisis outreach work is indicated in the following circumstances:

- When a crisis situation cannot be adequately assessed by telephone. For example, the caller is being interrupted by an extremely upset family member, making telephone assessment impossible.
- When the police or rescue squad is inappropriate, refused by the caller, or not an option. For example, the following tragedy occurred in one community that depended only on police for crisis outreach service. A man with psychiatric symptoms was brought to a hospital emergency department by two police officers for psychiatric examination. On the way out of the car, the man grabbed the gun of one officer and shot him. The other officer in turn shot the patient. The patient died instantly, and the police officer died a few hours later. Although this man had a psychiatric history, he carried no lethal weapons at the time of the police investigation. If crisis outreach workers had been available to this family, they might have prevented two unnecessary deaths.
- When immediate assistance is needed to avoid acute family disruption and possible forced removal of a person from the home.
- When there is acute danger of suicide and the person cannot or will not come to a clinic or hospital for help. This implies thorough assessment

according to established criteria, including policies for collaborative intervention with police.

- When there is possible danger of violence toward others. By initial telephone assessment, a crisis counselor should determine if lethal weapons are involved. If so, the case should be handled collaboratively with the police. This implies that prior working relationships with the police have been developed to avoid possible crisis escalation by police presence. Police officers should not be called to assist in life-threatening crisis situations and then be advised by mental health professionals on how to conduct themselves. If crisis workers have suggestions for police officers about handling such scenarios, they should be made in the context of in-service training or consultation programs *prior* to, *not during*, acute crisis situations. At *no time* should mental health crisis workers be expected to place themselves in situations that are openly dangerous to their own lives. Unfortunately, many are, as murders of shelter and group home workers readily attest.

A trained group of crisis workers capable of such community outreach work can prevent many possible destructive outcomes of crisis. *At no time should a crisis worker be expected to staff a walk-in crisis center alone or make crisis outreach visits alone.* This principle also applies to paraprofessional personnel working with vulnerable psychiatric patients housed in the community. Some of these clients have histories of assault which may not have been addressed on admission to the service. Any staff member requested to work alone, for whatever reason (such as staffing or funding shortage), should vigorously refuse. Although most distressed people are not dangerous, inattention to this precaution has resulted in loss of life.

People doing specialized crisis work in outreach situations should be highly skilled in assessing risk for suicide and violence toward others and working with police and other emergency services (see Hoff et al., 2009, chs. 9, 11, and 12). They should also be capable of mobilizing emergency housing facilities and have authority to make hospitalization arrangements (including certification for involuntary psychiatric treatment) when necessary. They also serve as consultants and supporters to frontline crisis workers such as physicians, social workers, nurses, police, rescue workers, and teachers. See Zealberg and Santos (1996) and Simakhodskaya, Haddad, Quintero, and Malavade (2009) for examples of mobile crisis intervention services.

Emergency Medical and Psychiatric Service

The initial step of this service element is carried out by specialized crisis workers, rescue workers, firefighters, and the police. Hospital emergency departments and emergency services of community mental health centers also play a large role in the complete delivery of this service element.

An effective crisis program must have reliable working relationships with psychiatric, medical, and hospital establishments. Physicians, preferably psychiatrists or psychiatric nurse practitioners, should be available as part of the team, at least as consultants, when medication and hospitalization are needed.

Example: Prevention and Life-Saving Collaboration

Police responded to neighbors' calls about the early-morning repeated disruptive behavior of a 33-year-old single parent with an 8-year history of psychiatric treatment for substance abuse and episodes attributed to her diagnosis of bipolar disorder. The two officers were greeted by the woman at her home wielding a large knife, which she used to stab and injure the officers. One of the officers responded by fatally shooting the woman with his authorized service firearm. Investigation of the incident revealed that only a few hours earlier—following a neighborhood disturbance—the woman was treated in the local hospital's emergency department (ED) at 3:00 a.m. and released to her home at 6:00 a.m. Records revealed no collaboration or follow-up by ED staff with the woman's psychiatric treatment team and no attempt to retain the patient in the ED as allowed by law without a court order in cases of danger to self or others upon release.

A case like this underscores the urgency of all health care providers and police officers' knowledge of basic life-saving measures and interagency collaboration around acute crisis situations regardless of time and staffing circumstances. In instances when medication and psychiatric hospitalization are indicated, neither should be delayed because of poor working relationships with the medical community.

Patients have reported considerable variability in attitudes toward and treatment of persons presenting in hospital emergency departments. Some hospitals have introduced initiatives to facilitate linkages and services with the community. One Canadian hospital in Alberta has a psychiatric nurse on call in the emergency department Monday to Friday from 6:00 p.m. to 10:00 p.m. to assess and triage individuals presenting with a crisis or psychiatric emergency. The service is already overextended, often running until midnight. The following is another illustration of hospital-based crisis work.

Example: Emergency and Crisis Care in a Metropolitan Trauma Center

Boston Medical Center is a major trauma center. It has long recognized crisis intervention as part of its mission to provide comprehensive and compassionate

> emergency medical and psychiatric services for adults and children. For 25 years, on all shifts, psychiatric nurse clinicians (collaborating with psychiatrists, social workers, and victim advocates) have not only attended to walk-in or referred psychiatric crises but also provided immediate crisis intervention to victims of violence (physical battery, domestic or sexual assault), traumatized persons, and their families. In such an integrated setting, where crisis intervention is valued, relevant, and promoted, every health care provider, student, or trainee comes face-to-face with the myriad challenges in everyday lives, as well as the terrible burdens of violence, trauma, addictions, and other harrowing experiences. And, the practice of crisis intervention continues with the graduates, who will return home, touch people's lives, and listen to their stories.

Community crisis centers and hospital emergency departments should have established agreements with shelters as an alternative to psychiatric hospitalization whenever it is impossible to maintain a person in crisis in his or her natural community.

The well-known overuse of the emergency department for crisis care is affirmed in Stefen's *Emergency Department Treatment of the Psychiatric Patient* (2006). As Stefen pointed out, the Emergency Medical Systems Act of 1973 paved the way for the use of EDs in crisis care, resulting in shouldering the brunt of the impact of deinstitutionalization. As a result, some EDs have avoided collaboration with community service providers for fear of additional referrals. As the modern era of psychiatry emerged in the 1980s, the ED became the chief entry point and gatekeeper to the public mental health system for the chronically mentally ill, the arbitrator for in-patient services, and a drop-off point for the problematic client and family. In response to this, there was an increase in the development of community crisis services in an attempt to ward off costly hospitalizations and compensate for the decrease in out-patient and in-patient benefits brought on by managed care (see Gwande, 2011; Hoff, 1993; Johnson, 1990).

Although the ED is an essential element in the crisis care continuum, efforts must be made to use community-based services when appropriate. Due to differences in operating philosophies, EDs are not always the most appropriate option for clients. Stefen (2006) noted the following:

- ED services are rated on speed, which is in direct opposition for people in crisis who sometimes just need the professional to slow down and listen.
- Due to reimbursement inequalities, there is little incentive for thorough assessment, and many EDs lack even basic standards with regard to evaluation and treatment.
- Patients' primary complaints with EDs are the use of force by security personnel (weapons, tazers, chemical restraint, searches) or ED professional staff (forced disrobing, involuntary medication, seclusion); ignoring or minimizing medical concerns; treating psychiatric emergencies with

> contempt or derision; lack of privacy and confidentiality; long delays; access issues for specific populations (deaf, history of trauma, service animals, different languages); accompaniment while waiting; and lack of effective grievance procedures or advocacy.

A study by Coristine, Hartford, Vingilis, and White (2007) in Canada found that social stressors (i.e., housing, finances, or relationship difficulties), not psychiatric illness, were the primary reason for many using the ED for mental health intervention. Many chose the ED due to the belief that other support services or natural support systems could not provide the assistance they needed. The design of a new medical and psychiatric triage program, with services delivered by a community mental health agency, resulted in positive outcomes for both patients and families, and the medical staff of the ED. Since EDs may be used even when subacute services are more appropriate and available, it is imperative that parents, teachers, police, and other gatekeepers are familiarized with available community-based services and convinced of the benefit of using them (see Chapter 6).

The inappropriate use of ED services is costly. In order for alternatives to crisis care in the ED to be more feasible, these services must be more broadly reimbursed—starting at the primary care level (Gwande, 2011; Kautz, Mauch, & Smith, 2008). For instance, Medicaid allows for billing for crisis services but only by professional staff, which can increase operating costs for crisis services. Some managed care organizations have negotiated capitated cost contracts with states, allowing for more flexibility in service delivery and thereby creating effective crisis alternatives. However, many successful crisis programs are state funded because they are not reimbursable by federal government or insurance companies due to a lack of ability to provide proof of effectiveness or credentialed providers. Most services are not proven effective simply because of lack of research in this area (Stefen, 2006).

Special Populations

People Who Are Homeless

Homelessness is fraught with crises, for individuals, communities, and the staff who provide shelter services. For example, in Boston and surrounding areas, shelter staff are responsible for the safety of several thousand people nightly. Rules are clearly posted. Random disturbances are not tolerated, and experienced staff avert crises before they happen. Clients with chronic substance abuse or disruptive behavior are barred from shelters.

At the more remote Long Island site of Boston's shelter system, staff experience more vulnerability than at a central city location. Screening for admission tends to be more restrictive. Staff are more affected by a crisis because the "problem client" must be escorted not just out the door but also off the island. A client who becomes psychotic or combative needs to be contained until the arrival of assistance. Other shelter clients are affected by this action. On any night, the staff in charge might be less inclined to risk escalation of offensive behavior at 1:00 a.m. and attempt to resolve the problem by sending the client by ambulance to the nearest emergency department for evaluation of "bizarre behavior." The client may be automatically barred from the referring shelter. In the Boston city system, a client who is disruptive with shelter staff or other shelter clients, or is in possession of alcohol, other drugs, or weapons of any kind, *is barred from all shelters*. Barring may be for 60 days or permanently.

A shelter system, such as Boston's Pine Street Inn, works with the mental health system to identify and serve mentally ill people. A separate shelter designated for these clients seeks to stabilize and rehabilitate those who are severely impaired. Clients may stay at the shelter to participate in programs, attend clinic appointments, learn survival skills, and earn the opportunity for self-reliance in a group home. The socialization and responsibility components prepare the client for a work program at an affiliated shelter. This program, incidentally, coincides with the original design of comprehensive community mental health care envisioned in the 1960s and essentially dismantled in the 1980s. In other words, *shelters are the new institutions displacing public hospitals for persons with serious and persistent mental illness*, though many lack adequate staffing by teams of mental health professionals (see Earley, 2006; Hoff, 1993; Levine, 1981).

Example: Shelter and Mental Health Services in Boston

Janice Cruz is a 32-year-old woman with low-normal intelligence and a chronic mental disorder. She graduated from a "protected" program to a kitchen job at the "regular" shelter. After 2 weeks, she was evicted from the shelter on a policy violation for "spending too much time in the bathroom" and the suspicion of "ingesting several pink and white capsules." Ms. Cruz's daily prescribed medication consisted of four lithium capsules taken nightly. Except for not taking her lithium for 2 days, no other discordant behavior was noted. Blood tests revealed that her lithium levels were within the therapeutic range. However, her return to the shelter was barred. Consequently, Ms. Cruz is again living on the streets. Having lost her residence, her job, and her locker at the shelter, she carries four bags of clothes with her. Even after the clinic conducted a medical evaluation and elaborated a service plan, shelter staff refused to take Ms. Cruz back until the following Monday, 3 days away, when her situation might be reconsidered. "She broke the rules," they contended, "but rules are rules, and they are the same for everybody." Shelter staff are often per diem workers, and with 200 people in a shelter, "you can't know everybody's story."

After a century's worth of accumulated knowledge and skill around the needs of mentally disabled members of society, it is a sad commentary that a scenario like the above could take place in a wealthy society like the United States. In light of situations like these, programs like the Gladys Ray Shelter (GRS) in Fargo, North Dakota, are embracing a new model of providing services to the "hardest to serve" among the homeless population. Shelter guests with chronic mental illness and substance dependence issues are not turned away but rather welcomed into a respectful and predictable environment where staff focus on developing relationships with the guests in an effort to help them access programs that will aid in increased independence. Many of the people have been denied by the traditional shelter system for not fitting into the various rules that govern the shelters. At GRS, the safety of all guests is the main consideration. The GRS staff have created a culture of respect that flows between guests and staff and allows for even the most chronically mentally ill and chemically dependent to cohabitate peacefully. If a guest's behavior creates a safety issue for other guests or staff, they are asked to leave for the night, knowing that the next day they get a fresh start. A guest who presents with severe intoxication levels is offered a bed in the attached detox facility and permitted to return the next morning.

Although there are numerous highly trained health professionals who are able and willing to provide services for persons like Janice Cruz, many are unable to do so because of budget cutbacks and unequal insurance coverage for the treatment of mental illness. Many, however, continue the struggle, often against great odds. The Victorian Order of Nurses (VON) in Edmonton, Alberta, for example, illustrates the integration of crisis and psychosocial care in its People In Crisis (PIC) program. The PIC program provides primary health care through nursing services to women, seniors, youth, and children living in shelters or special homes, who are victims of abuse and neglect. The services operate under the following client-driven principles:

- Recognition of the client as expert on his or her own life
- Collaborative relationships between client and provider
- Client identification of the problem
- Shared continuous needs assessment, information gathering, and evaluation of outcomes
- Client decision making (see Hoff et al., 2009, ch. 4)

Working in collaboration, registered nurses help clients make healthy lifestyle changes. Empowerment of the clients through regaining control of their health and their lives is the first step toward developing healthy residents and healthy communities.

Example: The Social Enterprise Intervention (SEI) for Youth

> The Social Enterprise Intervention seeks to engage homeless youth in vocational training and mental health services in an effort to enhance mental health, prosocial behaviors, social support, and service utilization. A pilot study done with 16 homeless youth in Los Angeles had five phases: youth outreach and engagement, vocational skills acquisition, business skills acquisition, cooperative formation, and clinical services. Youth who participated showed improvement in life satisfaction, family contact, peer social support, and depressive symptoms (Ferguson & Xie, 2008).

Older Adults

Older adults are the fastest growing segment of our population. Planning and implementing crisis and psychosocial services for the aging population need special attention. Of special concern are the unmet needs of older adults with severe mental illness (Levine & Miya, 2008) and the often unrecognized mental health needs of nursing home residents during crises such as disasters (Brown et al., 2009; see also Hoff & Morgan, 2011, ch. 12; Melillo & Houde, 2011).

Physical ailments often go hand-in-hand with aging. As physical ailments increase, mental well-being often decreases (Snowden, Dhingra, Keyes, & Anderson, 2010). When mental health concerns are present, older adults are more likely to consult with a family physician than with a traditional mental health provider, but physical health concerns often precipitate this help seeking. Aging Caucasians, who tend to be more somatically focused in their concerns and less likely to share mental health concerns, are more likely to utilize professional mental health providers when referred. Family physicians, therefore, are crucial to the identification, management, and treatment of mental health concerns among the aging population (Dupree, Watson, & Schneider, 2005).

Older African Americans who need mental health services are more likely to talk with a member of the clergy than with traditional mental health providers about their concerns. Developing partnerships with church organizations and members of the clergy may increase the likelihood of accessing the community mental health system. It is imperative, then, that education is provided to both the medical and faith communities to heighten awareness of mental health concerns among older adults. A joint collaboration between the health, mental health, and aging services could produce a comprehensive service delivery system that addresses needs in a culturally sensitive manner (Dupree et al., 2005).

Veterans and Their Families

Veterans deal with the horrors of war, longer and multiple deployments, uncertainty about lengths of deployments, and the constant tension of counterinsurgency warfare. Traumatic stress responses are prevalent within this population. Data from the Substance Abuse and Mental Health Services Administration's (SAMHSA) 2004–2006 National Survey on Drug Use and Health (NSDUH) indicated that more than 20% of veterans age 18 to 25 suffered serious psychological distress, with females being more vulnerable than males. In addition, nearly one quarter of veterans age 25 and under had suffered from substance abuse disorders, with those from low-income families especially vulnerable (SAMHSA, 2008). Female veterans also report sexual assault by their peers and inadequate prevention and support services from military superiors.

There has been a tendency toward the liberal use of the posttraumatic stress disorder (PTSD) diagnosis with combat veterans. Veterans deserve necessary support and treatment services (without a psychiatric label) when suffering from what should be considered a "normal" response after exposure to the extraordinary horrors of war experiences falling well beyond the ordinary range of the average person's life (Hoff et al., 2009). Even more shocking than the use of PTSD is the substitution of the diagnosis of "personality disorder," which can be seen as justification to deny disability benefits to veterans (Priest & Hull, 2007; Sennott, 2007). The difficulty for Vietnam War veterans in gaining benefits for health damage believed to result from exposure to the defoliant Agent Orange has been well documented. Veterans of the Gulf War (Desert Storm) received compensation for damage from unidentified agents during warfare only after testimony to Congress from sick veterans and their advocates. Veterans of the Iraq War face similar challenges in obtaining care (Kors, 2008).

Family members and others affected by deployment or by issues related to the return of their loved ones may also need mental health and substance abuse services. In many cases, when a military member is deployed, their significant other is left behind to pick up the pieces and develop a new routine in order to continue with daily life. The stress of additional duties, worry over the safety of their family member, and the range of emotions that go along with this enormous lifestyle change can lead to a variety of coping behaviors. Often, just as roles are redefined and families acclimate to their new lifestyle, the veteran returns, prompting a new adjustment.

Example: Traditional Roles Redefined

Tamara and John were married for 2 years before John was deployed for one year to the Middle East with his National Guard unit. Prior to deployment, John worked out of the home and was responsible for all financial decisions and home maintenance. Tamara had left her job after the birth of their first child and spent her days in their house enjoying her duties as wife and mother. When John deployed, Tamara was required to take on additional duties, such as paying the bills and maintaining the house and family vehicle. Although a struggle at first, Tamara came to thrive on her newfound independence. She joined a family support group, started working part-time to "get out of the house," and enjoyed having more control over her daily life. Upon John's return one year later, she was expected to quickly return to her more traditional role, and her marriage struggled and depression ensued. Despite the personal growth that Tamara had experienced, her husband was not supportive of the changes she had made and just wanted life to "go back to normal."

The lives of children of deployed veterans are also upset by military service. Research by Huebner, Mancini, Wilcox, Grass, and Grass (2007) on the effects of children of deployed parents, showed three areas of boundary ambiguity: routines, responsibilities, and reintegration of the parent upon return. These adolescents showed an increase in behavior changes and a lower threshold for emotional outbursts, and depression and anxiety were common due to the uncertainty of their parents' status. During deployment, adolescents were required to assume, and then relinquish, various roles and responsibilities, thereby adding to confusion regarding their place in the family system, and suggesting that reunification with the deployed parent was more difficult than the actual absence. Adolescents were also acutely aware of changes in the emotional state and personal resilience of the nondeployed parents.

The U.S. Department of Veterans Affairs has developed the Office of Mental Health Services, which oversees a wide range of crisis and psychosocial care options for military veterans and their families. Particular attention is given to suicide and violence prevention and intervention due to the high rate of suicidal and other violent behaviors among this population. Reintegration services aim to create a smooth transition from military to civilian life. Each group of veterans forms a special "brotherhood" with its own language, set of experiences, and feeling of community; therefore, effective services must take into account each generation's unique experiences. A veteran's ability to talk to others, decompress, and feel understood can prevent isolation, self-medicating, or engaging in other harmful behaviors. Providers must have some familiarity with the military culture and not be afraid to ask veterans to help them understand their experiences. Further complicating this issue is the fact that many veterans do not seek out services, in part because they have been taught to be strong, and help seeking is perceived as a sign of weakness. Considering the fact that some benefits for National Guard and Reserve members are time limited, immediacy of appropriate services is crucial (SAMHSA, 2008).

Community Linkage and Coordination Network

Effective and comprehensive crisis work in a community includes establishing clear working agreements and referral procedures with *all involved agencies*, including providers of the same services in different locations. In practice, this means that referral procedures and contact information should be available to all relevant agencies. Referral files should include the resource name, location, phone number, email address, URL, automated answering information, hours of operation, services offered, and eligibility requirements, as well as the date that the information was last updated (preferably no more than one year between updates). As technology improves, this has become increasingly less complicated to maintain. For instance, the 2-1-1 system allows access to this referral information to anyone with internet access. Information can be easily obtained by simply entering a city or state into the system search tool. Information cards or other literature describing local crisis counseling services and contact information should be made available to clients of hospital emergency departments and offices of primary care providers. This is especially important for persons who have made suicide attempts or have been victimized by crime and still receive *only* medical treatment in some general hospitals (see Hoff & Morgan, 2011). Most police departments now also distribute such information. This process may assist in minimizing the number of clients who fall between the cracks.

Example: The Need for Networking

Nina Valez, a 36-year-old Latina with a history of asthma, is found in respiratory arrest at home. Advanced life support measures at the scene and prolonged efforts in the hospital trauma center were fruitless. Ms. Valez died on a Saturday night, leaving two daughters, ages 12 and 16, stunned and desolate beside her lifeless body in the trauma room. A great-grandmother, living in Barbados and in poor health, was identified as next of kin. Her telephone number and address are in the meager housing project apartment where the trio survived on Nina's Social Security disability payments.

The local part-time crisis center is closed for the weekend, and telephone calls are transferred to the psychiatric emergency service at the trauma hospital. A report is made to the state Department of Social Services (DSS) hotline. Because the daughters are physically fine and have a neighbor available to them, DSS will make a home visit next week. The hospital chaplains do not respond to beeper pages, and messages are left on both home answering machines. The hospital administrator works with the psychiatric nurse trying to arrange resources. After several hours of crisis intervention, the girls and neighbor were anxious to get home. The neighbor agreed to spend the night with the girls. They were given a list of telephone numbers and instructions, including indigent burial help, and a long-distance telephone card. Messages were left on answering machines at the neighborhood health center, churches, the hospital's adolescent center, and the social work department. The only living persons to be reached were DSS (not helpful) and the mayor's hotline, which would follow up. The girls will undoubtedly lose home, schools, financial support, and friends, and may even be separated from each other. But this evening it is mainly answering machines recording their disaster.

Hazardous events like Nina Valez's death cannot be neatly scheduled to occur during the 8:00 a.m. to 5:00 p.m. time slot. This underscores a central message of this book, which advocates 24/7 availability of basic crisis services.

In another example, a battered women's shelter accepts a client who, in time, is found to have paranoid delusions with no actual battering danger. The woman refuses referral to mental health providers and so is asked to leave the shelter. Soon she appears at another shelter, and the cycle repeats. This client's needs are not being met, and shelter staff feel frustrated and ineffectual. Communication between shelters could promote a needs assessment and improve services to the client.

A formal written agreement is certainly not a guarantee against interagency communication problems. However, such agreements provide a context for workers to resolve some of the problems and misunderstandings that occur in crisis work—not to mention the obstacle of reaching only answering machines during a crisis such as Nina Valez's death on a Saturday night. The larger the community, the more important formal agreements become.

Example: Contracts and Managed Care

Chester Community Counseling, formerly a community mental health center, is now contracted to Large Managed Care Corporation (LMCC). It agrees to provide walk-in and crisis service for the area served. However, the contract does not include nights or weekends. After-hours calls are automatically referred to the Area Emergency Services Team or the Psychiatric Emergency Service at Bean Medical Center (BMC). Both of these resources are prepared for medical and psychiatric emergencies but have few after-hours links to community resources. The hospital's former after-hours links have been drastically cut in budget decisions precipitated in part by years of inattention to cost overruns and the need to survive and compete in the U.S. health care marketplace. The Ecumenical Center across the street provided 24-hour chaplain coverage for years. New BMC managers did not view this as an essential service, nor was it reimbursable. A Catholic nun and a Protestant chaplain are available weekdays and on call by beeper after hours. Neither person is reimbursed for the on-call time. Both live a good distance from the hospital. Because crises are unpredictable regarding length of stay in the emergency department, family resources, and other factors, it is usually unrealistic to seek out either pastoral counselor after hours.

Generally, bureaucracy is less complicated in smaller communities. Working relationships are usually more closely knit, thereby minimizing the "systems problems" prevalent in metropolitan communities.

A systems problem occurs when the network of community agencies does not work together in a cohesive manner to help people in crisis. Formal agreements, which include a review process, can reduce this hazard to effective crisis work. This concept is demonstrated in the emergency department of a Canadian hospital which has developed an acute adult psychiatry home support program. With a view to community-hospital linkages for persons in crisis, this program assists patients with postdischarge referrals to community resources. Vital to this program is community-wide coordination of crisis services through the agency known as The Support Network.

Example: The Support Network

The Support Network provides 2-1-1 service for Edmonton and surrounding cities, offering round-the-clock referral information for over 1,000 agencies in the capital region; operates the round-the-clock Distress Line and Seniors Abuse Help Line; provides referrals to Mobile Mental Health Crisis Intervention Services; offers a telephone follow-up service for callers affected by suicide or seniors abuse; provides training for its volunteers in responding to clients in distress, bereavement work, and fundraising; provides crisis response training and debriefing to community agencies and groups on request; offers groups for suicide bereavement; offers caregiver services for individuals supporting a person-at-risk; offers online support using a Live Crisis Chat program; offers individual counseling on a sliding-fee scale; and issues a number of publications, including the *Tough Times Handbook,* a mini-directory of basic needs–related services.

Example: FirstLink

FirstLink is a local 24/7 support line linking people to the assistance and caring resources they need. FirstLink focuses on community resources with emphasis on suicide awareness and volunteerism. FirstLink provides 2-1-1 service for the state of North Dakota and for Clay County, Minnesota, offering 24-hour information and referral for over 6,000 nonprofit human service programs and listening and support to callers. FirstLink operates a 24-hour Suicide Lifeline that is networked with nearly 150 crisis centers in the United States through the National Suicide Prevention Lifeline. The crisis centers in the national network provide consistent telephone support to people who are suicidal and to people who are concerned about someone at risk of suicide. FirstLink operates a separate crisis line providing after-hours telephone support for contracted agencies by screening calls. Call specialists will connect the caller to the agency's on-call person if necessary. All call specialists are trained in active listening, crisis intervention, suicide and violence intervention, farm and ranch support, and military and veteran support. In addition, FirstLink offers a number of services focused on suicide awareness such as a monthly support group for survivors of suicide loss, providing suicide prevention and suicide intervention training to professionals such as law enforcement and hospital employees, facilitating Applied Suicide Intervention Skills Training (ASIST), and providing suicide education outreach to junior high students in Cass County, North Dakota, and Clay County, Minnesota. FirstLink also runs a Volunteer Center which offers a number of services such as connecting people to nonprofits, promoting volunteering, and building local volunteer capacity.

FirstLink's strengths are managing call centers and managing groups of volunteers. FirstLink is contracted by the cities of Fargo, Moorhead, and West Fargo, and the counties of Cass and Clay to coordinate volunteers in a disaster. In the 2009 Flood, FirstLink ran a call center that answered approximately 55,000 calls and coordinated over 100,000 volunteers in Cass and Clay Counties. FirstLink is a member of many coalitions and collaborative groups such as Homeless Coalition, Voluntary Organizations Active in Disaster (VOAD), and Child Abduction Response Team (CART).

References

Brown, L. M., Bruce, M. L., Hyer, K., Mills, W. I., Vongxaiburana, E., & Polivka-West, L. (2009). A pilot study evaluating the feasibility of psychological first aid for nursing home residents. *Clinical Gerontologist, 32*, 293–308.

Coristine, R. W., Hartford, K., Vingilis, E., & White, D. (2007). Mental health triage in the ER: A qualitative study. *Journal of Evaluation in Clinical Practice, 13*, 303–309.

Dupree, L. W., Watson, M. A., & Schneider, M. G. (2005). Preferences for mental health care: A comparison of older African Americans and older Caucasians. *Journal of Applied Gerontology, 24*(3), 196–210.

Earley, P. (2006). *Crazy: A father's search through America's mental health madness*. New York, NY: Berkley Books.

Farberow, N. L., & Shneidman, E. S. (Eds.). (1961). *The cry for help*. New York, NY: McGraw-Hill.

Ferguson, K. M., & Xie, B. (2008). Feasibility study of the social enterprise intervention with homeless youth. *Research on Social Work Practice, 18*(1), 5–19.

France, K. (2007). *Crisis intervention: A handbook of immediate person-to-person help* (5th ed.). Springfield, IL: Charles C. Thompson.

Gwande, A. (2011, January). The hot spotters: Can we lower medical costs by giving the neediest patients better care? *The New Yorker*, 41–51.

Hoff, L. A. (1993). Review essay: Health policy and the plight of the mentally ill. *Psychiatry, 56*(4), 400–419.

Hoff, L. A., Hallisey, B. J., & Hoff, M. (2009). *People in crisis: Clinical and diversity perspectives*. (6th ed.). New York, NY: Routledge.

Hoff, L. A., & Morgan, B. D. (2011). *Psychiatric and mental health essentials in primary care*. London, UK: Routledge.

Huebner, A. J., Mancini, J. A., Wilcox, R. M., Grass, S. R., & Grass, G. A. (2007). Parental deployment and youth in military families: Exploring uncertainty and ambiguous loss. *Family Relations, 56*, 112–122.

Johnson, A. B. (1990). *Out of bedlam: The truth about deinstitutionalization*. New York, NY: Basic Books.

Kautz, C., Mauch, D., & Smith, S. A. (2008). Reimbursement of mental health services in primary care settings. (HHS Pub. No. SMA 084324). Rockville, MD: Center for Mental Health Services, Substance Abuse and Mental Health Services Administration.

Kors, J. (2008, September 18). How the VA abandons our vets. *The Nation*, 13–21.

Levine, M. (1981). *The history and politics of community mental health*. New York, NY: Oxford University Press.

Levine, S., & Miya, K. (2008). Is PACT a viable model for older adults with severe mental illnesses? An exploratory analysis of service use and outcomes. *Clinical Gerontologist, 31*(3), 67–73.

Melillo, K. D., & Houde, S. C. (Eds.). (2011). *Geropsychiatric and mental health nursing* (2nd ed.). Sudbury, MA: Jones & Bartlett.

Priest, D., & Hull, A. (2007, December 2). Mental health problems still stigmatized in the military. *Boston Globe*, p. A23.

Rosenfeld, L. B., Caye, J. S., Ayalon, O., & Lahad, M. (2005). *When their world falls apart: Helping families and children manage the effects of disasters*. Washington, DC: NASW Press.

Sennott, C. M. (2007, February 11). Told to wait, a marine dies. *Boston Globe*, pp. A1, A10.

Shneidman, E. S., & Farberow, N. L. (Eds.). (1957). *Clues to suicide*. New York, NY: McGraw-Hill.

Simakhodskaya, Z., Haddad, F., Quintero, M., & Malavade, K. (2009). Innovative use of crisis intervention services with psychiatric emergency room patients. *Primary Psychiatry, 16*(9), 60–65.

Snowden, M., Dhingra, S. S., Keyes, C. L. M., & Anderson, L. A. (2010). Changes in mental well-being in the transition to late life: Findings from MIDUS I and II. *American Journal of Public Health, 100*(12), 2385–2388.

Stefen, S. (2006). *Emergency department treatment of the psychiatric patient: Policy issues and legal requirements*. New York, NY: Oxford University Press.

Substance Abuse and Mental Health Services Administration (SAMHSA). (2008). Veterans and their families: A SAMHSA Priority. *SAMHSA News, 16*(1), 1–5.

Teller, J. L. S., Munetz, M. R., Gil, K. M., & Ritter, C. (2006). Crisis intervention team training for police officers responding to mental disturbance calls. *Psychiatric Services, 57*(2), 232–237.

Watson, A. C., Morabito, M. S., Draine, J., & Ottati, V. (2008). Improving police response to persons with mental illness: A multi-level conceptualization of CIT. *International Journal of Law and Psychiatry, 31*(4), 359–368.

Zealberg, J. J., & Santos, A. (1996). *Comprehensive emergency mental health care*. New York, NY: Norton.

Chapter 8

Program Management and Evaluation

Chapter Outline

Staff Screening and Selection
Staffing Patterns
Team Relationships in Crisis Work
Role of Volunteers
Qualifications of Clinical Supervisors
Differentiating Supervision From Related Functions
Maintaining a Program
Data Collection and Utilization
Evaluation

Many components work together to ensure a successful crisis program: an organizational structure that is clearly defined and working in coordination with other community services; a governing body that provides direction and an evolving vision as to the purpose and impact of crisis and psychosocial care; and a staff that provide skilled and knowledgeable intervention to a vulnerable consumer population in a timely, collaborative, and focused manner. All of these factors complement one another—but it is the caliber of individuals working in the program and the manner in which they are organized and supported that are critical to the well-being of a crisis program and the clients it serves.

This chapter describes the principle program features required to meet consumer needs for crisis and psychosocial care. Each section deals with a unique aspect of organizational strength. Together they contribute to an infrastructure that promotes excellence and minimizes detrimental consequences, including burnout.

Staff Screening and Selection

The success of a crisis program depends heavily on the selection of appropriate staff. The extensive experience of crisis trainers and supervisors clearly reveals that not everyone is suited to do crisis work. The crisis arena offers many rewards, challenges, and continuous excitement, but also considerable stress, increasing isolation, and some danger. These factors must be kept in mind in the recruitment, training, and supervision of crisis workers. Experience working in the crisis field may satisfy a hiring criterion, but alone it is not indicative of an effective crisis worker. A person whose tolerance for stress is low, whose attitude is unsuitable, or who feels forced into an unwanted assignment will be part of the problem rather than the solution in acute crisis situations. Individuals with a "rescue" perspective or the need to "feel good" as well as counselors with unresolved personal issues will undermine the basic principles of crisis work.

On the other hand, a person who is self-starting and independent yet works collaboratively will contribute to comprehensive and timely interventions. People who do well in crisis work are focused yet flexible, creative while balanced, not easily distracted under pressure, and mindful of client empowerment as pivotal in positive crisis resolution. Crisis workers must have a high tolerance for ambiguity. They need to be patiently near the consumer's experience, distinguish their own thoughts and feelings from that of the client, and must be able to allow meaning to be established by the client (Cavaiola & Colford, 2006). Crisis workers who have successfully navigated their own life crises and are mature, optimistic, well trained, and persistent are likely to reap the rewards of successful crisis work.

Precautionary measures must be taken during the hiring process. Inquiring about convictions for criminal offenses, sexual or physical abuse (especially of children and adolescents), and any moving violations on driving records can screen out potentially dangerous applicants. Both asking for and actually checking references are important steps in the hiring process. Background checks need to be completed uniformly to avoid discrimination lawsuits (Van Pelt & Hancock, 2007). If staff members are appropriately selected, trained, supervised, and supported, there will be no shortage of people willing and able to do the job. Therefore, the job should not be forced on anyone who does not want it.

Recognition of this major staff screening principle will eliminate many problems stemming from staff ineffectiveness or poor attitudes. It will also save many dollars in training time, staff turnover, and perhaps even losses from lawsuits by injured or dissatisfied clients. At best, it is short-sighted to expect ill-suited or unwilling people to do crisis work. At worst, the lack of staff screening can result in an inadequate crisis program for those entitled to it—all members of a community.

Staffing Patterns

Staffing should be determined by the kind and extent of service the agency offers. People doing crisis work need the support of a clearly defined staffing arrangement. Crisis workers must know who their teammates are and whom to call for consultation or other assistance. For example, an effective system was developed by the social work crisis intervention team in the emergency department of the Ottawa General Hospital. A staffing schedule was prepared and posted one month in advance. Staff were encouraged to schedule themselves and ensure equitable distribution of shifts. Double staffing was built into each day to accommodate short-term follow-up with clients, recording, consultation, and community liaison (Adamowski, Dickinson, Weitzman, Roessler, & Carter-Snell, 1993).

Crisis counselors and mental health professionals doing crisis work must possess an attitude of flexibility about their work schedule and be physically and emotionally able to cope with extended work hours. Workers responsible for consultation and outreach must be willing to be "on call." However, a crisis worker should not be expected to be on call more than one or two nights a week, the ideal being once every 10 to 14 days, depending on staff size and volume of service.

Mechanical devices such as a beeper system or cell phone should be part of any well-run crisis program, including primary care services, which are often the first to see highly distressed people. This increases the reliability of the call system and frees workers from remaining beside a telephone during the entire call period. It can reduce the prospect of staff burnout from being on call. Also useful are clearly defined high-risk indicators profiling potential crisis situations which enable staff to assess accurately, respond quickly, and thus eliminate unnecessary backup consultations.

Staffing arrangements must be flexible and include provision for staff to take time off when they have worked into the evening and night hours on crisis outreach. This is unnecessary in agencies that are sufficiently budgeted to pay staff for on-call time, even when no calls are made. However, many crisis programs do not have the budget for such reimbursement. As such, it is imperative that a clearly defined and feasible compensation mechanism for staff be identified and implemented (time off in lieu of pay, for example). Similarly, staff must recognize the value of earned vacation time and be encouraged to take regularly scheduled leave rather than accumulate these hours.

General hospitals that do not already have mental health specialists with crisis expertise routinely available to emergency department staff should make every effort to develop such a program. Boston Medical Center has had a program like this for years (staffed primarily by psychiatric nurses), and some hospitals have social work crisis intervention teams. Health providers who do not have this assistance will be more stressed handling crisis situations in hospital emergency settings.

Team Relationships in Crisis Work

Team relationships are important in carrying out any human service function. In crisis work, team relationships are critical. The effective use of social network techniques in crisis intervention demands that we relate with clarity and effectiveness to other people who are helping. Social network techniques demand a minimum of two people for constructive outcomes (See Hoff, Hallisey, & Hoff, 2009, ch. 5). In high-risk suicidal or homicidal situations in the home or elsewhere, the presence of *at least two team members* is essential as a resource and for safety.

However, today this ideal is often compromised, exposing staff to danger as increasing numbers of crisis workers and other providers function in isolation. Similarly, there are settings where the program focus does not necessitate the presence of two workers (as in telephone work) or the volume of work requires that each worker juggle several client groupings simultaneously (as in hospital emergency departments). Many crisis programs have experienced drastic funding cuts, eliminating all but maintenance staffing. As such, team relationships become of paramount importance, and trust is pivotal.

When distressed people come to an agency for help, they should be informed that the entire program team is available to them. The emergency telephone number of the agency, *never* the counselor's home number, should be given to the person. Giving someone a personal telephone number for emergencies implies that the counselor will be available for all possible emergencies. If a distressed person calls and the counselor is not there, a serious credibility problem can result. Counselors cannot and should not attempt to provide round-the-clock crisis services single-handed. To do so not only violates the basic principle of setting boundaries with clients but also may result in burnout—after 6 months or so, the counselor ends up so exhausted and overspent as to contemplate abandoning crisis work altogether. However, people in crisis do need easy access to 24/7 service. This can only be provided by an agency or community plan designed for such continuous service. Twenty-four-hour emergency coverage demands that all program staff members collaborate as a team.

Teamwork is also vital for offering encouragement to partners while working with clients. Stress is inevitable when dealing regularly with life-and-death matters as well as other critical life events. For example, if a person who is receiving counseling dies by suicide, the counselor is one of the survivors who needs someone to talk with about the traumatic experience. *Counselors are people too.* Their supply of energy is not inexhaustible. For example, within the homeless population at the Gladys Ray Shelter, multiple deaths and suicides have occurred among shelter guests. The staff and other shelter guests, who have essentially functioned as family for the deceased, are left to grieve. This has prompted the executive director to begin forming a network of local providers who are willing to process with guests and staff after such tragic incidents. As history of the crisis field shows, many programs function as the direct result of dedicated volunteers. One of their sources of "refueling" for more crisis work is the support and active cooperation of fellow team members. Some mechanisms to accomplish this may include a formal debriefing process, regular supervision sessions, consultation with a backup person, and meeting with other team members after a shift, daily rounds, and weekly team meetings. Scheduled team sessions also provide an ideal forum for resolution of conflicts around disagreements over treatment plans, personality issues, and other matters. (See Hoff et al., 2009, ch. 10, "Helping Survivors in Crisis," pp. 358–364.)

Role of Volunteers

In spite of the fact that volunteers are the backbone of various crisis programs (suicide prevention, drug hotlines, battered women's shelters, rape crisis centers), they are sometimes treated as inferiors. For example, some volunteer telephone counselors are not permitted to counsel clients face-to-face. Allegedly, the telephone counselor is not sufficiently skilled for the task. This practice is ironic on several counts. First, it implies that a caller in crisis is in worse shape *after* the telephone intervention than before, when the opposite is usually true. If people in crisis use the telephone at all, they usually use it at the peak of their distress.

Second, helping a person in crisis by telephone intervention can require *more* skill than counseling on a face-to-face basis. The telephone counselor relies on verbal and voice cues only, and has less opportunity to manage the counseling situation by directing client/helper interaction. The caller can always hang up, leaving the counselor very frustrated. In contrast, face-to-face counseling allows for visual signals as well.

Finally, whether over the telephone or face-to-face, *crisis intervention is crisis intervention.* The telephone is one of the many devices available to a crisis worker. A crisis volunteer who is trained to help people express feelings and understand their crisis situation, assess risk to life, and develop and implement a plan for crisis resolution can practice those techniques in various situations.

Perhaps one reason for not allowing telephone counselors to work with clients face-to-face is that in some settings such work is really psychotherapy, not crisis intervention. Most crisis workers are not trained to do psychotherapy, and many professional psychotherapists are not trained to do crisis intervention. Optimally, health and social service workers should do only what they are trained to do, but not be prevented from doing it fully. The "telephone versus face-to-face" distinction is also a hollow one as applied to emergency medical and nonpsychiatric primary care providers such as physicians and nurse practitioners. These providers integrate crisis and psychosocial care into routine practice and consult with crisis specialists—whether by telephone or in office and trauma settings (see Hoff & Morgan, 2011). The telephone versus face-to-face dichotomy is also counterproductive for those telephone staffers who seek certification as crisis workers. Success in the certification examination requires that workers can apply the general principles and strategies of crisis work in a variety of situations and settings, not just in the telephone framework.

All of us do formal or informal crisis intervention in our everyday lives. People who *formally* help other people in crisis are referred to as "crisis workers" or "crisis counselors." No distinction should be made between those who do crisis work as volunteers and those who work for financial remuneration. Volunteer crisis workers are the thousands of women and men who make up a majority of the staff of 24/7 telephone crisis services throughout many countries. Some of these same volunteers do outreach work and face-to-face counseling with distressed people. These crisis workers are often referred to as the "real professionals" in the crisis field.

Individuals who volunteer their time in crisis care do so because of their dedication and interest in this work as their chosen way of helping others. Most volunteers also claim that the experience promotes personal growth. This often depends on the training they receive, the nature of team relationships, and the quality of supervision. Volunteer crisis workers earn their living as accountants, teachers, writers, psychologists, homemakers, nurses, and secretaries. They work several hours weekly or monthly. They are not paid and do not rely on the work as a means of supporting themselves. "Paid" crisis workers may be full-time crisis specialists but also include nurses, physicians, social workers, police, and rescue workers constantly in contact with people needing crisis and psychosocial care.

Another group of crisis workers are paid or volunteer fire fighters and rescue workers. Their vital work in many communities is often taken for granted. Although their immediate concern is to put out fires and provide physical support before the person is brought to a hospital, such workers are not always included in the development of a community's comprehensive crisis services. Yet fire fighters and rescue workers respond to many emergency situations and often are left with the task of consoling the survivors of accidents or the relatives of heart attack victims. Such situations certainly require crisis intervention skills. In addition to consoling others, these emergency workers, especially paramedics, are exposed to all sorts of trauma. Frequently the events that lead to distress are "quiet events" that connect in some way with the emergency responder on an emotional level. Workers can be re-traumatized by quality assurance review in the absence of proper organizational support. It is also important to acknowledge the tremendous stress endured by emergency workers' loved ones regarding the emergency worker's safety and reaction to trauma (Regehr & Bober, 2005).

These volunteers should not be neglected as part of the total community "staff" of crisis workers. In addition, they may themselves need assistance when they have worked with a particularly difficult situation, such as an accident or abuse resulting in the death of a child. It is now commonplace in police departments, Red Cross disaster relief programs, federal law enforcement organizations (such as the Federal Bureau of Investigation and the Royal Canadian Mounted Police), to provide debriefing or emotional first aid and support sessions for workers who witness and deal with the results of gruesome crimes and catastrophic loss (such as the 9/11 terrorist bombing in New York, the Southeast Asia tsunami, hurricane Katrina, and the BP oil spill in the Gulf of Mexico). Failure to do so increases the probability of posttraumatic stress, inappropriate coping strategies, and burnout.

Qualifications of Clinical Supervisors

Although some people seem to have innate abilities as leaders, there are some identifiable qualifications and skills that a supervisor needs. A good supervisor thinks of supervisees as persons. This includes an attitude of respect and concern and an appreciation of the person's basic needs and growth goals. An effective supervisor also values and respects the supervisory role. The supervisor should possess leadership skills and managerial competence in several areas:

- Interest in being an active supervisor and willingness to devote time to the task
- Ability to establish and maintain a consistent and focused supervisory process
- Knowledge and skill in the area to supervise or consult (in this case, crisis and psychosocial care)
- Ability to share these skills with another in a nonthreatening way (for example, suggesting a well-established approach to a problem presented by a supervisee by saying, "What do you think about trying … ?")
- Ability to assess a worker's skills and needs (as when supervisor and supervisee meet to explore problem areas for which the worker requires help, such as clinical issues, overextension, or early signs of burnout)
- Ability to involve the worker in the supervisory process (as by asking, "Considering your experience in working with this person, what do you think about the approach we've discussed?")
- Ability to offer recognition, support, and pats on the back when indicated ("You did a great job")
- Ability to provide clear and concrete direction when indicated ("I suggest you call the rescue squad immediately")
- Ability to institute an open-door policy and being available in emergencies
- Visionary about how a program and its staff can achieve and maintain excellence, and respond to changing needs

The people who are supervised or need consultation should also possess certain attitudes if they are to obtain the greatest benefit from inspired leaders and the supervisory process:

- Self-confidence regarding one's abilities, needs, and potential for growth
- An attitude of openness toward learning, the supervisor, and the supervisory process
- Acceptance of the program's mission and goals
- A sense of shared responsibility for problem solving
- Acceptance of one's role in the program once appropriately defined in relation to one's skills and experience (some workers end up in trouble because of a very unrealistic concept of themselves and the skills they possess)

Administrative structures, including written policies and procedures that clearly spell out authority and consultative roles, can also eliminate many problems. Authority roles are either *ascribed* or *achieved*. An ascribed authority role is acquired by a legitimate administrative appointment. Achieved authority is acquired by virtue of experience, wisdom, and skill in one's field that has earned respect. People with achieved authority are often recruited for their leadership ability. Some people, unfortunately, function with *responsibility* to supervise but possess neither ascribed nor achieved authority. Such a situation is problematic and unproductive for both the supervisor and the worker. People supervised by an unqualified person have a hard time accepting the directions and suggestions of the supervisor. Any supervisors who find themselves in this untenable position should take steps to have it remedied. The supervisory responsibility can be refused, or the authority that should accompany the function can be insisted on.

Differentiating Supervision From Related Functions

One of the frequent problems encountered in the supervisory process is the failure to distinguish sharply between supervision, consultation, teaching, training, counseling and therapy, crisis intervention, and friendship. This is often referred to as a *boundary issue*. For example, a supervisor relying on personal relationships with supervisees for friendship may experience difficulty in shifting back and forth in these roles. Friendship with a supervisee is not out of the question, but the roles must be clear at all times. Supervisors must ensure that a particular job—in this case, crisis care—is done in a fashion worthy of the people served. As a bonus, friendship may emerge in the process but must be kept on a professional level in the workplace. Be aware that some supervisory functions can engender dislike or even hostility, such as taking corrective action for the worker who is consistently late or absent from scheduled work without notice.

Another problem that can interfere in the supervisory function is a supervisor's tendency to play therapist with a worker who either has or is *perceived* to have personal problems. Also, workers with personal problems sometimes try to use the supervisor as a therapist. This is best handled by focusing on the worker's actual performance. Keeping notes of the supervisory sessions is helpful—thus keeping everyone on track and focused. A principled supervisor will always discuss items of concern *directly* with the worker *before* documenting them in the worker's personnel file. If and when personal problems interfere with job performance, the supervisor should point this out to the worker. Outside counseling sources may be recommended. Being attentive and supportive to a personally distressed worker and doing crisis intervention for that person is appropriate; "therapizing" is not. There is an art to being accessible or inaccessible and knowing when and how to apply either way of helping another. These same principles apply to student–teacher (or clinical preceptor) relationships.

Workshops and engaging a mentor are useful strategies for supervisors wishing to evaluate and improve their style and effectiveness. Table 8.1 differentiates the various roles that sometimes get blurred. Continuing education programs on

Table 8.1 Supervision and Related Functions

Interactional Process	*Objective*	*Person Directed Toward*	*Method or Techniques*	*Relationship*
Supervision: clinical and administrative	To ensure quality control and agency accountability for service to clients; to ensure survival of the agency	Staff members (paid and volunteer)	Goal and problem assessment and clarification; demonstration and role modeling; concrete direction; constructive criticism; recognition and support	Line (authority)
Consultation	To offer necessary assistance in the delivery of crisis and mental health services	Staff member or other agency staff member	Problem and goal clarification; suggestions and recommendations	Staff (nonauthority): may be contractual
Teaching	To convey knowledge in a defined subject area	Student in a formal education program	Lecture or discussion; demonstration or role-play; reading; audiovisual methods; special assignments and projects	Contractual between student and teacher concerning subject areas only
Training	To convey knowledge, skills, and attitudes specific to a defined functional task (such as crisis management)	Staff member assigned to perform a specific job function (for example, a crisis worker)	Lecture or discussion; demonstration or role play; reading; audiovisual methods; special assignments and projects; role modeling	Contractual between a trainee and trainer concerning training module only
Counseling and therapy	To assist another individual or family to resolve personal or other life problems	Client	Individual, group, or marital or family therapy or counseling, as indicated by client's needs	Contractual between client and counselor or agency
Crisis intervention	To help people in crisis resolve their crisis constructively	Anyone in crisis	Crisis management on individual, family, or group basis; decision counseling	Contractual between crisis worker and person in crisis
Friendship	To provide personal needs for support, intimacy, and social attachments	Anyone	Communication, sharing of feelings and commonly enjoyed activities	Reciprocal, mutual attachment or intimacy

Source: Hoff and Miller (1987). Reprinted with permission.

supervision and consultation are valuable means of elaborating on these human interaction processes in the crisis field.

Maintaining a Program

It is imperative to provide as supportive a working climate as possible for people engaged in any high-stress work. Human services work, especially that incorporating crisis and psychosocial care, frequently involves long hours, evening work, and shift work taking one away from home and family. Decisions can involve life safety. Arranging time for paperwork and meetings is difficult because the worker must be prepared for interruptions at any moment. Clients are not always cooperative and pleasant, especially if it is necessary to provide trace, rescue, or psychiatric in-patient services. And the demand often exceeds the worker's capacity to respond.

Furthermore, for people situated at the entry point, like telephone crisis counselors or emergency service dispatchers, there is frequently no sure way to know the outcome of a crisis situation if the call is prematurely terminated or if the caller refuses to provide identifying information that makes follow-up possible. The worker is left with uncertainties about his or her performance and the results of a contact. Crisis workers may rush to the obituary page of the local newspaper, especially if they have been working with a client whose safety is of great concern. Such workers will probably need assistance around issues of responsibility, boundaries, self-care, and related matters.

For paid staff, salaries, as in most human service agency work, are often low. Unfortunately, crisis work seldom has high status in the community, and upward mobility may be limited unless the worker has an opportunity to gain some administrative skills. These staffing patterns often still include significant gender and racial bias. Also, human service organizations tend to offer the greatest financial incentive to those in managerial roles while neglecting those who consistently provide excellent clinical service. This is discouraging, as many frontline workers choose to remain in a frontline capacity due to a great sense of job satisfaction.

Addressing Staff Burnout and Vicarious Traumatization

Today, crisis workers face formidable obstacles in carrying out their work. They are increasingly challenged with both the volume and complexity of client needs—a situation sometimes compounded by the constraints of managed care systems. Multiple or simultaneous demands of various clients necessitate skillful prioritization in a timely fashion. Diminishing community resources and supports increase the volatility and critical nature of many situations; staff frustration follows when they cannot implement appropriate maintenance, preventive, or treatment measures. And many workers function in isolation with little opportunity for consultation or having their practical needs met (breaks, meals, and the like). Inadequate supervision contributes to burnout (Ullman & Townsend, 2007). Incongruence between the worker's professional values and job demands increase the risk of burnout. Stressful job demands, difficult clients, high workload, and unsupportive work environments compound the issue (Acker & Lawrence, 2009). The intensity of crisis work is stressful. Although stress is a common component of daily life, accumulated stress that has no outlet can lead to serious reactions, inappropriate ways of coping, and burnout.

Agencies must respond to the threat of staff burnout at two levels, *preventively* and *reactively*. Low salaries frequently contribute to staff turnover (Ullman & Townsend, 2007). The agency must provide sufficient compensatory time (the executive director should monitor the staff to ensure that they take it) for extra hours worked. Though pay scales are often relatively low, the governing body should provide as attractive a benefits package as possible, including paid holidays and adequate vacation and sick leave. Personal days off may be included as part of the sick leave package; these should be considered "mental health" days, requiring no justification. Few crisis workers abuse any privileges; most bring to their work a high level of idealism and commitment. The agency is protecting them, and itself, against their burnout and possible "compassion fatigue." A valuable resource for addressing burnout issues in crisis and psychosocial care are employee and family assistance programs (EAP) for workers and families. Supervisors should not be reluctant to "counsel out" or even terminate employees who are burned out or negatively affecting clients and other staff. Retaining ineffective workers creates an unhealthy atmosphere for others. Supervisory inaction in these situations can be perceived as weakness or favoritism by staff and can lead to destructive staff relationships.

Another burnout prevention strategy is to rotate crisis workers so that they are scheduled for a period of time, then switched to other activities to obtain relief from pressure. In agencies offering crisis care as well as traditional psychotherapy and counseling services, burnout may be prevented and job satisfaction increased if crisis work and on-call assignments are divided among *all* staff. Such a staffing arrangement *requires crisis intervention training as a prerequisite* as well as the cooperation and screening of all staff. This arrangement can also enhance continuity of care for psychotherapy clients who call after hours.

The director, coordinator of volunteers, or whoever is in the appropriate position must be sensitive to the experience of the worker. Some situations elicit particularly strong feelings, like working with a child victim of sexual abuse.

Given that most crisis workers are women, the chances that a worker herself is a survivor of violence are quite good, so she may be dealing with unresolved issues of her own. The supportive person's door must remain open to the worker, who should sense a clear message of availability and accessibility. Open communication is as necessary to the functioning of the crisis program as it is to the person in crisis. Adequate consultation for the worker is essential. In fact, it is not unlike the message the agency wishes to convey to the public. The agency must itself provide, or arrange to have available, needed professional consultation on any difficult issue that the worker cannot handle alone, for example, violence or verbal abuse by clients.

Closely related to burnout is the prospect of vicarious traumatization and the attention it requires for staff support. Vicarious traumatization is the feeling of distress and psychological trauma experienced especially by persons working with victim-survivors of violence and abuse whose job entails listening with empathy to a particularly gruesome story of violence, or to similar stories of clients repeated over hours, days, or months in a job. It refers to the absorption of the trauma into one's own psyche which, without attention to its source and appropriate support and self-care, can lead to burnout and other psychological or social problems (Hoff et al., 2009, p. 499; see also Hoff, 2010, ch. 12; Ullman & Townsend, 2007).

Elisabeth Kübler-Ross (1969) has written about the need grieving people have for a "screaming room"—most crisis workers could benefit from a supportive place to discharge their tensions and sometimes, their anger. Other strategies that promote worker health and safety include maintaining good communication with supervisors and regular debriefing sessions which assist staff with positive resolution of the cumulative impact of their work (as in vicarious traumatization). The formation of staff problem-solving committees promotes worker empowerment. Staff meetings should be scheduled on a regular basis, and staff retreats are a worthwhile tool for long-range planning and problem solving. These are best conducted out of the office, away from telephones and other interruptions.

Staff cohesiveness and support are crucial to the prevention of burnout and vicarious traumatization. Acker and Lawrence (2009) found that workers who felt competent in their abilities to handle the demands of their job had lower levels of burnout than those who perceived themselves as incompetent. Social support was associated with an increased perceived competence. In-service training is another method for combating burnout. It provides a sense that the agency cares enough about its staff to invest time and money in continued learning. It also strengthens the capacity of workers to deal with stressful situations and plan together how to maintain normal operations during in-service or retreats.

The executive director can also prevent burnout by actively responding to workers' concerns. For example, a worker assesses a client as highly suicidal and persuades the client to go to the emergency department where a cursory assessment is made. The worker is not consulted and the client is not admitted. The crisis program director must be prepared to make contact with the emergency department, to obtain needed information about the experience, and, when appropriate, to advocate for the staff member. There is considerably less burnout among staff who experience their director and, at a greater distance, their governing body as supportive, for example in dealing with sudden death (Adamowski et al., 1993).

Nurturing resilience in crisis professionals can help them deal with the highly stressful and complex world of crisis care. Resilience can help volunteers and professionals develop the confidence necessary to deal with constant changes, reframe negative experiences into positive and self-enhancing ones and create positive outcomes. Resilience can be fostered through having non-work-related support and interests; professional development; having insight into one's work; having a sense of faith, morality, and advocacy; having a sense of humor; support and processing at work; keeping work life separate from home life; and taking care of oneself through diet, exercise, and adequate rest. Resilience is a product of experience, clinical expertise, a sense of autonomy, responsibility, and confidence (Edward, 2005; Hoff, 2005). Clearly, it is time to acknowledge staff as *the* most valuable resource of a crisis service. Contemporary crisis programs must make an active commitment to include worker health and safety issues as critical components in program planning, implementation, and maintenance.

Special Issue: Chronicity

Anyone who has ever attended a conference of crisis program staff has probably noted the substantial number of papers, discussion sessions, and general conversations about the problem of chronicity. *Chronicity* refers to the behavior of a small group of persons who *chronically* (repeatedly) use crisis services as a substitute for a natural support network. Crisis programs—appropriately—do not see themselves in the business of maintaining lonely people through long chats on the telephone or working for years and years with clients who cycle in and out of institutional care. Furthermore, there are real concerns about people who become addicted to the crisis service, as others do to call-in radio shows or social-networking websites.

From our perspective, there are two major issues that need to be considered with regard to chronicity: the impact on the client and the impact on the staff. Clients who demand repeat service over an extended period of time are probably not truly appropriate for a crisis program. The "warm line" at FirstLink as discussed in Chapter 7 is one approach to this problem. Few agencies can provide the kind of ongoing support available through a 24/7 service and staffed by enough different crisis workers so that the burnout factor for an individual worker is minimized. This is particularly true of telephone crisis services that tend to attract an ongoing clientele who then become problematic for the agency. The problem of chronicity is most troublesome when telephone crisis services are not effectively integrated with face-to-face counseling programs and continued care, especially for callers who are mentally ill.

For some clients, repeated contact with the crisis service may be counterproductive. They may use the service to defuse rising tensions, rather than make the commitment to psychotherapy, which may be needed to change long-standing behavior patterns. Or they may use the service to contravene the work they are doing in therapy, and attempt to pit therapist and crisis service against each other. In addition, they may be in contact with numerous other helping agencies, thoroughly confusing themselves by participating in too many plans and programs. Records reveal that numerous suicidal clients already in therapy are making contact with crisis services to discuss their suicidal feelings. When asked if their therapist is aware of their self-destructive mood, the response too often is "Oh no, I couldn't tell my therapist about that." It is difficult to know if the therapist has conveyed a subtle message that it is not okay for the client to discuss suicide or if the client is being either untruthful or unnecessarily timid. In either case, it is the responsibility of the worker to assess risk and attempt to facilitate open communication between client and therapist.

In addition, a crisis service can unwittingly promote a subliminal message. When a client is in crisis, everything stops to provide support and immediate access to service. Family members may be encouraged to help the individual through the crisis. Employers may be advised to back off for a period of time. And the general support structure may be strengthened. But without effective crisis management, which includes post-crisis planning for continued care, it is entirely possible that once the danger is past, the support may be withdrawn. The message may be that only when in acute trouble or threatening suicide can a person get needed help—which is similar to a client's suicidal presentation as a "ticket" to hospital admission.

Frequently, chronicity is a problem for people diagnosed as having borderline personality disorder, minimal interpersonal skills, or marginal ability to cope with life's daily stressors. Some programs refuse repeated contact with these clients, denying them access to the crisis line; others set firm limits; and still others accept all calls from all callers. One of the most useful directions to take with a repeat client is to develop a *clear action plan* as early as possible. This may be achieved manually or through technology. One facility established a "frequent visitor book" that logged the names of persons who contacted the service often. In it, the clients' plan was outlined, and all contacts were logged. When the client called, the book was reviewed, and the clients' plan was implemented or followed up. Continuity of care was thereby maintained. FirstLink, in Fargo, North Dakota, has gone as far as to set up calling limitations (a maximum number of calls per day) with certain high-frequency callers. All crisis workers are aware of the plan, and a log is kept of the calls to maintain boundaries with chronic callers.

Another strategy, especially for a multiservice user, is to call a case conference with the *client's collaboration* and participation in *all steps of the process*. A representative from all agencies in the individual's network should be invited. A useful question for the convener to ask is what the client thinks he or she needs from each agency represented and then ask the agency to respond to the expressed need. A plan for appropriate use of service can be developed with the client as a central and willing participant. An agreed-upon service plan is drawn up and distributed. This may alleviate the pitting of one agency against another, which is detrimental to the client and unproductive for all agencies involved. The positive results of such client-centered networking may appear "miraculous" in dealing with very challenging clients, but its strategies are grounded in the principles of social psychiatry (Garrison, 1974; Polak, 1971). For social network strategies, see Hoff et al. (2009, ch. 5, pp. 154–160).

Further, there may be some individuals for whom the ability to contact the crisis service, primarily through its hotline, may make the difference between maintaining themselves in the community or returning to the hospital. These might include people who suffer from hallucinations and call the service as a way of regaining control, using it as a touchstone on reality. Also, a caller who has a thought disorder (as in schizophrenia) or who sees a primary care provider in health clinics might just be "touching base" about hallucinations, and may need only general support and assurance as that may be all the person can tolerate; that is, the "intimacy" of a one-hour psychotherapy session can be overwhelming or threatening to such an individual. Others might be people who suffer from frequent panic attacks and for whom the ability to connect with a calm, soothing presence, capable of careful assessment, makes a world of difference.

Some repeat callers to crisis services abuse the line for the purpose of sexual excitation. Most agencies have a policy about these calls. For many, the policy is to deny the caller access to the service while engaged in sexually explicit description or masturbation. In these instances, it is important to provide workers with clear guidelines consistently adhered to by the program. In fact, *consistency* is a crucial element in working with all "chronic" or, less pejoratively, "maintenance" clients.

Data Collection and Utilization

Increasingly, the collection of data is on the minds of administrators and governing bodies. Information and referral databases are designed for agencies to document and store data about provided services. IRis, for example, is the client–server database management application used by many of the 2-1-1 services nationwide. Other package database systems include iCarol, Alice, and Efforts to Outcome. Many crisis providers build their own system to meet specific needs.

It is important for a crisis program to determine what type of information it needs to collect and for what purpose. There is often a strong temptation to collect more than is needed simply because of the capacity to do so. One must examine not only utility but also the human resources required to maintain data input and analysis. In addition, confidentiality of electronic records must be taken into consideration, and appropriate safety nets put in place.

Complete data provide documentation about the use of the crisis program. Data collection is an effective tool for funders, governing bodies, and staff to understand the nature of the program's work (answering the question "Why do we exist?"). In addition, an effective data collection mechanism can give the program focus ("What are we doing?"). Databases also collect information on unmet needs, which can then be passed on to community leaders and funders in order to bridge the gap between needs and services. Finally, data provide a basis for program evaluation ("How well are we doing?").

Example: Identifying Victims of Domestic Violence

At one Canadian hospital, a protocol for the identification and treatment of victims of intimate partner violence was initiated in the emergency department when staff noted a statistical discrepancy; research data indicated approximately one woman in six is the victim of violence and seeks medical care, yet the emergency department's statistics did not reflect this reality.

At the Boston Medical Center a retrospective chart review revealed that among the 100 to 120 women who presented per month for treatment of injuries traced to partner abuse, only 20% had self-disclosed, indicating the need for protocols that include routine questions about abuse.

Another evaluation focus would compare the agency's actual population to the target group. For example, if males between the ages of 23 and 30 are the highest risk group for suicide in a given community but females between the ages of 50 and 59 are the primary callers to the agency, this may indicate a need for more effective outreach efforts. Data can be used to justify certain funding requests, such as the appropriateness of funding a service that can document use by young people or military veterans.

In addition, the database is able to query things like the number of calls on a specific day of the week or time of day, which can be used to measure the effectiveness and efficiency of staffing patterns. For example, are there periods when the agency should strive to make more staff available? Would the hiring of administrative staff provide crisis workers with more client time?

Computerized data collection facilitates data entry by crisis workers, thus ensuring timely input as well as an abundance of information for research purposes. Technology can also allow for inter-agency networking. For instance, in Massachusetts, Jane Doe Inc.—the Massachusetts Coalition Against Sexual Assault and Domestic Violence—has developed a database that all member programs have the option to use. The database will also provide statewide data on who is being served and what services are available and will also allow member programs to easily report statistics to state funders.

The kinds of data useful to collect include date, sex, age, marital status, current living situation, city the call is being made from, primary problem, victimization, danger to self or others, intensity of crisis, response time of hotline service, duration of contact, referral, insurance information, and employment status. Along with collecting these forms of data, Emmerson et al. (2007) encourage the routine documentation of critical incidents. With the vast amount of information that can be collected, a particular category of information should be examined for its significance. For example, in Ithaca, New York, for a number of years, employment status was a collected item. Ithaca is a high-employment area in which education is its primary industry, and the unemployment rate, one of the lowest in New York State, fluctuates very little. Over the years, the data revealed nothing significant. However, subjective impressions were that a number of people were underemployed. A change made in the data collection process revealed that in this academic community, the partners of graduate students and faculty were often forced to turn to employment below their level of ability, and that role generated a special kind of stress. See www.crisisprograms.org for sample data collection tools.

Data should play a role in shaping the training program as well as any in-service teaching programs. An analysis of statistics will reveal the nature of the presenting problems. Major issues that the agency works with should be part of the initial training program. If a crisis program receives a significant number of repeat visits from psychiatric patients who have been discharged into the community, special attention should be given to understanding their needs (Gwande, 2011). At the same time, one can use data to eliminate from training those issues that do not surface in the program's operation. Furthermore, data can be used for supervisory analysis and program evaluation. A comparison of risk levels and duration of contact can indicate if the program is expending its resources on the clients who are at greatest risk.

Evaluation

One of the most important uses of data is program evaluation, which should be an integral part of agency functioning.

The Centrality of Program Evaluation

As Figure 1.2 in Chapter 1 illustrates, an agency's "philosophy" is the foundation for evaluating service programs. The essential elements of a comprehensive crisis program—crisis assessment and psychosocial support, and intervention and counseling via telephone, internet, face-to-face, and outreach methods—must be based on what the service providers (or governing body) believe about crisis service, the community's needs, and particular obligations to meet these needs. Ideally, a program should be based on the characteristics and needs of particular communities. Consequently, although *immediate access* is a basic element in all programs, avenues for assuring access and program relevance will vary from rural and reservation to urban settings and from suburban to inner-city areas. For example, the specifics of crisis response to rural farmers and ranchers reeling from flood-related losses differ from that of an inner-city neighborhood facing gang-related youth violence, but the principles of 24/7 access, physical safety, emotional support, and linkage to essential resources inform all effective crisis programs.

These contextual considerations imply two things. First, a person contemplating a crisis education, training, or service program needs to have a thorough knowledge of the philosophy, needs, resources, and constraints operating in their agency and community. Second, if such knowledge is lacking, then the needs and resources must be assessed formally—a fundamental step in the planning process (see Chapters 6 and 9).

Program evaluation involves governing bodies, staff, and consumers. Evaluation can be rigorous and formal, conducted by an outside agency, or it can be internal and informal. Depending on political and other sensitive issues, a strategic step might be to contract with an objective outside source for the assessment. Many agencies are located near universities, rich potential resources for assistance with program evaluation. Graduate students, under supervision of faculty, are often looking for a hands-on evaluation project. Their interests can be tailored to fit agency needs for information about itself. Some faculty members may have an interest in some aspect of the program's function and be willing to conduct an evaluation. It may be useful to involve and familiarize a member of a psychology or sociology faculty on the agency's governing body to introduce new energy and resources for evaluation.

The governing body may assign the task of program evaluation to its own program committee. Their strategies may include personal interviews with relevant staff and representatives of other agencies, review of data indicating use of services and other factors, review of service costs, or written or electronic questionnaires. Such evaluation requires a committed, sensitive, and capable group of volunteers, and probably, one member from the agency's paid staff to serve as a resource person.

Measurable program objectives simplify such evaluations. Some agencies have used the principles of Total Quality Management, Quality Assurance, Continuous Quality Improvement, and Service Process Quality Management with great success. This quality assurance process consists of three core activities—defining quality, measuring quality, and improving quality—and work synergistically to ensure quality care. Quality assurance promotes decision making based on accurate and timely data rather than assumptions (Silimperi, van Zanten, & Franco, 2004). Cost containment issues in health care systems and the requirements of managed care suggest serious attention to evaluation designs and resources that measure whether a program actually works as intended. For example, an agency might assess how effectively mobile outreach interventions diverted clients away from unnecessary (and expensive) emergency department visits or how crisis intervention with rape victims helped them deal emotionally with the trauma and avoid or reduce coping through suicide attempts, substance abuse, unplanned absences from work, and other responses. In addition to such measureable service outcomes, an agency might consider implementing procedures that delight both clients and funders—for example, every telephone call will be answered by a *human being* by the fifth ring or every sexual assault victim presenting at a hospital emergency department will be seen by a crisis counselor within 30 minutes.

Though it is difficult to evaluate an anonymous and confidential telephone service, it behooves all of us to establish quality monitors and measurable outcomes. Telephone access reports can provide information regarding availability of the service and inform hotline management regarding the need for additional telephone staff or lines. Caller satisfaction surveys can be implemented in various fashions—for example, asking callers at the end of a call to comment on the quality of intervention, calling back the caller at another time, requesting that the caller leave feedback on an answering machine, and asking telephone workers their subjective response to a completed call.

Accreditation of Crisis Programs

One of the most fruitful avenues for assessing the functioning of a crisis service is through the accreditation process offered by either the American Association of Suicidology (AAS) or Distress Centres Ontario. Because consumers are increasingly conscious of the desire for (and, many would argue, their right to) appropriate service, all crisis trainers and service providers should be aware of available accreditation programs and take steps toward providing service that conforms to international standards. Program administrators must ensure that all persons working with the program are included in this process. For example, crisis intervention may include the services of an interpreter. If they are to be used for formal evaluation of medical, psychiatric, or social services, it is important that interpreters be certified to ensure an accurate analysis of information as well as respect for boundaries and client confidentiality.

Besides the humanistic value of assuring minimum standards of service for persons in crisis, there are other advantages to accreditation (AAS, 2011; Hoff & Wells, 1989):

- Validates service delivery programs that performs according to internationally recognized standards.
- Examiners offer consultation tailored to the needs of an individual program, its staff, and board.
- Access to accrediting organizations best practices resources.
- Increased visibility and credibility of an accredited program provide opportunities for modeling of program excellence to other agencies and professionals.
- Provides a morale boost for staff working in the field of crisis intervention.
- Additional credibility with funding agencies and insurance companies.
- Access to criteria for systematic, ongoing self-evaluation.
- People in life-threatening and other crises obtaining service from certified programs are assured that staff have seriously examined their commitment to providing service according to recognized standards.

Agencies eligible for certification include independent crisis centers, emergency mental health programs operating within community mental health centers or general hospitals, branches of the Samaritans, various professional psychiatric agencies, and comparable groups offering crisis services.

References

Acker, G. M., & Lawrence, D. (2009). Social work and managed care: Measuring competence, burnout, and role stress of workers providing mental health services in a managed care era. *Journal of Social Work, 9*(3), 269–283.

Adamowski, K., Dickinson, G., Weitzman, B., Roessler, C., & Carter-Snell, C. (1993). Sudden unexpected death in the emergency department: Caring for the survivors. *Canadian Medical Association Journal, 149*, 1445–1451.

American Association of Suicidology. (2011). *Organization accreditation standards manual* (10th ed.). Retrieved from http://www.suicidology.org/c/document_library/get_file?folderId=234&name=DLFE-306.pdf

Cavaiola, A. A., & Colford, J. E. (2006). *A practical guide to crisis intervention.* Boston, MA: Lahaska Press/Houghton Mifflin.

Edward, K. (2005). The phenomenon of resilience in crisis care mental health clinicians. *International Journal of Mental Health Nursing, 14,* 142–148.

Emmerson, B., Fawcett, L., Ward, W., Catts, S., Ng, A., & Frost, A. (2007). Contemporary management of aggression in an inner city mental health service. *Australian Psychiatry, 15*(2), 115–119.

Garrison, J. (1974). Network techniques: Case studies in the screening-linking-planning conference method. *Family Process, 13,* 337–353.

Gwande, A. (2011, January). The hot spotters: Can we lower medical costs by giving the neediest patients better care? *The New Yorker*, 41–51.

Hoff, L. A. (2010). *Violence and abuse issues: Cross-cultural perspectives for health and social services.* London, UK: Routledge.

Hoff, L. A., Hallisey, B. J., & Hoff, M. (2009). *People in crisis: Clinical and diversity perspectives* (6th ed.). New York, NY: Routledge.

Hoff, L. A., & Miller, N. (1987). *Programs for people in crisis: A guide for educators, administrators, and clinical trainers.* Boston, MA: Northeastern University Custom Book Program.

Hoff, L. A., & Morgan, B. D. (2011). *Psychiatric and mental health essentials in primary care.* London, UK: Routledge.

Hoff, L. A., & Wells, J. O. (Eds.). (1989). *Certification standards manual* (4th ed.). Washington, DC: American Association of Suicidology.

Hoff, M. (2005). Resilience: A paradigm of promise. Unpublished master's thesis, North Dakota State University, Department of Counselor Education.

Kübler-Ross, E. (1969). *On death and dying.* New York, NY: Macmillan.

Polak, P. (1971). Social systems intervention. *Archives of General Psychiatry, 25,* 110–117.

Regehr, C., & Bober, T. (2005). *In the line of fire: Trauma in the emergency services.* New York, NY: Oxford University Press.

Silimperi, D. R., van Zanten, T. V., & Franco, L. M. (2004). Framework for institutionalizing quality assurance. In A. R. Roberts and K. R. Yeager (Eds.), *Evidence-based practice manual: Research and outcome measures in health and human services.* Oxford, UK: Oxford University Press.

Ullman, S. E., & Townsend, S. M. (2007). Barriers to working with sexual assault survivors: A qualitative study of rape crisis center workers. *Violence Against Women, 13*(4), 412–443.

Van Pelt, R., & Hancock, J. (2007). *The youth worker's guide to helping teenagers in crisis.* Grand Rapids, MI: Zondervan.

IV

CLOSING THE GAP BETWEEN ESSENTIAL KNOWLEDGE, ATTITUDES, AND SERVICE DELIVERY SKILLS

The two chapters in this section elaborate on themes introduced earlier. Specialized service and interdisciplinary education models are presented and the role of consultation and community education is highlighted—serving to address some of the fragmentation in the crisis field. We hope that these exemplary models will inspire readers, teachers, administrators, and students in the tasks demanded for moving forward together in the vital concern of crisis care and its key role in comprehensive mental health service delivery worldwide.

Chapter 9

From Classroom to Interdisciplinary Service Models: Diversity Perspectives

Chapter Outline

Distinct and Complementary Missions of Education and Service Providers
Curriculum Issues: Generalists, Undergraduate, and Graduate Education
Interdisciplinary Graduate Certification Program: Violence, Crisis, and Human Rights
Crisis Program Models

We have come full circle from our overview in Chapter 1 citing decades of education, clinical training, and service delivery on behalf of people in crisis. As Figure 1.1 illustrates 24/7 crisis care is not just an *essential* element of comprehensive mental health services within the overall health care system. It also provides the greatest return in terms of a person's independence and wholeness, and is most cost-effective when provided through community-based supports during crisis.

This chapter offers ideas and strategies for closing the gap between formal education arenas and on-site clinical training for ideal crisis service delivery. It builds on the successful and inspiring work of pioneers in the crisis field who have paved the way for systematic rather than incidental attention to the topic of crisis care within health and social services degree programs. We elaborate on examples introduced in Parts 2 and 3 of this book, and distinguish further the "generalist" and "specialist" roles in crisis care. Finally, we present an interdisciplinary graduate certificate program model designed to meet the continuing education needs of diverse crisis workers. We think this and similar models can help close the gap between essential *knowledge, attitudes, and skills* required in this important practice field. As things stand today, it is not unusual for health and social services faculty to work in relative isolation from the service delivery arenas in which their graduates will eventually practice. We hope that the vision and models we share will help to bring formal classroom instruction alive through encounters with distressed people in supportive learning environments staffed by experienced clinical supervisors.

Distinct and Complementary Missions of Education and Service Providers

By definition, the formal preparation of future health and social service providers is rooted in and driven by requirements of the publicly regulated service sector. Although inextricably connected, time and curricular constraints can put a damper on the collaborative education and training process so vital to success in this challenging field. Closing the gap between classroom and on-site instruction for ideal student and trainee outcomes entails clarity about the distinct but complementary institutional missions:

- Health and social service agencies: To *provide service* in accordance with government bodies that regulate staffing and other facets of safe and competent service on behalf of diverse people in distress
- Faculty of health and social service degree programs: To *prepare future providers* for such expert service delivery, teaching, research, and consultation

When preservice curricular deficits in college and university programs occur, one result—besides shortchanging students—is that service agencies must compensate by default to assure practice competency on crisis and violence issues. The time spent to make up for such formal education deficits might otherwise be spent in service for clients in crisis or high-risk circumstances. Several factors complicate this education and clinical training issue. First, crisis, violence, and suicide by definition are interdisciplinary topics, yet university departments typically function as separate disciplines (psychology, nursing, social work, criminal justice, sociology, etc.). These higher education structures challenge faculty in the necessary interdepartmental bridge building on an already demanding topic. Second, many faculty and future practitioners do not feel adequately prepared to teach on crisis and violence issues. A notable exception is among those faculty who also dedicate regular time in direct practice with clients in crisis or related health and social issues. Third, the required "clinical practicum" and/or intern experiences of future practitioners demand a smooth collaborative education/clinical training process between faculty and licensed on-site supervisors. This arrangement is embedded in accreditation standards for the degree-granting institutions, as well as in national examinations for licensure and/or certification for practice. It also involves differences in the preparation of undergraduate and graduate students and implications for varying levels of clinical expertise required in the service sector. Together these factors involve curriculum and practicum content that recognizes both "generalist" and "specialist" roles in diverse practice arenas.

Listening to Students About Educational Goals and Career Mission

Addressing these complex issues invites consideration of parallels between the teaching/learning process, the healthy resolution of emotional crisis, and a key concept in crisis theory: *isolation.* If a person in crisis from disaster, significant loss, and/or victimization is alone and lacking social supports, probable outcomes may be coping with alcohol or other drugs, depression, suicide, or violence toward others. Understanding of and empathy with the pain of social isolation and often, fear for one's life, is pivotal to the process of assisting a person in crisis, for example, a victimized person needing healing and the complex transition to a violence-free life.

In the learning arena, the most lasting part usually occurs *not* in the lecture hall, but in the student's often lonely wrestling with the connections between the professor's wisdom, critical reading, and, in the case of a human service provider, one's *firsthand experience* with people in physical and emotional pain. This translates to the carefully planned and supervised clinical practicum or internship providing a meaningful link between theory and practice.

While recognizing the struggles of the learning process, in no way can it be compared with the lonely and frightening consideration of whether to live or die, or the loneliness of victimization trauma. As noted earlier, researchers, teachers, and clinical supervisors also note the experience of "vicarious traumatization" among some students and human service providers who study this topic and work with victim-survivors of abuse (Hoff, 2010a, pp. 199–201). Also, some students embarking on the study of crisis and violence are themselves victims of abuse; for them, the challenge may be balancing this individual lonely effort with the necessity of interaction and support from fellow human beings to garner the most fruitful learning outcomes. In a similar vein, early crisis hotline development revealed that some would-be volunteers, motivated to help others in acute distress, were not yet healed from their own bout with suicidal crisis (discussed further in the "Interdisciplinary Graduate Certificate Program" section of this chapter).

Example: Teaching Undergraduate Nursing Students About Incest

> A professor teaching child and family health nursing observed this pattern over a 3-year period: When the topic of "incest" was addressed, two or three students would abruptly leave the class without excuse. Although the professor knew this was "essential" content, her background in this topical area was very limited. She therefore sought consultation from a colleague specializing in crisis and violence issues, and asked the colleague to observe and critique her approach to the topic. After a brief introduction, the professor relied heavily on a film demonstrating the psychotherapeutic process with a teenage client who was deeply traumatized by years of incest. The students' self-dismissal from the class suggests the probability of incest in their own history, including perhaps some unhealed wounds. The consultant noted that use of such a film is contraindicated for this student-learning level and recommended instead to focus on triage, basic crisis assessment, and appropriate referral skills (as illustrated in Tables 9.1 and 9.2). In general, such graphic content should be reserved for graduate-level teaching of mental health professionals for whom self-examination and often psychotherapy are part of the learning process for successful advanced practice.

This example brings us to further consideration of essential content at different levels of practice—that is, for generalists (what *every* health and social service provider needs to know) versus the requirements for crisis specialists.

Curriculum Issues: Generalists, Undergraduate, and Graduate Education

Despite decades of progress on interdisciplinary research, publication, teaching, and clinical practice standards in the crisis field, its attention in formal curricula

Table 9.1 Comprehensive Service Components by Discipline

Service Component	Discipline
1. Prevention	All
2. Treatment of physical injury	Medicine, dentistry, nursing, physical therapy
3. Crisis management	
a. Identification/triage	All
b. Comprehensive crisis assessment	Crisis specialists, family medicine, nurse practitioner, psychiatric nursing, psychiatry, psychology, social work
c. Crisis counseling	Crisis specialists, mental health professionals
d. Referral	All, depending on mission and crisis situation
4. Follow-up counseling and treatment	Medicine, nursing, mental health professionals, physical therapy, occupational therapy, dentistry, specialists such as substance abuse counselors (depending on assessment needs)

Source: Hoff (2010a). Reprinted with permission.

is still often tied to individual faculty interest versus designation as *essential* curriculum content. In some instances, it consists of a few hours at most in formal classroom discussion; further, it typically lacks *planned* clinical practicum experience in crisis care, unless particular students express a career interest in crisis practice, such as with sexual assault victims ensuing from their work as a volunteer on a crisis line. Several decades ago, national mental health survey data in the United States revealed that for *any* problem or crisis, the first contact for many is one's doctor or clergy person (Congressional Joint Commission, 1961). This situation is dramatized by the fact that typically, the *first* contacts for someone who has made a suicide attempt or is injured by violence are police, physicians and nurses, with follow-up contacts usually by a crisis or mental health specialist.

Considering these facts and epidemiological data about incidence of medical and life-threatening crisis situations, the "incidental" coverage of *essential knowledge, attitudes, and skills* required for competent crisis care is striking. Yet, health professions educators face several stark and challenging factors in moving from incidental to systematic coverage of these essentials:

Table 9.2 Comprehensive Service Components by Student Level

Service Component	**Focus at Various Student Levels**			
	Beginning	*Intermediate*	*Advanced*	*Graduate and Crisis Specialist*
1. Prevention	Personal and family life	Individual and families in crisis	Community and population groups at risk	Teaching and counseling; community education
2. Treatment of physical injury	Observe and assist as directed	Perform with immediate assistance of preceptor or supervisor	Perform with assistance or supervision on-site	Perform with preceptor available on-site
3. Crisis management				
a. Identification and triage	X	X	X	X
b. Comprehensive crisis assessment	O	O	Assist	Perform with supervision
c. Crisis counseling	O	O	Observe or perform with supervision	Perform with supervision
d. Referral	X	X	X	Depends on particular needs and mission
4. Follow-up counseling and/or treatment	O	O	O	According to needs assessment and mission

Key: X: do perform; O: do *not* perform.

Source: Hoff (2010a). Reprinted with permission.

1. The knowledge and technology explosions which demand attention in the preparation of health professionals.
2. The dubious practice of an "add-on" curriculum response to each request for inclusion of new and important topics versus strategic connecting links to major concepts.
3. Health professionals' earlier collusion (if only by silence and inattention) in traditional definitions of violence as a "private matter" rather than its current widespread acceptance as a major public health issue (Hoff, 2010a; Hoff & Ross, 1995, p. 137; Ross & Hoff, 1995).

These challenges point to the need for curriculum revision drawing on effective linkages with crisis experts in the practice arena, and careful attention to social change strategies. Students new to the enormous implications for the health of individuals in crisis, or with personal histories of abuse and suicidal risk, may express shock and impatience at the pace of action to correct inadequate or damaging responses to people in crisis.

Yet, the reality is that change around such value-laden topics like suicide and violence is deeply embedded in centuries of tradition, social structures, and diverse belief systems. *Knowledge* about strategies for needed change on urgent and often life-or-death issues helps students to become *part of the solution* rather than giving in to a sense of helplessness and desperation around the enormity and urgency of the problem. It also speaks to the earlier point of loneliness and these realities: (a) The sociocultural parameters of emotional crisis demands more than an individual solution; and (b) a key principle in high-risk crisis care is *to never work alone*—teamwork is absolutely essential (for social change strategies, see Hoff, Hallisey, & Hoff, 2009, pp. 60–63).

The strategic use of epidemiological data is also instructive in the challenge of curriculum corrections regarding crisis content, time limitations, and avoiding an "add-on" approach. Consider this example illustrating CORE content.

Example: Evidence-Based Essential Content

A woman is hospitalized for complications of pregnancy. Among risk factors to be considered with this woman are gestational diabetes and abuse by her spouse. Epidemiologically speaking, the risk of gestational diabetes, a medical condition—albeit with psychosocial implications, as is true for any diagnosis—is 2–6%; the risk of current or past history of intimate partner abuse is around 25% (McFarlane, Parker, Soeken, & Bullock, 1992; Rodgers, 1994; Stewart, 1993). Each risk factor comprises essential (CORE) content in medical and nursing curricula.

Most nursing and medical educators would concede that gestational diabetes is less complex for student mastery than the issue of intimate partner

> abuse. Thus, when considering these two content areas in curriculum development, decisions can more easily be made about learning activities against the standard of *essential knowledge, attitudes, and skills* (see Section II of this volume). Unlike battering, gestational diabetes is not embedded in values and myths which may affect both the practitioner's ability to broach the subject in routine assessment, and the woman's willingness to disclose. Rarely would such factors complicate a physician's or nurse's assessment and teaching around diabetes. Accordingly, this example suggests that curriculum planners allocate relatively less time for diabetes than for partner abuse; in fact, gestational diabetes might be covered in reading and self-directed learning, whereas intimate partner abuse almost certainly requires teacher-facilitated classroom discussion (Hoff, 2010a, p. 45, reprinted with permission).

Undergraduate Education as Foundation

This learner category encompasses college students in the humanities and other required courses for a bachelor's degree, including premed, nursing, social work, and clinical or counseling psychology. It also serves as a recruiting ground for crisis hotline volunteers whose experience can help them in career goals and further studies toward an envisioned future as a physician, professional nurse, or psychotherapist. For example, courses in Developmental Psychology or Social Issues typically include content such as the crisis potential of major life transitions, youth violence, sexual assault, vulnerability of war refugees, and so on. A guest lecture by an expert in these fields or a related "elective" course can spark interest and inspire students toward realizing their "dream" career. Another fruitful avenue is placement in health and social service agencies for "co-op" experience as part of required course credit—a "mini-internship" of sorts on the way toward professional practice. These examples illustrate a key pedagogical principle: The most effective teaching method involves active learner collaboration, whereas the least effective is lecture. To quote William Butler Yeats, "Teaching is not the filling of the pail but the lighting of the fire."

Professional Education, Accreditation, and Licensure Requirements

A well-established tradition for health and human services professionals is assurance that their college or university degree is approved by state and regional accreditation boards as a "quality control factor" contributing to publicly recognized safe practice by its graduates. This includes verification that clinical supervisors' licensure credentials are in order for the supervisors' tasks of "practicum" or "internship" placements, for example, in nursing an RN, and in social work an LICSW.

An additional public recognition of qualifications for some clinical supervisors is appointment to "adjunct faculty" status in respective degree-granting programs. The actual experience of some, however, suggests a certain "disconnect" between college and university course professors and the on-site experts they rely on for clinical supervision of their students. Agency practice reviews also reveal overlap, repetition, and a lack of coordination between campus and agency-led seminars for students focusing on discussion, critique, and sharing their real-life learning experiences. Some supervisors also note only occasional faculty visits to the experiential learning sites of their students. Ideally, such site visits should be routinely scheduled rather than "occasional." Also, clinical supervisors might be invited to join their faculty cohorts for taking full advantage of seminar linkages and their potential for maximum learning benefits, or faculty participation in clinical site seminars.

One avenue for addressing these issues is the practice of "dual" appointments, a long-established pattern in medicine, and other professions as well as a great aid for avoiding "out-of-touch" teaching about practice issues, which students learning in the "real" world quickly recognize and may rightly criticize. The downside, of course, is heavy faculty workloads. One solution is clinical volunteer work. Despite these challenges of teaching in practice disciplines, most on-site agency supervisors welcome student interns not only for their enthusiasm and fresh ideas, but also for their considerable contribution toward agency workloads and service delivery requirements. Some of these decision points regarding classroom and supervised clinical experience are illustrated in Tables 9.1 and 9.2.

Interdisciplinary Graduate Certificate Program: Violence, Crisis, and Human Rights

These issues and constraints across several dimensions of clinical practice might be addressed in a pilot-tested model of a graduate certificate program on crisis and violence issues. It incorporates "blended" or "hybrid" learning formats—that is, a planned and strategically linked teaching and learning model using traditional classroom or "in-person" instruction and "online" learning. It resembles the widely expanding online certificate programs offered by many universities on an equally wide range of topics.

Unique Challenges of Online Learning on Value-Laden Topics

The inherent sociocultural and political facets of crisis and violence issues requires consideration of online learning around points already touched on (e.g., loneliness, or student histories of abuse)—points including challenges less easily mastered online than, say, in scientific, fact-laden, or technology-focused courses such as biology or website construction.

If this is true, then how can distance learning afford a viable format in topical areas where face-to-face interaction with another human being is critical to relieving one's isolation or desperation during crisis? In other words, because communication skills are an essential component of a health provider's repertoire of qualifications, practicing communication with another human being is essential to the learning process. Some of this communication can occur in online chat rooms; but some of it *must* occur in face-to-face seminars or through individual contact, as discussed in Chapter 4. This is because the medical and psychosocial care offered to assist victims in the healing process occurs primarily in person-to-person interaction. Interactive learning includes refinement of a practitioner's sensitivity to verbal and visual cues, and application of these skills to the service arenas in which survivors seek treatment and support.

The vision is that online or distance learning formats are a *part* of the picture, but not sufficient to achieve the goals of the international interdisciplinary graduate certificate program we envision. Cross-cultural research and training, as well as international UN-sponsored Women's Conferences underscore the *commonalities* as well as *differences* vis-à-vis violence against women and children in diverse societies. As the global village shrinks via the internet, international travel, and the flow of immigrants and refugees between countries, the commonalities and theoretical frameworks shared cross-culturally can be addressed via distance learning formats, including student–student and faculty–student chat room interaction.

Also, major metropolitan areas like New York, Los Angeles, Boston, and the Minneapolis–St. Paul area are typical magnets for immigrants, asylum seekers, and/or victims of torture or human trafficking where specialized crisis care and resettlement programs are offered. Most major cities in the United States, Canada, and the European Union have programs such as the International Institute of Boston and New England that focus on the special needs of refugees (see www.iine.us). Finally, in U.S. Western and Midwestern universities (for example, University of North Dakota), Indian studies programs are common and provide natural linkages for interdisciplinary studies that include the serious crises rooted in the suppression of indigenous populations and related poverty, violence, and substance abuse rampant on reservations.

Cultural differences and their distinct local application, however, require traditional face-to-face opportunities to process with a tutor-seminar leader and fellow learners in one's language group the controversial points, attitudinal issues, and complex problems encountered in cross-cultural practice arenas. A truism of educational theory underscores the pairing in this program of two teaching–learning methods to enhance achievement of curriculum objectives: (a) the learner's intense involvement in the enquiry-based learning (EBL) model, and (b) critique and reinforcement of individual study and practice in face-to-face small group seminars. Herewith, then, is such a program pilot-tested in Portugal in the early 2000s.

Program Description

This certificate program was developed and implemented at the Institute for Applied Psychology (Instituto Superior de Psicologia Aplicada, or ISPA) in Lisbon, Portugal, which recently achieved university status in the European Union. Its title at ISPA was *Genero, Poder e Violencia* (Gender, Power, and Violence). One of the unique features in its development was the formal partnership between ISPA and the *Associacao de Mulheres Contra Violencia*, a nongovernmental organization (NGO) and the first shelter program for abused women in Lisbon, led by Margarida Martins. Three of the students included women in this NGO seeking an academic credential for their work and future career goals. Major factors underpinning the program initiation include the following:

- The global epidemic of violence, especially toward women and children.
- Recognition of the key role of health and social service professionals in addressing this epidemic.
- Research findings revealing that most health care faculty and practitioners do not feel adequately prepared on this topic, because existing curricula have only recently begun to address it.
- National and international survey data revealing that violence-related content is addressed only incidentally in curricula preparing future health and social service professionals.
- The need for health and social service agencies to compensate for these curricular deficits through in-service training time that might otherwise be used for direct service to clients at risk of or injured by violence.
- Evidence of need for a university/college credential on the topic by some social service personnel working in community-based grassroots agencies on violence issues. Some of these agencies rely very heavily on helpers who may have had minimal formal instruction on the topic prior to their volunteer positions.

Purpose and Significance

The broad purpose of this certificate program is designed to prepare health, mental health, and social service professionals for teaching, expert practice, consultation, and research on violence prevention and the care of victim-survivors. It aims to increase interprofessional attention to the worldwide epidemic of violence against women and children. The purpose for individual students may vary in relation to educational background, experience, and career goals. For example, some may take only a single course for "generalist" practice, whereas others may complete the entire program, which would qualify them for "specialty" practice, teaching, or research on the topic (see the "Diversity of Learning Goals" section of this chapter).

Significantly, the program provides an opportunity for individuals and organizations across disciplines to learn together about violence issues in flexible adult learning formats. An expected outcome is that health and social service educators will be better prepared to include violence content in established curricula. The certificate program would thereby contribute toward tapping the enormous potential of health and social service providers to positively influence violence prevention, detection, and intervention around interpersonal injuries and their negative health and social sequelae. From a research perspective (i.e., education as intervention), it provides data-based opportunities for assessing the outcomes of systematic interdisciplinary education on violence issues; that is, we expect it to improve providers' competence in violence prevention and intervention for individuals, families, and communities in reducing the human and other costs of violence and abuse.

Background and Sources of Development

This graduate education project was developed from the following sources (see www.crisisprograms.org):

1. National survey data from health sciences faculties and health professions students in Canada and the United States
2. Evaluation data from curriculum development surveys and workshops in five Canadian health sciences faculties
3. Results of Canadian and U.S. students' competency assessments regarding violence prevention, detection, and intervention
4. Assessment of in-service training sessions, special seminars, and graduate education programs in Portugal, London, and Lowell, Massachusetts

The program corresponds in general to the standard length of certificate programs, that is, the equivalent of one year's graduate study in blended format (i.e., traditional classroom and distance learning) adapted to student interests and available study time up to 3 years. Course content draws on these disciplines:

public health; social, cultural, and health and mental health sciences; criminal justice and forensic medicine; trauma theory and rehabilitation sciences; and public education and curriculum development theory.

Theoretical Assumptions Underpinning the Program

Moving beyond an individualistic focus in some education and practice arenas, this program underscores these evidence-based concepts:

- Violence is widely recognized as a human rights issue across cultures.
- The importance of building bridges and partnerships: across cultures, NGOs, and professional groups, theory and practice, feminist and mainstream perspectives.
- Violence is viewed as a *continuum* from interpersonal to global levels.
- Roots of violence: cultural values, social structures, unfair policies, and vulnerabilities of both victim-survivors and perpetrators based on race, class, gender, and sexual identity.
- The need to recognize commonalities and distinctions regarding violence cross-culturally, without excusing violence on cultural grounds (i.e., cultural relativism).
- Interconnectedness of interpersonal violence across the life span.
- Violence is an interdisciplinary topic.
- Violence is an abuse of power: *collaboration* (vs. co-optation and control) models how *not* to abuse power.
- Violence defined in *moral*, social action terms, *not* as psychopathology or madness.
- Students have a right to be taught in their own language.
- Health care and social service providers have enormous (sometimes untapped) potential to stem the tide of violence.

Course (or Module) Requirements for Certificate(s) on Violence, Crisis and Human Rights

The course (or module) requirements include completion of eight courses (two or three credits each) fulfilling 240 to 280 didactic hours. The assumption is that the full-time equivalent is four 2- or 3-credit courses (30 or 35 hours per course) per semester over a 1-year period with the option to space coursework out over a 3-year period. Required credit and didactic hours may vary and be adapted among universities.

The courses fall into four categories and include the following:

1. Clinical/Direct Care Courses:
   a. Emergency and Crisis Response to Violence and Abuse
   b. Criminal Justice and Psychosocial Follow-up Service
2. Social Science and Prevention Courses:
   a. Historical and Sociocultural Roots of Violence
   b. Public Education and Community Organization regarding Violence
3. Teaching and Service Program Development Courses:
   a. Pre-service Curriculum and In-service Training Development
   b. Development and Evaluation of Service and Prevention Programs
4. Courses Geared Toward Student Background and Career Goals:
   a. Elective or Independent Study (e.g., Medical/Forensic Protocols; Research Strategies: Critique and Community Collaboration; Literary Sources Addressing Violence; Self-Care and Mind/Body Connections; Workplace Violence and Abuse; and Programs for Perpetrators of Violence)
   b. Project (practice, teaching, consultation, or research) and Synthesis Seminar

Diversity of Learning Goals

Considering student education records and career goals, plus university requirements, these courses or specific modules can be taken with several learning goals in mind:

- To achieve the certificate upon completion of eight required courses or modules.
- To enhance existing knowledge and skills in particular content/practice areas (e.g., clinical care or community prevention programs).
- To earn credit toward a professional degree (e.g., in counseling psychology, advanced practice nursing, or social work).
- To earn continuing education credits in one's professional field by those already holding a graduate degree and license to practice, but whose formal education was lacking in this topical area; such persons might choose selected courses, but not the full certificate program.

Given this diversity, not only of learning goals, but also the variety of "certificates" granted in formal and continuing education arenas, a university or college offering a program such as this may also award a "certificate" that specifies attendance, say, of a 6-hour or 3-day workshop on topics of current or special interest in the crisis field (e.g., workplace violence, sexual assault, or group counseling for abusive men). See www.crisisprograms.org for course descriptions and two sample syllabi for this Certificate Program.

At City University, London, UK, there is a variation of offering university-approved course credit toward a degree, based on successful examination of content mastery or evaluation of supervised clinical experience. Faculty there have adapted and expanded the certificate program to a graduate degree status: MSc in Interprofessional Practice: Violence, Society and Practice, and Civil Emergency Management. The department sponsor is the School of Community and Health Sciences, Department of Interdisciplinary Studies for Professional Practice. Besides degrees, it offers continuing professional education for health and social services professionals, police, and emergency medical practitioners working with victim-survivors of violence and their communities, following injury from violence.

Building on our graduate certificate example, we seek other university collaborators for expansion and cross-cultural adaptation of this program envisioning an international university-consortium that would link with extensive online infrastructures already in existence in many universities. With foundation or other support, many more learners could be reached, and the rich resources of wealthy countries can be shared with poorer nations, for example engaging native speakers in, say, Chile, Brazil, or Senegal to work with faculty members as adjunct clinical supervisors of their students enrolled in an online class at Boston University, for instance, or the five-campus University of Massachusetts system—both with already extensive distance learning programs in place. The crisis program models presented in the next section might also be linked to such a consortium. We hope this certificate program will "stoke the fire" and incentives needed to move from incidental to systematic attention to this topic in the preparation of health and social service professionals for practice.

Following is the mantra for possibilities of what this certificate program might actualize for students committed toward action to address the global epidemic of violence and urgency of crisis care:

VISION FOR INTERNATIONAL DEVELOPMENT

A vision without a task is but a dream
A task without a vision is but drudgery
A vision with a task can change the world

Global Cooperation for a Better World, India (1989)

Crisis Program Models

Complementing this certificate program model, we present examples of several crisis and violence prevention programs. Inspiration for this section came from two sources. First, a 2-week internship program in Metropolitan Boston arranged for Dr. Raquel Correia, a fifth-year resident in psychiatry from her university in Oporto, Portugal. This request arose from Dr. Correia's awareness that, as she moved toward completion of her residency, her *formal* education had less than she needed to know about crisis and violence issues for competent psychiatry practice—as discussed above regarding "incidental" inclusion of such content. Second, follow-up site visits and interviews with key staff were conducted in the agencies that hosted Dr. Correia in the summer of 2010, with a view to include major facets of these ideal programs for this part of "closing the gap." Several of the programs were also featured in a presentation at the WHO 2010 World Conference on Injury and Violence Prevention in London, "Violence Issues: Education as Prevention and Intervention" (Hoff, 2010b).

These programs serve diverse clientele, as do many others across the United States and elsewhere. They either serve as formalized clinical internships for future licensed professionals (e.g., social workers, psychologists, and nurses) or offer CE workshops and guest lecturers for an array of students-in-training or professionals seeking CE credits for continued licensure. They also highlight the overlap between "generalist" and "specialist" roles in the field, illustrating, for example, that much more than basic "crisis intervention" is called for in the expert care and treatment of victims of torture or human trafficking, although every health and social service professional should know how to detect such persons, offer them immediate support, and refer them to specialists.

Following is a brief summary of these model programs, including contact information. We recognize that comparable programs exist worldwide, and encourage educators, administrators, and clinical trainers to seek out and develop partnerships with these types of programs.

Boston Center for Refugee Health and Human Rights

This collaborative project, founded in 1996, includes the following sponsors: the Boston University Schools of Medicine, Public Health, Dentistry, and Law; the National Center for PTSD; Global Lawyers and Physicians; the National Center for Tortured and Trafficked Persons (NCTTP); resettlement agencies; and the refugee and legal communities.

The project's mission is fourfold: (a) to provide comprehensive health care for refugees and survivors of torture and related trauma coordinated with legal aid and social services; (b) to educate and train agencies and professionals who serve these communities; (c) to advocate for the promotion of health and human rights in the United States and worldwide; and (d) to conduct clinical, epidemiological, and legal research for better understanding and promotion of health and quality of life for survivors of torture and related trauma.

Its target groups include refugees, torture victims, and asylum seekers from around the world; women survivors of sexual assault as a weapon of war; medical students and residents of the Boston University School of Medicine; and NGOs working with victims of war. Services draw on traditional social service and comprehensive crisis case management strategies adapted to this very vulnerable population. Social work interns are a key facet of this project. Services include primary health care and mental health services for adults; referrals for medical specialties, dental care, neuropsychiatric evaluation, and legal service; case management and career development services; English as a Second Language courses and support groups; and psychological and medical evaluation for asylum cases.

Two of the project programs are as follows:

1. *Ujambo!: African Women's Good Health Project*: DVD and guidebook for immigrant women, available in several languages. This program is a component of medical residency training and interdisciplinary continuing education, with these key features:
   - Developed from community-based focus groups with immigrant women and men
   - Highlights challenges and barriers African women face in access to health care in the United States
   - Basic medical context and videography—fruitful avenues for teaching about health care (e.g., mammography and pap smears)
   - Serves as an avenue for revelation of sexual assault history and attendant shame and reluctance to disclose
   - Highlights importance of mental health care for sexual assault survivors stigmatized by their communities
   - Underscores sexual violence as a crime and the importance of supporting survivors in healing from such trauma

   The *Ujambo!* DVD has been dubbed from English into French, Lingala, Somali, and Swahili. It is accompanied by a guidebook and translated handouts. Workshops using the DVD underscore the promise of a culturally and linguistically attuned vehicle of health promotion for a vulnerable and difficult-to-reach population.
2. Refugee Patient Navigation (RPN) is one of about 200 such programs across the United States, but is distinctive for its primary target on the

> refugee and asylum-seeker population. Among the clients served, the majority are new to the U.S. health care system, and have language barriers. Many have complex immigration and legal issues and have endured great hardships and trauma such as torture, and they suffer the physical and psychological effects of torture and loss before arrival to the United States.

Services are offered in multiple languages (the most common are English, French/Haitian Creole, Swahili, Somali, Luganda, Arabic, and Spanish). It is partially funded by the Office of Refugee Resettlement, U.S. Department of Health and Human Services. It relies heavily on volunteer service, including training and awareness of refugee issues among future health care workers, for example, students in public health, nursing, medicine, and international relations.

Contact: Linda Piwowarczyk, MD, MPH, and Erica Hastings, www.bcrhhr.org.

Emerge: Counseling and Group Education to Stop Domestic Violence

Emerge, Inc., an NGO, was established in 1977 by a group of men at the request of women who were working in a battered women's program in the Boston area. Many victim advocates had argued that men must join women in their work with victim-survivors of intimate partner violence—not only to communicate the message that violence against women is a human rights issue of equal importance to men, but also to play a unique role in educating and confronting men who abuse women. The founders included social workers, counselors, a teacher, a community organizer, a lawyer, and a cab driver.

As the first of its kind, Emerge is one of the most widely emulated abuser education models in the world, having provided trainings of group leaders and government officials in 45 states and 24 nations. Since its founding, at least 1,500 programs for abusive men exist in the United States alone, with growing numbers developing internationally. Because of controversy among some professionals about the principles guiding services for abusive men, here we underscore the Emerge program's emphasis on *accountability* and prevention of violence. Although recognizing that offenders have *individual* problems such as alcohol abuse, these problems should not serve as an excuse for abuse of their partners. Complementing this point is that counseling and education sessions are conducted in *groups* with a male–female team as coleaders. This arrangement facilitates discussion of gender-tinged attitudes regarding violence which might be less likely to occur with a single-sex leader. A majority of clients attending these sessions are court-ordered in lieu of incarceration for conviction of violence against their partners (see Adams, 2007; Adams & Cayouette, 2002; Seck & Hoff, 2010, ch. 10).

Emerge has played a central role in promulgating this important mission worldwide: to eliminate violence toward women through international training and resources on batterer interventions. Its aims are to educate individual men who batter, prevent young people from learning to accept violence in their relationships, improve institutional responses to domestic violence, increase public awareness about causes and solutions regarding violence against women, and help men to become more responsible parents.

Emerge's pioneering role in the prevention of violence includes its innovative collaborations with programs for battered women (e.g., preventive education for teens, community outreach, training of police and courts, and targeted outreach to communities of faith). Other key features include the following:

- First abuser education groups in Spanish, Vietnamese, and Khmer
- One of the earliest programs to provide services for abusers in same-sex relationships
- Conducts continuing education (CE) workshops for health and human services professionals
- Provides national and international trainings on danger assessment
- Founded the Responsible Fatherhood Program geared for fathers with histories of domestic violence
- Publishes research on intimate partner homicides, abuser program outcomes, attitudinal correlates to domestic violence, and childhood antecedents among men who batter

Contact: www.emergedv.com, dadams9@aol.com, and tedgermanemerge@gmail.com.

Psychiatry and Mental Health: Oporto, Portugal

This interdisciplinary postgraduate degree and continuing education program is sponsored by the Medical School, Oporto University, and St. John's Hospital, both in Oporto, Portugal. The program offers postgraduate clinical training for mental health professionals, including crisis and violence prevention. Target groups include medicine—psychiatry, nursing, psychology, social work, and occupational therapy. Its interdisciplinary student population and continuing education and online options afford ample opportunity for student–professional interaction in a postgraduate learning context. Following Dr. Correia's internship in Metropolitan Boston, as noted above, a vision of the program graduates is the development of crisis specialty services such as the models noted in this chapter.

Contacts: Dr. António Roma Torres, director of psychiatry services, St. John's Hospital, Oporto, psiquiatria@hsjoao.min-saude.pt; Professor Rui Coelho, director of psychiatry and mental health, Medical School, Oporto University, psiquiatria@med.up.pt; and Raquel Correia, psychiatry resident, St. John's Hospital, Oporto, rscorreia@med.up.pt.

Child Witness to Violence Project (CWVP)

This project is sponsored by Boston Medical Center (BMC), Department of Developmental and Behavioral Pediatrics. It was established in 1992 as an intervention and prevention program to support the needs of hidden victims of violence: young children and their families who are bystanders to community and domestic violence. The project is dedicated to helping these children and families heal by providing therapeutic services, family advocacy, community outreach, public policy initiatives, and comprehensive training for their network of professional caregivers. It offers brief supportive counseling, as well as longer term services, ranging from a few sessions up to 4 or 6 months. For children still in need after 8 months, the therapist discusses options with the parents.

The Child Witness to Violence Project is staffed by a multicultural, multilingual team of social workers, psychologists, early childhood specialists, and a consulting pediatrician. Therapists have graduate training in child development and trauma-focused counseling, plus specialized experience in working with very young children (see Tables 9.1 and 9.2).

As one of four sites focusing on early childhood trauma in the National Child Traumatic Stress Network, the CWVP is well known for its expertise in treating children age 8 and younger, and working with children and families affected by domestic violence. Approximately 80% of referrals originate from domestic violence incidents affecting children; 60% of referrals are for children age 6 or younger. Services include the following:

- Trauma-focused counseling to young children and parents, using highly skilled mental health clinicians trained in trauma intervention and early childhood development
- Oversight to the BMC Department of Pediatrics for all cases of suspected abuse and neglect seen at the hospital
- Development of training curricula for police, early care and education providers, mental health clinicians, and health professionals on identifying

and working with young children affected by trauma (see Groves, 2002; Van Horn & Groves, 2006)

- Training professional and community caregivers to identify and intervene with young children affected by violence
- Collaboration with the courts and legal system to provide evaluations for children affected by violence, and training for judges and lawyers
- Consultation and technical assistance to NGOs, other institutions, and state and federal government agencies: U.S. Department of Justice, Safe Start Initiative; National Council of Juvenile and Family Court Judges; Massachusetts Department of Social Services; Massachusetts Trial Courts; Boston Police Department; and Pennsylvania Coalition against Domestic Violence
- Action to influence local and national policy on children, domestic violence, and abuse

Contact: www.childwitnesstoviolence.org.

Boston Area Rape Crisis Center (BARCC)

The Boston Area Rape Crisis Center is the only one of its kind in the greater Boston area. Their vision is to end sexual violence through healing and social change. Founded in 1973, BARCC is a national leader in providing confidential and free services for people of all ages 12 and older. It is dedicated to healing and advocating for change. Clients helped by BARCC include survivors, their family and friends, and professionals through the following services:

- 24-hour crisis hotline
- Medical advocacy
- Legal resources
- Counseling and case management
- Community awareness, education, and prevention
- Professional training

In addition to hotline and office-based services, BARCC provides a wealth of information on its very extensive website—a particularly valuable resource, given the often experienced but misplaced self-blame and shame among sexual assault survivors who face very difficult medical and legal decisions. The user-friendly site offers links and information specific to the *survivor, parent of a survivor, and/or friend of a survivor*, including, for example, immediate steps to be taken, and what will happen if one chooses to go or is taken to the hospital. Other features of BARCC's extensive service repertoire are web links specific to a teenage survivor, friend or family member of a survivor, college student survivor, male survivor, and gay, lesbian, bisexual, or transgender (GLBT) survivor.

Like other ideal models noted in this chapter, BARCC also is the host and professional training site for social work student interns envisioning career specialization in victim-survivor crisis and follow-up counseling services.

Contact: www.barcc.org.

Casa Myrna Vazquez: Metropolitan Service for Abused Women

Casa Myrna Vazquez is greater Boston's largest NGO providing shelter and supportive services to women and children made homeless by domestic violence. It was founded by grassroots activists and street workers in Boston's South End community during the mid-1970s. These folks found themselves listening with outrage and frustration as neighborhood women confided their beatings and abuse by husbands or partners, while children talked about the abuse of their mothers. As the campaign to help them took form, activists from the Villa Victoria housing development, United South End Settlements, and the South End Project Area Committee helped to establish Casa Myrna. Other church, health, and social service groups jointed their efforts.

The agency's vibrant and passionate work reflected its diverse community. Latinas were a significant presence, one of whom was Myrna Vazquez, a renowned actress in her native Puerto Rico. Her unwavering belief in the restorative power of the arts and culture inspired a community beset by many inner-city problems such as crack cocaine, speculative redevelopment, and violence. Following Myrna's sudden death in 1976, the group named their first shelter—and the organization—in her honor. A first shelter of its kind was an eight-bedroom brownstone in Boston's South End, staffed entirely by volunteers. It has remained in continuous operation since opening and is now Casa Myrna's emergency shelter program, offering the following programs:

- *SafeLink*: The only 24/7 statewide toll-free domestic violence hotline in Massachusetts, staffed by advocates fluent in English, Spanish, and Portuguese. Casa Myrna's Legal Advocacy Program includes a legal help line, advice, assistance, and representation on issues ranging from restraining orders to family court matters. This program offers accredited internships to law students from area universities who help staff the program throughout the year.
- *Counseling*: This service provides individual counseling and support groups on-site and in other community locations in both Spanish and

English. It is directed by a licensed clinician, offers accredited internships, and is staffed primarily by interns majoring in psychology and social work degree programs.

- *Residential programs*: (a) The Mary Foreman Emergency Program provides safety and shelter for 10 women and 13 children made homeless by domestic violence; (b) the Transitional Living Program offers post-emergency longer term housing for six women seeking permanent housing and professional development assistance up to 18 months; (c) the Adolescent Transitional Living Program addresses the needs of pregnant and parenting teen victims of abuse up to 18 months; and (d) Family Services focuses on the complex needs of children who have witnessed the abuse of their mothers.
- *Education and prevention*: An education and prevention specialist works with youth groups, college students, business groups, places of worship, and adults across health and social service settings to learn about patterns of control that lead to abuse, gender stereotypes, street violence, the media's influence in promoting violence and disrespect, domestic violence, and how abusive language can contribute to violence in the family. An interactive workshop focuses on warning signs of controlling, abusive, and potentially violent relationships, and provides resources for violence prevention and help in crisis situations.
- *Supportive services*: These multilingual programs include legal advocacy; counseling; housing advocacy; community advocacy (with district courts, a justice center, and the Boston Police Department); and Stability, Opportunity, Achievement, Results (SOAR), a program providing workshops and individual counseling focused on helping victim-survivors learn to review their credit histories, repair bad credit, open savings or checking accounts, and master the realities of budgeting and sound financial planning aimed at avoiding economic dependency as one of the hazards of staying in abusive relationships. Casa Myrna also provides on-site advocacy for women identified for being in an abusive relationship and referred by medical practitioners at the South End Community Health Center.

Contact: www.casamyrna.org.

Workplace Violence Prevention for Nurses

This program is sponsored by Vida Health Communications, Inc., a health education research organization, through a Small Business Innovative Research (SBIR) Phase II grant from the U.S. National Institute of Occupational Safety and Health (NIOSH) in collaboration with the American Nurses Association.

Supported by federal funding, this web-based multimedia continuing education program addresses the burden and costs of workplace violence and abuse directed toward nursing staff. It aims to provide essential knowledge, attitudinal, and skills content including individual, institutional, policy, and professional responses for prevention and intervention. The program builds on epidemiological data revealing nursing as an occupation at high risk of injury or death at work—comparable to police and firefighters.

The targeted audience includes staff nurses in the front lines delivering direct care, nurse managers, staff development departments of health care agencies, employee assistance programs, and nurse educators in colleges and universities.

The program includes three intersecting modules:

Module 1. Manifestations and Consequences of Workplace Violence in Health Care Settings

- Prevalence and extent of the problem
- Workplace violence typology
- Manifestations of workplace violence
- Consequences to the individual, organization, and society

Module 2. Case Studies in Workplace Violence

- Police deliver a psych patient to a hospital emergency department
- Family member of patient assaults labor and delivery nurse; nurse's history of abuse
- Patient threatens violence in a home care setting
- Geriatric patients in a long-term care facility
- Patient's angry outbursts toward and sexual harassment of nurse
- Worker-on-worker violence and abuse

Module 3. Workplace Violence Prevention Policies and Their Implementation

- Components of a workplace violence prevention program
- Advocating for a safer workplace

Major implications of this program for health practitioners at risk include *knowledge as power*; the obligations of administrators to provide a safe work environment; and, for nurse educators preparing future practitioners, *education as prevention*. Internationally, an implication is the gender-based vulnerability of women health care workers cross-culturally.

Contact: John Craine, MS, MBA, principal investigator, chief operating officer, John.Craine@vida-health.com; and Lee Ann Hoff, leeannhoff@comcast.net.

In conclusion, we hope these models and the issues discussed in this chapter serve as incentives for more formalized partnerships between existing health and social services degree programs and the service agencies supporting ideal and very diverse practice on behalf of people in crisis and other very vulnerable populations. The "generalists" and "specialists" in the broad crisis field can all benefit by continuing to close the gaps between essential knowledge, attitudes, and service delivery skills, as these education and service delivery examples portend. An adage applies here: Know what you really *need* to know and master for your level of practice, recognize what you *don't* know and refer to others, and don't tread on thin ice leading to burnout or drowning!

References

Adams, D. (2007). *Why do they kill? Men who murder their intimate partners.* Nashville, TN: Vanderbilt University Press.

Adams, D., & Caayouette, S. (2002). Emerge: A group education model for abusers. In E. Aldarondo & F. Mederos (Eds.), *Programs for men who batter: Intervention and prevention strategies in a diverse society* (pp. 4-1–4-23). New York, NY: Civic Research.

Congressional Joint Commission on Mental Illness and Health. (1961). *Action for mental health.* New York, NY: Basic Books.

Groves, B. (2002). *Children who see too much: Lessons from the child witness to violence project.* Boston, MA: Beacon Press.

Hoff, L. A. (2010a). *Violence and abuse issues: Cross-cultural perspectives for health and social services.* London, UK: Routledge.

Hoff, L. A. (2010b). Violence issues: Education as prevention and intervention. Poster presentation at the WHO Safety 2010 World Conference, London, UK, September 21–24.

Hoff, L. A., Hallisey, B. J., & Hoff, M. (2009). *People in crisis: Clinical and diversity perspectives* (6th ed.). New York, NY: Routledge.

Hoff, L. A., & Ross, M. (1995). Violence content in nursing curricula: Strategic issues and implementation. *Journal of Advanced Nursing, 21*, 137–142.

McFarlane, J., Parker, B., Soeken, K., & Bullock, L. (1992). Assessing for abuse during pregnancy: Severity and frequency of injuries and associated entry into prenatal care. *Journal of the American Medical Association, 267*(23), 3176–3178.

Rodgers, K. (1994). Wife assault: The findings of a national survey. In *Juristat Service Bulletin.* Ottawa, Canada: Canadian Centre for Justice Statistics.

Ross, M., & Hoff, L. A. (1995). Education of health professionals: Interdisciplinary curriculum guidelines related to abuse and neglect of older Canadians. In M. J. MacLean (Ed.), *Abuse and neglect of older Canadians: Strategies for change* (pp. 95–106). Toronto, Canada: Thompson Educational.

Seck, M., & Hoff, L. A. (2010). Perpetrators of abuse and violence: Individuals and states. In L. A. Hoff (Ed.), *Violence and abuse issues* (pp. 149–168). London, UK: Routledge.

Stewart, D. E. (1993). Physical abuse in pregnancy. *Canadian Medical Association Journal, 149*(9), 1257.

Van Horn, P., & Groves, B. (2006, Winter). Children exposed to domestic violence: Making trauma-informed custody and visitation decisions. *Juvenile and Family Court Journal*, 51–60.

Chapter 10

Crisis Consultation and Community Education

Chapter Outline

This chapter presents the general features of consultation and community education programs in crisis and psychosocial care. It also provides guidelines to develop such programs systematically as an integral facet of comprehensive mental health care. This book assumes an established body of knowledge in crisis and psychosocial care and the need for specialists to deal with high-risk crises and psychiatric emergencies. But uncoordinated service and practice symbolizing the traditional mind–body split are often the basis for many client complaints about health care delivery. This chapter builds on Figure 1.1 depicting the continuum of mental health services in relation to cost and client independence (see Chapter 1). It also assumes the ideal partnership of university and college health and human service faculty and clinical experts in practicum and internship programs who supervise future practitioners' competency in crisis care gained in model crisis programs, as addressed in Chapter 9.

The current emphasis on primary care and realities of fiscal constraint imply a better understanding of the consultative process to assure access to all mental health specialty services needed, yet refrain from pressuring primary care health providers and frontline workers (such as police and rescue staff) to be "all things to all people." For example, a physician or nurse practitioner may *know* that prescribing psychotropic medication after only 10 minutes with a client is not ideal practice, but if mental health and crisis consultation are not readily available, it may be the expedient way of managing a heavy client load and the scheduling demands of a for-profit health care organization whose primary obligation is to its stockholders.

Consultation: Nature and Purposes

Consultation is an excellent means of assuring that clients in crisis do not suffer because a worker lacks extensive experience in solving complex human problems. In health and other human service fields, consultation has been widely used to bring the fullest possible range of knowledge to bear upon a person's particular health problem. In the community mental health movement and in Caplan's *Principles of Preventive Psychiatry* (1964), consultation is considered to have an equally important function in the mental health and crisis fields. Additionally, consultation is extremely important where primary care and mental health intersect, such as with the influx of children with behavioral problems and mental health concerns into the primary care setting (Hoff & Morgan, 2011). Goodfriend, Bryant, Livingood, and Goldhagen (2006) found that utilizing child psychiatrists (a rare commodity in the primary care setting) to train and consult with pediatricians showed an increase in attending to and properly diagnosing children and adolescents.

Consultation provides a powerful process in which consultees can harness their skills and traits and rise to the challenge of providing appropriate services for clients' ever-changing needs (Knotek, 2006). Consultation can take place between a crisis worker (volunteer or paid) and designated consultant, between a crisis worker and a supervisor, or between a crisis specialist and another service worker such as a nurse, physician, police officer, teacher, pastor, or agency administrator. Many supervisors prefer to function in a consultative role with workers concerning clinical matters, rather than in their appointed authority role as supervisor (see Table 8.1 for distinctions between these roles). The exception to this usually occurs when the worker's level of skill is insufficient to allow complete freedom to accept or reject the recommendations of the supervisor, a freedom that characterizes the consultative relationship. The focus of consultation can be either on problems working with an individual client ("case consultation") or on an entire program. Even though case consultation is more common, program consultation (for example, developing suicide prevention or antibullying programs in schools) might prevent crises and other problems if it were engaged in more frequently.

The Consultative Relationship

Even though a consultant offers suggestions and recommendations to the consultee, the consultee is free to accept or reject the information offered (except in special instances between a worker and supervisor, as noted earlier). However, along with the *freedom* to accept or reject the information, the consultee has the *responsibility* for the quality of service to the client. If the consultee agrees that certain action should be taken on behalf of a client, it is his or her responsibility to carry it out. Actually, although there is high status in the consultant role, there is no line or "ascribed" authority (as in a supervisory relationship). Instead, a consultant has "achieved" authority (personal wisdom acquired through education and experience), which, it must be remembered, the consultee can accept or reject. Misunderstanding or nonacceptance of this fact by consultants can be the source of many problems in consultative relationships.

Many qualifications of a good supervisor, discussed in Chapter 8, apply to the consulting role as well. Also, effective supervisors often use a consulting style even though they possess ascribed or line authority over supervisees. In general, it takes time and patience to develop productive consultative relationships with various caregivers and administrators. People who take on consultative roles should be very experienced and confident in the crisis field without appearing arrogant. A superior attitude does little to foster meaningful consultative relationships. No matter how skilled or confident a consultant is, there is always something to be learned from the people we consult with and supervise. Consultants should also be sufficiently secure in themselves to sustain possible rejections of suggestions or recommendations without experiencing severe blows to self-esteem.

A professional degree in a mental health field may or may not be one of the qualifications of an effective consultant. Rather, crisis consultants' success depends on their expertise as crisis workers. Unfortunately, consultants in some suicide prevention and crisis programs have had no special training in crisis intervention or suicide and homicide risk assessment, and many have never made a crisis outreach visit with police officers—for example, relying instead on traditional psychiatric training. Crisis workers and the people they serve are bound to be cheated by this kind of consultative arrangement. Extensive knowledge and field experience in the community-based crisis arena are undisputed means of avoiding many problems in the consultative process.

Depending on the attitude of the consultant, a consultee may find it either humiliating or rewarding to work with a consultant on a problem. A crisis worker or administrator should never feel inferior or demeaned from the necessity of seeking help from a consultant. If, and when, this happens, no one benefits—not the client, the consultee, or the consultant. Instead, it is useful to view the relationship as a *partnership* for the benefit of the consumer. When communication breaks down in consultative relationships, the consultant should assume leadership in trying to resolve the problem.

Criteria and Procedures for Crisis Consultation

There are many reasons why crisis workers (paid or volunteer) and community caretakers should seek consultation. *Accountability* is at the forefront inasmuch as all workers are accountable to someone: the executive director to the governing body; crisis workers to a program clinical director, appointed supervisor, chief of service, or unit manager; all of us to the consumers (people in crisis) whom we serve; and an agency or governing body to its funding source or to legislators who are accountable to the electorate.

In crisis work, there will be many times when we need the support of a colleague, especially in very stressful situations. For example, when dealing with a highly suicidal or dangerous person, we should *always* work on a team or consultative basis, including with a peer. The responsibility and risks involved in doing otherwise are too great and may cost lives. Crisis workers should obtain consultation from a senior-level crisis worker in the following kinds of situations:

- Circumstances where there is significant danger of suicide, assault, or homicide.
- Situations in which psychotropic medication or psychiatric hospitalization may be indicated.
- Situations with legal or ethical implications, other factors involving the worker or agency in court, or other legal or public proceedings.
- Situations in which the client has a grievance about the service received.
- Instances in which a medical or neuropsychiatric diagnosis is needed.
- Any circumstance where the crisis worker is uncertain about what to do to help the client more effectively.
- Any situation in which the worker's own issues interfere with an objective response to a client's needs.
- Any occasion where there is a dispute among team members as to the most appropriate intervention plan for a client.

Once a worker—crisis counselor, nurse, or teacher—has decided that he or she needs consultation, the following steps should be taken:

- The consultee should clearly define, verbally and/or in writing, specific questions to be asked of the consultant and explicit information desired or expectation of recommendations concerning identified problems areas.
- In the instance of client consultation, the consultant and consultee should determine if the client should be seen directly by the consultant.
- If it is determined that the client will be seen directly by the consultant, the consultee will prepare the client for that conference.
- The outcomes of the consultation should be recorded on appropriate agency forms.

Client Consultation Illustrations

The following examples illustrate some of the uses of client consultation by crisis workers.

A particular human service worker, in this case a police officer, may wish to provide a service for a person in crisis in which he or she is not particularly skilled.

Example: Acute Psychiatric Disturbance

A police officer called a local crisis clinic from the Monroe home when he saw that he was unable to handle Jeffrey Monroe's irrational, upsetting behavior. Although Mr. Monroe was violent, throwing things and breaking furniture, the officer could tell that he was also suffering from psychiatric symptoms. (Mr. Monroe stated that he was afraid that his wife and others were plotting against him.) The crisis worker came to the home and acted as a consultant to the officer, who by this time had established some rapport with the family. Together, they convinced Mr. Monroe to seek help at an emergency mental health clinic.

A crisis worker wants to obtain a broader perspective and help with a complex crisis situation that involves many people.

Example: Diabetic Patient Paranoid About Insulin

Janet Orley, age 29, has diabetes but neglects to take her insulin. She believes it is contaminated after each use of the vial and refuses to let her mother or the community health nurse administer it. Ms. Orley is also picked up occasionally by the police for vagrancy and public intoxication. She has a crisis counselor who has assisted her through several incidents, but without much change in her underlying lifestyle. Ms. Orley refuses psychiatric treatment regarding her unreasonable ideas about the insulin. One day the nurse called the crisis counselor after discovering Ms. Orley in a diabetic coma. An ambulance was dispatched, and Ms. Orley was hospitalized. When Ms. Orley recovered from her medical crisis, the crisis counselor sought consultation from the program director of the crisis clinic about the next steps in helping the woman. Among the suggestions that the supervisor made was an interagency planning conference, including Ms. Orley as an active participant (see the "Community Linkage and Coordinaton" section of Chapter 7; and Hoff, Hallisey, & Hoff, 2009, ch. 5).

Someone in a supervisory position needs advice from a crisis specialist concerning a staff problem.

Example: Government Administrator

A federal department administrator, Ms. Patti Boyd, calls a crisis worker for help with a staff member who becomes suicidal. Because the supervisor is personally concerned about the staff member and has her own fears about suicide and death, she wants the help of an outside consultant to avoid an overly subjective approach to dealing with the problem.

A mental health provider, in this case a psychologist in a university counseling office, needs assistance on how to address substance abuse issues that her client reported.

Example: Depressed Student Abusing Alcohol

The psychologist has been working with an undergraduate student, Tom, who presents with depressive symptoms and suicidal thoughts. Over the course of several sessions it becomes apparent that Tom's use of alcohol is abusive and contributing to depressive symptoms, suicidal thoughts, and poor academic performance. The psychologist requests the advice of a substance abuse specialist regarding how to address Tom's substance abuse issues, what treatment options are available, and how best to assist the student in seeking necessary services.

A member of the community, in this case a teacher, wants to gain a broader knowledge base in working with someone who may be suicidal.

Example: Student, Teacher, and Themes of Violence Toward Self and Others

During a consulting session with a crisis specialist, a high school teacher explains that a student is writing essays about violence, suicide, and death. An agreement is reached about the next steps to take, and the teacher receives suggestions about how to respond to the student's dangerous thinking and writing and facilitate confidence in openly discussing the problem. Subsequent steps for a referral process may be worked out, or the situation may be discussed in a follow-up consultation session, depending on the particular circumstances of the situation: How much information does the teacher already have? How much danger of suicide or harming others is there based on the information available? Is the student perhaps a victim of bullying from classmates and feels helpless to stop it? What other information is needed, and what is the best way of obtaining it in order to decide on next steps (for example, a conference with parents or the school administrator)?

A community mental health agency works with school staff concerning an assaultive student.

Example: Abusive Student

Dennis Fleeton, age 15, was referred by a community mental health agency to a school for children and adolescents with emotional and psychiatric difficulties. His grades were passable, but he was physically abusive to other children and sometimes struck out at teachers. During one of his fights with another boy, he knocked out both the boy and the teacher who tried to intervene. Dennis was immediately expelled from the school. Dennis also had outbursts of uncontrolled behavior at home. While he was on home instruction, the mental health counselor initiated consultation sessions with the school in an effort to get Dennis reinstated. In fact, Dennis' upsets in school coincided with his mother's hospitalization for heart disease. Family crisis counseling sessions were held, supplemented by individual sessions for Dennis. He was able to verbalize many of his fears about his mother's heart disease and possible death. Gradually, he learned how to express his feelings in less destructive ways. After several family conferences at school, Dennis was reinstated. Teachers and the guidance counselor stated that they had learned a great deal about adolescent behavior and the role of the family (in this case, the mother's illness) in an adolescent's problems. The school decided to continue regular consultative sessions with the mental health agency, even though earlier attempts of the agency to establish a regular consultative relationship had been refused.

Program Consultation

Though used much less frequently than case consultation, program consultation is also important. However, as the examples above illustrate, there is a tendency to wait for a specific crisis before examining an entire program and institutional practices that contribute to individual crisis situations. This is known as *learning from crisis* as opposed to *learning for crisis*—in which an agency attempts to prevent crisis, be better prepared, and avoid simply reacting to the crisis (Smith & Elliot, 2007). For example, some nursing homes have a staffing arrangement whereby staff rotate ward assignments biweekly. This approach to staffing contributes to the adjustment problems (and possibly crises) of older people whose age makes it difficult to accommodate such rapid changes. It also prevents older people and staff from establishing stable relationships with one another, which could prevent individual crisis situations. The tendency to focus on individual cases and neglect the *preventive* approach implied in program consultation conforms to the general inattention given to primary care.

The concept of program consultation is often resisted most strongly by the very institutions that could use it most productively—hospitals, nursing homes, and schools. An administrative consult may be used to effect change across the organization by focusing not only on improving programs but also by strengthening the role of professional consultation within specific programs. One option is using internal consultants who can provide administrative crisis consultation based on their intimate knowledge of the agency's internal dynamics (Knotek, 2006). When internal consultants are not an available (or the best) option, the most effective way to proceed against resistance is through community education efforts and the availability of consultation regarding individual crisis cases. When administrators see the positive results of consultation concerning individual stress situations, they are often more open to the possibility of program consultation. Also, a resistive institution is often more receptive to program consultation shortly after a crisis has occurred. However, new knowledge must be translated into changed behavior that in turn creates a cultural shift within the agency for organizational learning to be sustained (Smith & Elliot, 2007).

Example: Human Resources Department and Job Loss

A social worker and crisis specialist assisted the Employee and Family Assistance program staff in a federal government department in understanding and helping colleagues of a woman who had committed suicide after receiving her job termination notice. After this experience, the director arranged for a regular consultative program with the social worker regarding the psychosocial impact and potential crisis following job loss, as well as an examination of policies and sometimes inhumane or punitive procedures around workplace termination notices.

Besides dealing with job loss itself, some employees complain that after years as a devoted worker, they are "treated like criminals" upon termination, as managers post a security guard at the door while the employee vacates an office. Understandably, the employer wants to prevent possible theft or sabotage by the dismissed employee. But, as recent tragedies illustrate, bullying by peers, insensitive dismissal procedures, and the lack of outplacement services can trigger violent responses by disgruntled former employees for whom job loss is literally the "last straw." Such dangerous responses are more probable among those already troubled and for whom the job was like family. These situations highlight the importance of consultation for Employee and Family Assistance staff to increase awareness of impending crises and skills in prevention and early intervention strategies (see Churchill, 1995; Hoff, 2010, ch. 10).

In general, program consultation is more challenging for the consultant and more threatening to the consultee than case consultation. This occurs because more is at stake in the possible exposure of leadership practices, vested interests, and perhaps the continuation of the agency itself if certain deeply rooted problems are exposed. But program consultation can be more rewarding because it leads to the necessary change and revitalization (or continuation, if shutdown is threatened) of an entire institution. And for cost-conscious governing bodies and executive directors, the *preventive* impact of consultation (in human and financial terms) cannot be overstated.

Crisis programs seeking certification from the American Association of Suicidology (AAS) report that one of the most beneficial aspects of the process is the program consultation they receive from the accreditation examiners. Such consultation is built into the feedback session to the agency director (and designated staff) at the conclusion of the accreditation site visit. Agencies preparing for accreditation may also arrange for pre–site visit program consultation if necessary.

Community Education

Because each community member is bound to experience a crisis at some time or will be called on to help someone else in crisis, everyone should know where and how to get community crisis services. A comprehensive community crisis program that meets national standards has a public relations program that gives all residents this vital information. There should be established channels of communication between community members and various service organizations. One of the AAS standards for crisis services is that residents have regular input to the governing body and administration. This is one important way to determine how well informed people are about their crisis service. Figure 10.1 suggests target groups that could benefit from various education programs in crisis and psychosocial care. All residents should know the following:

- What services are available
- How they can contact the crisis program
- How long it takes to get help in an emergency

Target Groups	a	b	c	d	e
Citizen boards of human service agencies	●				●
Senior citizen clubs	●		●		●
Business associations	●				●
Church groups	●		●		●
Parent-teacher associations	●		●		●
Town boards, supervisors, councils	●				●
Media (TV, radio, newspapers)	●		●		●
Bartenders, hairdressers, disk jockeys	●	●	●		●
Service clubs (Lions, Kiwanis, etc.)	●				●
Youth boards	●		●		●
Voluntary agencies (Mental Health Association, Help Your Neighbor, Welcome Wagon)	●	●	●		●
Traveler's Aid, International Institute	●	●	●	●	
Salvation Army	●	●	●	●	●
Police	●	●	●	●	●
Teachers, residential staff	●	●	●	●	●
Clergy	●	●	●	●	●
Social service workers	●	●	●	●	●
Victim advocates	●	●	●	●	●
Physicians	●	●	●	●	●
Nurses	●	●	●	●	●
Rescue workers	●	●	●	●	●
Psychiatrists	●		●	●	●
Psychiatric nurses	●		●	●	●
Social workers	●		●	●	●
Clinical psychologists	●		●	●	●
Counselors	●		●	●	●

Types of Programs: a–e

Citizen and Consumer Group | Community Service Groups | Caretakers | Health Providers | Mental Health Providers

Target Groups

Key
a. General information about crisis service.
b. Consultation concerning specific crisis situations.
c. Community resources and interagency referral system.
d. Crisis management.
e. Special topics.
* If and when these groups are trained and experience in crisis management, they should be able to serve as community educators, consultants, and trainers for others.

Figure 10.1 Community education. Target groups that could benefit from various education programs in crisis and psychosocial care. (From Hoff and Miller (1987). With permission.)

- Who is eligible for the service
- What, if anything, it will cost to use the service—which should be publicly supported
- If client confidentiality will be observed

All residents should know the answers to these questions. A public relations committee of the community crisis program has several available avenues for publicizing the answers. At the same time, the committee can offer information to help people recognize and understand better the common signs of crisis, risk of suicide, and assault; learn how to help themselves and others through new ways of problem solving; and generally improve their mental health. This would also include information to discourage destructive ways of problem solving such as resorting to alcohol and other drug abuse, violence toward others, or suicide attempts.

Some of the basic tasks involved in a community education program are as follows:

- Appoint a director or coordinator of public relations with experience in crisis intervention and community education work. This person should select committee members who are willing and able to work on behalf of the program.
- Identify the specific educational needs of the local community being served. This can be done by contacting governing body members; citizen advisory and planning groups; caretakers such as police, teachers, and rescue squads; service clubs (Lions, Elks, Kiwanis, and so on); churches; and other community groups.
- Develop education materials such as brochures and posters that illustrate crises in families, alcohol and other drug use, bullying, aging, suicide, HIV/AIDS, violence, divorce, illness, job loss, and other transition states.
- Organize a systematic means of distributing these materials—for example, develop working agreements with primary health clinics, hospitals, mental health providers, public and private schools, and college counseling offices for making brochures and business cards available in lobbies, offices, and other high-frequency areas and a routine mechanism for replenishing or updating the supply. Churches and service clubs are also good places to distribute crisis information.
- Organize a speaker's bureau with people who can discuss various topics pertinent to crisis and psychosocial care. Speakers could appear at service clubs, churches, and other community groups; in the local media; and before special groups such as senior citizens and school health and social science classes. Speaker's bureau activities can often be developed cooperatively with the local Mental Health Association or public speaking organizations such as Toastmasters International.

- Develop a program for systematic and periodic contact with the media. Less than 1% of the total U.S. population does not have television, and even fewer people have no radio. In poor countries, radios and cell phones are available even in remote rural areas. The Suicide Information and Education Collection (SIEC) and the AAS are valuable sources for promoting public information regarding suicide and how to get help in crisis situations. Victim assistance programs, women's centers, the National Organization for Victim Assistance (NOVA), and the YWCA have information about what to do if victimized by crime. These are valuable resources for every public relations coordinator of a crisis program.
- Work with the local telephone company to ensure listing of the crisis telephone numbers along with emergency telephone numbers at the front of the directory, if this has not already been done.
- Develop a system for monitoring and evaluating the outcome of the public relations program. For example, conduct a random survey to find out what percentage of residents has appropriate information about local crisis programs. Decades ago, such a survey in Great Britain revealed that 92% of the population had knowledge of the Samaritans.

A strong community education program not only gives people the information they need about crisis programs but also helps keep the program on a firmer financial foundation. People who are informed and actively involved with a program important to them will make sure that the program makes vital use of their tax dollars.

Crisis work is demanding, unpredictable, and emotionally intense. But it is also highly rewarding in its potential to make an immediate and lasting difference—sometimes between life and death—for distressed or traumatized persons. When crisis workers are trained, collaborate with community networks, and receive the supports they need, the rewards are even greater. Without such preparation, support, and interdisciplinary links, the best intentions and expertise of clinicians on behalf of the very persons most in need of crisis service may be compromised.

The mission of crisis and psychosocial care—especially in an era of fiscal constraint and global change—speaks far beyond individuals in distress or despair. As the preventive facet of psychosocial care, crisis intervention empowers its recipients and benefits all of society far in excess of its financial costs—keeping children in school and adults in jobs, finding homes for the homeless, and preventing violence and premature death by suicide.

We are convinced that timely and coordinated delivery of crisis care during episodes of loss, trauma, illness, and other hazardous events is a wise investment for any community concerned about cost containment *and* quality of service.

References

Caplan, G. (1964). *Principles of preventive psychiatry*. New York, NY: Basic Books.

Churchill, J. (1995, November). CISD policy development and implementation. *Employee Assistance*, 11–16.

Goodfriend, M., Bryant, T., III, Livingood, W., & Goldhagen, J. (2006). A model for training paediatricians to expand mental health services in the community practice setting. *Clinical Pediatrics*, *45*, 649–654.

Hoff, L. A. (2010). *Violence and abuse issues: Cross-cultural perspectives for health and social services*. London, UK: Routledge.

Hoff, L. A., Hallisey, B. J., & Hoff, M. (2009). *People in crisis: Clinical and diversity perspectives*. (6th ed.). New York, NY: Routledge.

Hoff, L. A., & Miller, N. (1987). *Programs for people in crisis: A guide for educators, administrators, and clinical trainers*. Boston, MA: Northeastern University Custom Book Program.

Hoff, L. A., & Morgan, B. D. (2011). *Psychiatric and mental health essentials in primary care*. London, UK: Routledge.

Knotek, S. (2006). Administrative crisis consultation after 9/11: A university's systems response. *Consulting Psychology Journal: Practice and Research*, *58*(3), 162–173.

Smith, D., & Elliot, D. (2007). Exploring the barriers to learning from crisis: Organizational learning and crisis. *Management Learning*, *38*(5), 519–538.

Glossary

burnout: A chronic condition manifested by cynicism, anger, resentment, and emotional exhaustion, usually stemming from work-related stressors. People suffering from burnout often do not connect their feelings and behavior with the chronic stress they are under.

chemical restraint: The temporary use of potent psychotropic medication to restrain an individual during acute psychiatric emergencies.

chronic condition: A condition that occurs over many months or years without complete resolution. Substance dependence, for instance, is usually considered a chronic condition. Incidents that occur in conjunction with this chronic condition can lead to crisis (e.g., domestic abuse, legal trouble, and job loss).

client: A person who uses the services provided by a crisis program. The client may be a brief "caller," a long-term mentally ill "patient," a victim of crime, or a homeless abused woman. In this book, *client* is sometimes used interchangeably with *consumer*.

collaborative service model: A model of human service delivery that focuses on working collaboratively with the identified client and supportive family members. This empowering approach is accomplished by fostering autonomy from rather than dependence on the service provider and takes into account the client's individual goals. Also known as *recovery orientation*.

core curriculum: Academic courses required of all students graduating from an educational institution, without which the educational goals would not be met.

correlate: One of two interrelated variables (e.g., depression is a correlate of suicide).

crisis: A state of acute emotional upset in which one's usual problem-solving ability fails. Crisis occurs in response to an identifiable traumatic event, such as an accident, victimization, death of a loved one, or divorce. Crisis states are self-limiting and short-lived, as the emotional pain of acute crisis demands early resolution, whether positive or negative.

crisis assessment: The first of four basic steps in crisis care—ascertaining the stressful or hazardous event, its origins, the precipitating factor, the person's vulnerability and response to what happened, and resources aiding positive crisis resolution. Assessment includes biopsychosocial factors and the recognized standard of *explicitly* ascertaining victimization trauma (current or past), risk of suicide, and risk of assault or homicide.

crisis counseling: An aspect of the crisis management and resolution process focusing on the emotional, cognitive, and behavioral ramifications of the crisis. A crisis worker with formal preparation in counseling techniques carries out this process. Typically it is limited to only a few sessions (six to 10).

crisis intervention: That aspect of the crisis care process focusing on immediate response to and resolution of an urgent problem—with particular attention to its life-threatening aspects—through use of personal, social, environmental, spiritual, and sometimes material resources. Crisis intervention includes but is not limited to debriefing. The process is carried out by a crisis worker, such as a nurse, police officer, social worker, physician, psychotherapist, counselor, or minister. Crisis intervention is related to but differs from psychotherapy.

crisis management: Consists of the entire process of working through one's crisis to its endpoint or resolution. It implies the active collaboration between the person or family in crisis and a human services provider. The emphasis is on empowerment and growth of the individual leading to mastery of life circumstances with timely support from others.

crisis program: Any of the various organized agencies that provide services, including emergency services of community mental health centers, suicide prevention centers, psychiatric or behavioral departments of emergency medical services, community health centers, shelters for runaway teenagers and the homeless, rape crisis centers, battered women's programs, and services for other victims of crime.

crisis stabilization: A term referring to the short-term treatment (12 to 72 hours) of an acute psychiatric emergency situation in a hospital setting, in which chemical restraint is often applied. Crisis counseling and a follow-up treatment plan are instituted when the disturbed person is more tranquil and can be engaged in problem solving.

crisis worker: A person, paid or volunteer, with the knowledge, skills, and attitudes required to assist a person or family in crisis (e.g., a police officer, mental health professional, clergy, nurse, physician, or social worker).

cultural competence: A popular term in health care literature referring to the development of adequate knowledge about various cultures, thereby allowing for the provision of culturally sensitive and appropriate services. This terminology presents a daunting challenge for providers who face a multitude of languages and belief systems among their clients. Though well intended, the term shortchanges the reality that most people will never *completely* understand or be "competent," except in their own ancestral culture with its language, values, behavioral norms, and so on. The term *cultural awareness and sensitivity*, which refers to the variety of diversity issues, is more inclusive and less demanding for well-intentioned providers in multicultural societies.

cultural relativism: Making a judgment about the acceptability of certain actions that are different from or relative to a particular culture, circumstance, or the like (e.g., excusing violence toward women as "part of their culture" in contrast to defining violence in a universal human rights framework).

curriculum: The complex array of learning activities, or a body of courses, organized to achieve specific educational goals.

diversity: A term denoting "difference," sensitivity to which aids our understanding and response to people across cultures in reference to their gender, race, class, language, ethnicity, sexual identity, age, values, religion, and citizenship status. Because health care is a major domain of all societies, health professionals in multicultural societies such as the United States and Canada must recognize differences in how clients experience emotional security; their varied responses to pain, ill health, and/or threats to personal safety; what diverse groups consider appropriate behaviors when expressing courtesy and respect, such as avoiding eye contact with a person of "higher authority"; or how traditional "gender roles" (e.g., in female-dominated nursing profession) might interfere in either the delivery and/or acceptance of health care, limit setting on abusive behavior, and so on.

emergency psychiatry: A branch of medicine that deals with acute behavioral disturbances related to severe cognitive impairment, emotional instability, or dysfunction in daily living and self-care. It includes crisis intervention but also implies the need for distinct *medical* intervention such as psychotropic medication or admission to an inpatient psychiatric facility. Elements of its practice are carried out by various members of the traditional mental health professions: psychiatry, psychiatric nursing, social work, and clinical psychology.

enquiry-based learning (EBL): an approach to learning that is driven by the students' process of enquiry, thus engaging them as partners in the learning process. EBL encourages students to draw upon their existing knowledge and then concentrate their efforts on where they need to undertake further work. Working collaboratively in small groups or with structured support from others, EBL promotes social interaction and cohesion that can be difficult to achieve in a larger educational setting.

esoteric: Something that is meant to be understood by a group of people with specific knowledge (e.g., medicine or psychiatry).

formal crisis care: That part of the helping process carried out by health and other human service providers on behalf of a person or family in crisis; also known as *crisis intervention*.

hierarchical service model: A model of human service delivery that indicates a power differential between provider and client. This model holds the potential to exploit clients and exacerbate powerlessness or feelings of being out of control. Treatment goals under this model are identified by the provider, minus active collaboration with the client.

iatrogenesis: A concept referring originally to disorders or injury caused by medical treatment, but now applied to injuries originating from any health, mental health, or social service provider's action or neglect. It also refers to serious complications from the injudicious use of psychotropic drugs.

managed care: A system of health service delivery in the United States emphasizing (a) coordination of care through a primary care provider and (b) containment of health care costs. While reducing unnecessary care, a hazard to clients in managed care systems (especially for-profit managed care organizations, or MCOs) is that providers may be pressured to provide less care as an avenue for stockholders' increased profits. This hazard has particular implications for individuals needing crisis and psychosocial care. Although life-saving interventions can be implemented in a few minutes by skilled crisis workers, comprehensive psychosocial care requires more than the 10- or 15-minute slot of time often allotted in primary care medical settings.

natural crisis care: That part of the helping process carried out by a friend or family member on behalf of a person in crisis.

open-dialogue therapy: A family and social network approach used for the treatment of first-episode psychosis. It was developed and refined by Jaakko Seikkula and associates in Finland. This approach establishes a dialogue with the client and provides immediate support and treatment planning. There is a decreased emphasis on the use of psychotropic medications, and research results indicate fewer hospitalizations and secondary episodes of psychosis.

palliative care: The management of the physical, psychosocial, and spiritual needs of patients with serious, life-limiting, or chronically debilitating illness. The focus is on symptom management to maximize quality of life. It can occur at any age or any point in the illness and differs from hospice care, which focuses solely on the care of a dying patient and their family.

paradigm: A model for explaining a complex process or idea that is accepted by most people in an intellectual community. In this book, based on research and clinical experience, a paradigm depicts the crisis experience from origin through resolution. Understanding this experience serves as an underpinning for natural and formal crisis intervention across a range of hazardous events and transition states to promote growth and avoid negative crisis outcomes, such as substance abuse or violence toward self or others.

parasuicide: Suicidal gestures or attempts, or self-harm, with no intent to die. It is a predictor of future suicidal behavior. It is most common among adolescents and young adults.

pharmacotherapy: The treatment of disease with medications. In cases of mental illness, the use of psychotropic medications (those that affect the mind) is prevalent. When indicated, psychotropic medications should be prescribed and monitored by a medical or psychiatric professional with specific training.

posttraumatic stress disorder (PTSD): A psychiatric term describing a chronic condition that may occur years after experiencing a trauma that is outside the normal range of life events. The term originated from work with survivors of concentration camps and the Vietnam War. The occurrence of posttraumatic stress often signifies that crisis care was inadequate when the traumatic event was experienced. The term *traumatic stress* signifies the essential "normality" of emotional response to horrific events, although psychiatric "disorder" may follow in the absence of early supportive response.

primary health care: Refers to the first or entry point to the health care system, with the emphasis on education and early detection of health problems and the pivotal role of primary care providers to coordinate the often complex facets of health service delivery. It assumes the psychosocial aspect of any health problem. It is a key concept in crisis care for its emphasis on preventive mental health and timely response to self-injury, abuse, and other critical life events.

psychosocial health care: The element of human service that recognizes and addresses the psychological and social factors inherent in most health, illness, and crisis phenomena. Systematic attention to psychosocial facets of care plays a pivotal role in *preventing* emotional crisis and buffering the impact and potential hazard of stressful life events.

psychotherapist: Someone specially trained (and with a minimum of a master's degree) to help people resolve underlying psychological and psychiatric problems. A person working with a mental health license: psychiatrist, clinical or counseling psychologist, licensed social worker, or advanced practice psychiatric nurse.

psychotherapy: A helping process directed toward changing a person's feelings and patterns of thought and behavior. In contrast to crisis intervention's focus on problem solving around hazardous events, it involves uncovering unconscious conflict leading to symptoms of distress.

resilience: The ability to recover quickly and thrive following setbacks or serious upsets. A dynamic process that results in psychological and social adaptation in the context of significant adversity.

social network: May consist of a person's family, friends, neighbors, relatives, employer, teacher, bartender, hairdresser—anyone with whom a person has regular social intercourse.

suicide: Self-intended, self-inflicted death.

suicide survivor: Those people left behind after a person has died by suicide. This can include family and friends, but also includes human service providers. This term does not describe someone who has attempted suicide but did not die.

traumatic stress debriefing: The first step in the crisis management process, initiated as soon as possible after a critical event, such as a suicide in school or by a hospital patient, police and emergency medical response at a crime scene, or loss by disaster. It typically involves listening, opportunity for catharsis, emotional and material support, psychoeducation about normal crisis response, and linkage to follow-up crisis counseling and psychiatric services based on assessed needs. It is sometimes also referred to as *critical incident stress debriefing* (CISD).

vicarious traumatization: The feeling of distress and psychological trauma experienced especially by persons working with victims or survivors of violence and abuse whose job entails listening with empathy to a particularly gruesome story of violence, or to similar stories of clients repeated over hours, days, or months in a job. It refers to the absorption of the trauma into one's own psyche, which, without attention to its source and appropriate support and self-care, can lead to burnout and other psychological or social problems.

victim-survivor: A term used to describe someone who has been victimized by abuse. The term acknowledges the person's victimization but simultaneously conveys potential for growth, development, and empowerment.

violence: Social action that inflicts harm, or even death, on another and for which one is accountable, except in cases of self-defense or insanity.

About the Authors

Miracle Hoff is a mental health and substance abuse professional. She holds a master's degree in counseling and guidance with an emphasis on community counseling. She is licensed as both a professional counselor and addiction counselor. Her clinical experience includes work with diverse clientele experiencing crisis situations associated with mental health disorders and substance abuse. Work settings include outpatient, residential, and correctional programs providing assessment, group, individual, and family counseling service. Her clinical practice is grounded in a strength-based and empowerment philosophy.

In addition to her direct clinical work, Miracle provides clinical supervision to other licensed professionals and undergraduate and graduate students in a variety of human service areas. She offers community education, preventive, and crisis services to students of all ages, family members, community members, and professional service providers. Miracle has also worked as an administrator within for-profit and not-for-profit agencies providing mental health, crisis, and substance abuse services.

Lee Ann Hoff is a nurse-anthropologist and crisis specialist, and the founding director of the Life Crisis Institute based in Boston. Dr. Hoff has extensive experience as an educator, consultant, clinician and crisis service manager. Her major publications include the award-winning book *People in Crisis: Clinical and Diversity Perspectives*, 6th ed. (Routledge, 2009), and *Violence and Abuse Issues: Cross-Cultural Perspectives for Health and Social Services* (Routledge, 2010). Currently, Dr. Hoff is adjunct professor, University of Ottawa, Faculty of Health Sciences; visiting professor, Institute for Applied Psychology (ISPA), Lisbon, Portugal; and consultant on workplace violence training at Vida Health, Cambridge, MA. Her teaching experience spans undergraduate, graduate, and continuing education programs across health, social service, women's studies, and police departments nationally and internationally. See www.crisisprograms.org for Dr. Hoff's other publications, educational background, and contact information for collaborative research, writing, and human rights projects.

Index